SEAN CONNERY

SEAN CONNERY

MICHAEL FEENEY CALLAN

STEIN AND DAY/*Publishers*/New York

First published in 1983
Copyright © 1983 by Michael Feeney Callan
All rights reserved, Stein and Day, Incorporated
Printed in the United States of America
STEIN AND DAY/*Publishers*
Scarborough House
Briarcliff Manor, N.Y. 10510

Library of Congress Cataloging in Publication Data

Callan, Michael Feeney
  Sean Connery

  Filmography: p.
  Includes index.
  1. Connery, Sean.   2. Moving-picture actors and
actresses—Great Britain—Biography.   I. Title.
PN2598.C76C3   1983   791.43′028′0924 [B]   83-42827
ISBN 0-8128-2932-8

Contents

Photographs

Introduction

SEAN AND I made a film together: *Zardoz*. Not a big hit, although it made its way. It was an ambitious, labyrinthine piece, an exercise in movie metaphysics expressed in Sci-fi spectacle. For Connery (as for me), it was risky and daring. My script required him to spend eight weeks in a scarlet diaper in an Irish spring (Arctic), to daub his body in white clay (it plucked out his considerable body hair when removed), to rape, pillage, dress as a bride (white organzas), quote T. S. Eliot, horse-ride and – a final ordeal – endure days of complex make-up for a final sequence in which we see him age, wither and die.

The picture was thick with special effects which are slow and tedious for an actor. We made the film for one million, one hundred dollars. Sean took almost no fee, contenting himself with a piece of the profits (as did I).

Sean said 'yes'. In the movie business 'yes' is hedged round with 'buts' and 'maybes'. Not so Connery. He stayed at my side. When the going got tough he got stronger. He is loyal and true. His masculine power is so evident that it gives him the confidence to expose his poetic, feminine side. He is a complete man, standing alone, making his own judgements, realized and balanced.

There is no bitterness about his deprived childhood. He looks upon it as an enriching experience. He suffered the customary humiliations of the British class system, but today moves up and down classes with tolerance and, above all, without modifying his own behaviour.

How did he achieve this? If this book throws light on that, then it will be worth reading.

1

I believe that Connery touches us because he personifies the best qualities that came out of the post-war upheavals, in Britain. The reform of education, the busting of the BBC's monopoly, and so on allowed a lot of talent to flourish. A revolution was produced in the theatre, in popular music with the Beatles, and in other fields. Much of it has withered and disappointed. But Connery is an archetype of what was best in those times. And that is his power. But like all archetypes, he also represents something timeless. His persona reaches back and touches a tradition in British life. I can best define that by suggesting characters that he could play better than anyone else:

CAPTAIN COOK   W. G. GRACE
THOMAS HARDY   KIER HARDIE
ISENBARD KINGDOM BRUNEL   DRAKE
TOM FINNEY

John Boorman

Author's Preface

SEAN CONNERY IS a serious man who wants to be seen as a serious actor. But finding the context for evaluation – the biographical backcloth, the thoughts and motivations – is difficult because he is primarily a man who craves privacy. Unlike virtually every star performer he has no publicist, hasn't had since the early Bond days. The reasons for his obsession – and that is probably the fairest word – are complex and vary according to the source you choose to plumb. Terence Young, director of a number of early Connery films, among them *Dr No* (1962), cites without hesitation the actor's reluctance to open up to non-intimates. In the beginning, he contends, the press were snide with Connery, seeing contradiction in the screen portrayal of a refined Etonian gadabout by an Edinburgh slum kid. After a year or two as Bond, when Connery was the worldwide number one box-office attraction, he punished the press with silence. Fending off swarming frustrated journalists during *Thunderball*, Young was obliged to tell them, 'Sean is not unpleasant. You started it, after all. You tried to make a monkey out of him and now he doesn't need you.' Connery himself has been similarly if more succinctly forthright. In 1964 he was telling American journalist Allyson Sloane in surly explanation, 'It's a known fact that most people come out of Scotland with vast superiority complexes.'

Connery has consciously endeavoured – unwisely, I'd venture – to allow his work to speak for itself. I stress unwisely because the shadow cast by the Bond boom was unnaturally dense and too far reaching. He *could*, I believe, have challenged it more vociferously and succeeded

3

better in exorcising the ghost. *The Offence* (1972) explicitly demonstrated his versatility, but it was badly packaged, wrongly timed and all but obliterated by its immediate predecessor, the colossal success *Diamonds Are Forever*.

Connery has often gone on record asserting he owes nothing to public or paymasters beyond an earnest performance, a full day on the set, utter professionalism.

But he does, I believe, owe more to himself.

Within the industry he is, it is true, widely regarded as a venerated giant, 'a *huge* personality,' to quote John Huston. Co-workers genuinely admire him, his sense of duty and drama is taken as read, his prospects viewed as exciting. But there are chinks in the burnished armour that surrounds him. Odd factors *do* beg analysis. 'He hasn't won an award worth mentioning,' a director colleague selflessly complained, 'Yet he was the backbone of the biggest grossing film series in history, and he's made a half dozen non-Bond gems. What's against him? The outmoded beefy looks? His image of constant stylistic exaggeration. . . ?'

The man himself?

It could be that Connery, with his Scots-cautious vision of the capricious film business, is his own worst enemy. But that is the trite and zippy explanation, the one that harks back to the jaundiced impatient off-set mood of *Thunderball*. I can promise no definitive answer to that central of all questions – what denies Connery the 'respectable' celebrity he so obviously deserves? The truth, as always, lies somewhere between, and is as hard to get to as the man himself. But detective work, the business of sniffing down, assessing and elucidating, is one of the great joys of biographical writing. So, in a sense, my pleasures in undertaking this task can be weighed in direct inverse proportion to the troubles Connery posed.

A considerable array of people, new friends and old, showbusiness denizens and fans, Connery admirers and cinema buffs, journalists and diarists, were generous with assistance of one sort or another in the preparation of this book.

It is pleasing to report that the vast majority of those I

4

approached over the months were responsive and kind. Sean Connery conveyed good wishes to me at the outset and his brother Neil, while admirably cautious, was equally charming. Extensive help, in either interview or archive-hunting, came from the following people, to whom I truly owe that hard-worn old debt of gratitude:

Michael Caine, Guy Hamilton, Kieron Moore, Honor Blackman, Dennis Selinger, Michael O'Herlihy, Robert Hardy, Zena Marshall, Alvin Rakoff, Alfie Bass, Michael Hayes, Robert Henderson, Molly Peters, Richard Lester, Brian Doyle, John Clive, Ivan Waterman, Sonia Eveleigh at Fred Zinnemann's office, Peter Vollebregt, Tony Crawley, Iain Campbell, Alistair Sutcliffe, Marjorie Bilbow, Bill Bryson, John Brady, Johnny Wallis, Ian Porteous, Jack Vinestock, Craigie Veitch, Fiona Perdesatt, Harry Band (United Artists), Paul Higginson (20th Century-Fox), and translators Marianne McGeehan and Clodagh Hourigan.

Also for contributions above and beyond the call, to those gentlemen adepts, Fred Zinnemann, Lewis Gilbert and Ian Bannen. Pat Perilli and the staff of the Information Section at the British Film Institute deserve commendations for patience and efficiency, as do Information and Library staff at *Screen International*, the *Guardian*, *Playboy*, the BBC, and Westminster Central Library. Gilbert Gibson and the Aquarius Agency proved helpful, as did the generous Mrs J. W. Gregson of British Actors' Equity. I am also grateful to my editor, Hilary Muray.

Special thanks to John Boorman and Seamus Smith, former managing director of the Irish National Film Studios, who gave so heartily of their time and advice. And, for unstinting brave support, to Bill Brady. Thanks too to Jane Judge for being unerringly faithful, and Ree for keeping me on course throughout the squalls.

Anonymity, where requested, has of course been honoured.

Michael Feeney Callan

CHAPTER ONE

Facing Back

AT CHRISTMAS 1981 Sean Connery came home for his first
serious break from work in more than a year to ponder a
question that had been on the lips of half the world's
movie-goers for seven years: would he don the Savile Row
mantle of James Bond again? Home, 'the sanatorium ran-
cho' by his wife Micheline's definition, was the place to
be during that bitter European winter. Balmy as a good
May in Britain, with hibiscus and lime trees to spice the
air, San Pedro de Alcantara in Southern Spain is a one-
time fishing village that has now absorbed an overspill of
nearby Marbella's beautiful people. The Casa Malibu, the
Connerys' low-slung stucco-and-tile villa, huddles on the
beach, a private nugget of peace that welcomes no journalist and precious few beautiful people. By Hollywood
and Fleet Street standards the Connerys rarely entertain.
But when they do throw open the studded doors of the
sprawling hacienda it is usually to greet low-scoring golf
buddies of Sean's from Aloha, Atalaya, Guadalmina or
one of the other dozen-odd courses that ring the coast
from Malaga to Gibraltar. Non-showbiz, no-nonsense,
true-hearted true-gritters only are favoured with the sight
of Jean Cocteau murals and Micheline's glittering impres-
sionist paintings.

'The world's number one bullshit detector' – as his
friend Michael Caine calls him – labours at keeping his
home unspoilt and sacrosanct, the ark in the relentless
movieland tempest. When the seas kick up doubly rough
and storm clouds darken furiously, the Connerys tend to
batten down with a vengeance. And such was the mood
as Christmas stretched towards the New Year. 1982 would

be, significantly, the twentieth anniversary of the incarnation of James Bond. Twenty years that had seen Sean Connery sweep from second-feature gypsy player to rock-solid superstar with a personal fortune calculated at £10 million. Twenty years, too, of running. But now, as Connery idled in the garden hammock or toiled at the yards-long office table, scribbling rejection signatures to Wardour Street offices with itchy scripts in dire need of a hype, the doppelgänger he'd been running from was back, shadowing the putting-green lawns, rapping at the door, touting a project that conceivably could recast the hardening mould of Connery's unsatisfactory future.

The past year had, for Connery, been personally distressing and professionally disappointing. A court action by his former trusted film accountant, Kenneth Richards, threatened to cost him more than £100,000 and an ongoing 2 per cent of some thirteen films Richards had worked on, which, with court expenses had Connery's counter-suit failed, would have amounted to a massive sum. Richards lost his claim, but Connery was shaken by his misreading of a key professional associate and by what was, not only on the face of it, a close-fought battle. Popularly lauded as a clever businessman with a maverick flair since he first screwed Jack Warner for $50,000 when *A Fine Madness* briefly overran its shooting schedule, Connery least likes to blunder in the business arena. A measure of his anguish about the November row was reflected in a *Daily Telegraph* headline: CONNERY NEAR TO TEARS AS HE WINS BOND FILM FIGHT, and the concurrent spray of articles that spoke of his torment and delight. 'It was certainly an ordeal,' Connery confessed. 'Something I don't want to go through again. It's much better on the film set.'

But on the film set for more than three years things had been anything but good. *Meteor* (1979), *Cuba* (1979) and to a lesser extent *Time Bandits* (1981) had been painstaking enterprises embarked on with customary gusto, drummed out with fanfare and drenched by the critics. 'Rugged Sean Connery Returns' bawled the *Cuba* press handouts; 'Rug-topped,' gibed the tabloids, celebrating the return of Connery's toupee after many years' absence. All fared badly at the box-office, *Meteor* – a catastrophe movie lagging jadedly behind every other big bang hopeful – proving worst of all, with a recorded loss of $15.8 million two years after release.* Disinclined to hitch on to another flop, Connery chose his next projects carefully. *Outland* and *Wrong is Right* were bountifully promising, offering 'hot' writer-directors Peter Hyams and Richard Brooks respectively. Hyams had just scored with *Capricorn One* and Brooks was distinguished for such minor classics as *In Cold Blood*. But disappointments loomed again. *Outland* was an arduous, fast shoot, made entirely at Pinewood Studios, with a coolly slick director and a general air of optimism. *Wrong is Right* staggered a bit under the boisterous Richard Brooks in New York, but seemed strong enough on story and style to carry. Neither did. By New Year '82, with Brook's movie in the can and *Outland* premiered and back-pedalling, Connery was in a difficult position. Both movies had their merits but neither, it was clear, would shake any positive box office records. 'Sean was, I think, much disappointed by *Outland*,' friend Ian Bannen, who co-starred in two of Connery's best films, speculated. 'He'd seen the recent trend in cinema, seen the Star Wars eruption, and thought that space-age *Outland* would make a fortune.'

There was reason to be disappointed, and alarmed. Rock-solid superstardom frequently gives way to stony petrification. Richard Burton can be farmed out to junk, Richard Harris to parody his own deliciously pernicious raucousness, Olivier to all comers. Star actors need to watch every step along the tightrope of celebrity, especially when the balance tilts, the rope slackens and miscalculations of adjustment are made.

So, disorientated by a run of bad luck and doubting his own judgements, Connery found himself taking time off and squarely facing James Bond, the alter ego he loved to hate, once again. Could Bond restore his flagging market

---

Meteor rates 7th in a recent authoritative Top Ten survey of all time flops. *Waterloo* (1969) with $23.6 million losses heads the list. (*Anatomy of the Movies*, ed: David Pirie, 1982)

appeal? Certainly, without doubt, he could hike Connery's 'purchase' price. The deal on his last Bond, *Diamonds Are Forever* (1971) had never been matched: $1.2 million from United Artists, plus a percentage and a choice of two further movie projects. Connery's recent fees had been nearer half a million, often somewhat less. Apart from elaborating the super-draw profile, what could 007 offer Connery in compensation for the risks and difficulties – at 52 years of age – of revival? $2 million? More?

The businessman in Connery was stirred by the factors working *for* a return to Bondage at this time. Above all, the proposed project, offered by producer Jack Schwartzman, was in direct competition with the Cubby Broccoli-Roger Moore Bonds. The course and purpose of the recent Moore Bonds was manifestly confused and audience indulgence was waning. *Moonraker* (1979), undistilled kids' fizz, grossed massively by turning tail totally on trademark Bond; its successor, *For Your Eyes Only* (1981) limped through twelve months before showing a satisfactory Bondian profit. But still Roger Moore could cruise on *Moonraker* and demand, as he did, $5 million for the upcoming Broccoli venture, *Octopussy*. Fine by Connery. If Moore was good for $5 million while the pre-sold Bond market was quivering uncertainly, Connery could bat against that figure and look for more. What of the quality of the new Bond property, though?

'Quality doesn't come into it, not in the purist sense,' Ian Bannen opines. 'I think Sean was crazy to give up Bond in the first place. When he quit he was riding high, but he could have gone higher. He could have done a Bond a year and said, to hell with it. Great, it's done, now I can go on and do Shakespeare or whatever *I* like. . .' Typecasting apart, Connery himself felt that Bond at his best was something to be proud of. With their multi-layered scripts, inventive direction and extraordinary production values, those early Connery Bonds minted a brand-new cinema genre and Connery, once you scratch the surface, has always basked in the pleasure of his part in the magic-making. Few understood, he felt, how much acting and art went into making Bond a world-beater.

Schwartzman's Bond had all the indications of the pedigree best. Schwartzman himself for a start was the kind of producer Connery liked to deal with: forthright, scrupulous, a fast decision-maker. He had been associated with Lorimar, producers of the TV hit *Dallas*, and had masterminded Peter Sellers's subtly wonderful *Being There*. Schwartzman's essential intention was to remake *Thunderball*, the rights of which, alone in the Bond corral with *Casino Royale* (made as a spy spoof and sullied forever by Charles Feldman and Jerry Bresler in 1967) did not belong to Cubby Broccoli's Eon Productions company. Based on a treatment by Ealing scriptwriter Jack Whittingham, part-time Irish producer Kevin McClory and Bond creator Ian Fleming, the original *Thunderball* was made by Broccoli and Harry Saltzman – the original Eon – in 1965 under arrangement with McClory who, after a court wrangle with Fleming, had won film rights. Specific in the arrangement was the condition that all rights to *Thunderball* would revert to McClory after ten years. This remarkable clause either demonstrates the shortsightedness of Eon or the bargaining strength of the blarney-rich McClory. Whichever way, as Bond sailed soundly into the seventies, the Irishman was left with a solid gold property – the script and characters of what many still reckon was one of the best sixties Bonds. Duly, early in 1975 when Connery was in America overseeing post-production on *The Wind and the Lion*, McClory presented his revival idea.

Connery demurred at first. But McClory was as bewitchingly persuasive as ever. 'He asked would I be interested in contributing in any way,' Connery explained, 'with all the experience that had been gained in the six previous ones I'd done. I thought about it and said, "It depends who you've got writing it." '

Blockbusting novelist Len Deighton, living in tax exile ninety miles away from McClory's Southern Ireland home, was lured in, Connery was appeased and an agreement reached. Connery, Deighton and McClory would write the new Bond. Connery flew to Ireland and took up residence at Blackrock, Co Louth, with Deighton. Twelve months passed, then a full-page advertisement in *Variety*, the sacred showbiz chronicle, announced production preparations for McClory's *James Bond of the Secret Service*, a Paradise Film Production. The electric addendum, 'One of the most exciting screenplays I have ever read,' signed Irving Paul Lazar, the top American agent, stamped marketworthiness on the whole thing. Speculation still flapped around Connery's possible portrayal of Bond (he was, in fact, quite keen to play the role), then suddenly McClory and Paradise Films fell dumb. The cause, quite simply, was Eon's wrath. Many claimed McClory was suffering the most fundamental problem – financial difficulties. But unofficial spokesmen from the Irishman's camp retorted with the sizzling reminder that the first *Thunderball* was (and still is) the biggest ever Bond grosser. In its cinema tour it took $27 million – allowing an inflation adjustment factor, an equivalent today of $67.5 million. And the law of the cinema is what rakes once can rake again. Connery defended the financial solidity of McClory:

'So many people were wanting to contribute to the picture with funds and what have you. There were no problems financially. But I was under the impression that it was totally clean. Free from any litigational problems. When we started to talk quite seriously about the possibility it became so complex. Och, the lawyers came out of the woodwork by the hundred. . . The legal factors were harder to face than making the film. Then the publicity started to work on it and I said, "That's enough!" And I walked away. . .'

Walking away entailed some anguish because 1975 was, for Connery, the *ideal* time to contemplate swooping back as Bond. At forty-five he was still fit and fast enough to appear credible with Berettas or in the boudoir. And the clutch of interestingly diverse and artistically successful pictures he had just made distanced him sufficiently from a too-ready character identification whilst allowing the challenge of developing Bond with some continuity. Roger Moore, commencing his third Bond for Broccoli, was consolidating a personal following, just enough to whet Connery's competitive appetite. 'Professionally there's no

11

more fierce competitor than Sean,' says Michael Caine – and Moore's blisteringly resonant challenge was, now, the happiest of motivators.

But Eon and United Artists, the Bond series' distributors, would allow McClory no leeway. Clearly they recognized Connery's power, resurrected at any time as Bond, to scotch their films. Court action began. Arthur B. Krim, head of UA, insisted that nothing other than a verbatim rehash of *Thunderball* was permissible, that a new script using 007 was illegal. McClory resisted, detailing his speculative screen work with Fleming back in '59, before Bond ever hit the big screen. *Thunderball* was not the only Bond treatment. There was *Latitude 78 West, Bond in the Bahamas* and others – any of which could legitimately be used as the basis for a McClory Bond film.

It was a borderline case but McClory's intentions were eventually seen to be honourable and legal enough, and Broccoli's intentions designed – for understandably commercial considerations – to obstruct and delay. Early in 1980 an Appeal Court decision in America cleared the path for McClory and in July of that year, while Connery's Los Angeles agents were negotiating *Outland*, an 'exclusive report' in British newspapers announced that the actor had at last signed a contract to return 'for a small salary, most of which will go to charity'.

In reality Connery had signed nothing. McClory had his clearance to do a Bond but, exhausted from wrangling, was beginning to arrange to offload. Already he had invested and lost a considerable sum in defending his Bond rights. Enter Schwartzman, fresh from the triumph of *Being There*, with a favourite writer, Lorenzo Semple, Jr., formerly of *Batman*, latterly *Three Days of the Condor* fame.

Protracted talks followed before a deal was settled upon, late in '81. Schwartzman inherited the Fleming-McClory concepts and the Deighton-Connery script and hefted the lot onto Semple's desk. Around the same time Schwartzman, in McClory's wake, decided only one actor could provide the proper pep for his dog-eared, wind-bashed property: Sean Connery. Before the respective producers' signatures had dried on what was then widely known as the *Warhead* contract, Schwartzman had Connery on the telephone – and Connery wasn't saying no. The initial response was equivocal but encouraging enough for Schwartzman to hurry out and start shuffling together a distribution deal and investments of the highest order which would afford Connery the kind of welcome the penny-conscious Scotsman was never likely to refuse. Schwartzman might have thought Connery could be seduced by $2 million. But Connery's vision of the movie marketplace and the quirks of Bondage was, and always has been, broader than most. And his sense of personal worth allied to Bond, and the limits of that worth, were roused. 1975 might well have been the ideal time for a seventh spin as Bond, but '82 was a sterling second best – possibly from a financial angle, if managed properly, the *key* time, the last-chance throw, the pension paymaster.

Connery, without doubt, watched closely as the to-fro exchanges between Cubby Broccoli and Roger Moore's management boomed loud during the early part of the New Year. Broccoli incurred Moore's expensive anger by scouting for a possible new Bond (Superman Christopher Reeve was considered as, reputedly, was Broccoli's daughter's boyfriend, an unknown American actor: it was that sort of inane press silly season). Finally, sensing multi-millions slip away from him with Broccoli's impatience, Moore settled for a salary of $4 million – ample enough to cover the daily consumption of Monte Cristo cigars at £9 a smoke or jet-hop trips back to Gstaad for the family when the din of Pinewood's sound stages wore thin. Connery, meanwhile, was allegedly drawing closer and closer to the Schwartzman camp. By April word had leaked that Irvin Kershner, a director Connery had already worked with and admired, had been engaged by Schwartzman – a sure sign for some that Connery, though perhaps still sitting on the fence fee-wise, was practically and interestedly involved. 'Sean might string this one along a bit,' a colleague expanded, 'but you can bet he'll have the measure of everything working for and against him. He'll be aware of the Broccoli plans, and every aspect of Schwartzman's finances.'

To understand Connery's reluctance to leap in feet first once the heavy legal artillery was withdrawn and the going got half-good, one must understand something of his attitude to his craft, and to money. The duality of his feelings for the character Bond swung between an actor's pride at the worth of his contribution and, on the negative side, spiralling alarm about the series' development. Later we will see the gradual transformation of the series that so irritated him. Couple this irritation with the agonies of typecasting and the argument for burying Bond forever comes clear. Above all, it must be seen, Connery has always loved competing, succeeding . . . but even these provisions lagged a bit behind his devotion to acting, his craft. In an interview with showbiz writer David Lewin in 1965 he explained his tardiness about arriving, at the relatively late age of thirty-two at the state of matrimony: 'When I was acting on stage I was so caught up in my work it would have been impossible for me to marry at all. Why, I was so isolated that I even gave up my bike. . . !' The success of Bond was a joy but even then, at the height of that success, the ideal of the dedicated actor was shining through. 'I was here before Bond came along,' he insisted often and defiantly, 'and will be here after he has gone. Really, I am detached from the success of the Bond films.' Bond was, and is, apparently, acceptable to Sean Connery – warts and all – provided a separation of personae is allowed. Once Bond can be judged by his fantasy merits and Connery by his craft, then Connery is content. The craft matters. After all, for nearly ten years before the breakthrough of *Dr No* Connery gave himself, night and day, body and soul, to 'the job'. Success then was defined as succeeding with the craft, succeeding in entertaining. The change today in that definition concerns money. Connery reckons he sweated out a long apprenticeship. Now he expects to be adequately compensated for the slings and arrows of serving the public.

Evaluating Connery's attitude to money-chasing not long ago, the writer George Feifer reckoned Connery

14

showed 'scant understanding that he himself exploits – in the sense that the entire industry does – as well as suffers exploitation'. True, Connery does resentfully assert that he has been exploited in the past by others; and, true, he does now jostle tirelessly for the 'right' fees. But a scale of exploitation of and by the industry should be drawn. In 1981 a conservative estimate put Bond movie earnings at around $260 million. It is unlikely Connery, the very life's breath of Bond-in-films, would have netted a fiftieth of that. Connery, probably rightfully, feels aggrieved. Bond was not one lucky-dice throw for him, rather a continuing commitment over nine years. He nurtured Bond, he worked; others laboured energetically, but Connery piloted, Connery created. . .

There was nothing of meanness in the bartering for several million to play Schwartzman's Bond. Connery simply weighed his position past and future, watched Moore and judged his own worth. Then he stuck by it. Meanness, his best friends say, is unknown to Connery, though he does cheerfully admit to a Scottish aversion to lavishness. He rarely tips, has never enthused about material possessions (up till the late sixties he never owned a new car), and exudes unease when the conversation turns on dollars and inch-long lines of noughts. Back home in the slum district of Edinburgh where he was born he is remembered as 'a canny Scot, no less than you'd expect', but a street mate of those days, John Brady, recalls, 'He was fair to a fault. Careful with his money, as we all had to be then. But when it was his turn for a round at the Fountain Bar, he was fast to his pocket. He didn't like meanness.'

In part, Connery had always been a financial hoarder. From the time he left school at fourteen to take up a first shaky fulltime occupation as a milk-roundsman he had been saving for inevitable Edinburgh rainy days. By the end of '71, with *Diamonds Are Forever* completed and a $1 million donation gone to the Scottish International Education Trust he had personally set up to assist the talented poor, he was in business with the industrialist Sir Iain Stewart, coining sweet diverse profits. Their investments included a Pall Mall bank – Dunbar & Co – and the PR company, Industrial Communications Ltd, which had the accomplished Ray Gunter as chairman. Stewart, a golf buddy and then director of BEA, Eagle Star Insurance, the Royal Bank of Scotland and Beaverbrook Press, granted Connery the ultimate accolade when their partnership was forged, telling the *Guardian*, 'He's got a good Scots head on his shoulders,' and stressing that he, Stewart, need not be regarded as business mentor or guide. Underlining the difficulty of keeping things in proportion as the stakes and earnings got higher, Connery told the *Daily Express*, 'Funnily enough I worry much more about small sums than big amounts. Blood and tears go into parting with £10 on the golf course – ask any of my friends. But when something like £40,000 is involved I am much more objective.' His friend the director John Boorman backs this up:

'Sean's surprisingly fussy about small matters. When he stays with me he'll be the perfect house guest, graceful, attentive to others, often the last up to bed. Then he'll go round the house checking each light switch, making sure everything's properly off . . . but then he's an incredibly generous man too.'

Essentially, as attested by the Bond revival story, the common touch seems never to have been lost. Remove him from the perch of success and Connery's the canny kid from the backstreets again, warily watching for tomorrow's troubles. A bit-part actor on the film *Ransom* (1974) expressed quixotic puzzlement when describing his working friendship with 'the star':

'I found Connery fine – courteous, tending to moodiness but very professional. Not, as many people find him, intimidating at all. Then there was an incident at a restaurant in Oslo. There was a break in shooting and I came in with a girl I wanted to impress. I didn't know Connery was lunching, but there he was with a lady friend, and he got up and beckoned us over. We had a good meal and he was quite extravagant and very open-handed, and we were all very flattered. Then when the meal ended – his meal, that is – he called for the bill and right in front of us all started to divide it up. 'Let's see: you had the fish, I had the veal. . .' Well, we hadn't *asked* to join him and maybe I'm assuming too much, but you'd imagine a guy with his fortune. . . ?'

Press accusations of penurious · behaviour have been matched only over the years with the largely untested suggestions of a dour and uncooperative personality. Connery in his hard-headed way does nothing to allay press suspicions. Occasionally, when he grants a rare in-depth interview, he word-plays with journalists, like a big cat toying with errant cubs, offhandedly embroidering his darker image – out of devilment perhaps – with spiky remarks about the importance of caution with money, repetitive bleak reminiscences of harder days.

But in the *Warhead* negotiations Connery had no time for play-acting or press hounding. Regardless of press bitching, he considered his objective to be a vital assessment of the project proper. There would, almost certainly, never be another realistic chance to tackle James Bond. Whatever deal he would do now must be the best of his career. For if the Bond revival failed and his market-footing slid further, opportunities to collect hefty cheques – even good lead parts – might diminish drastically.

According to sources in Marbella, a positive commitment to do Schwartzman's film was signed in Los Angeles by Connery on May 18th, a few weeks after *Wrong is Right* opened to universally poor notices in the States. Location shooting was scheduled for the Bahamas and Ireland (though this was altered once confirmed news that the Irish government was closing its National Film Studios came through) late in the summer. Irvin Kershner flew to Britain and studio time was booked at the EMI Elstree complex, not too many miles down the road from Pinewood where the whole Bond business had begun and where, on August 16th, Roger Moore knuckled down to start sixteen weeks on the rival *Octopussy*.

Kershner, Schwartzman and Connery stayed tight-

17

lipped about fee arrangements but, presumably, Connery was happy. Late in July when I queried a major director friend who holds Connery's confidence I was told, 'I won't say Sean's madly looking forward to Bond, but he's looking forward to the $5 million it will earn for him.'

There were still ruffles to be ironed out. Broccoli's solicitors intended a last minute Appeal Court objection, hoping to retard Schwartzman's now precisely-set plans – but with only a marginal chance of success. The biggest ruffle, the real worry, rested squarely in the lap of Sean Connery: how does one dust off the 'dream hero of all our yesterdays', re-dress him for today and coach him to hit the jackpot another time?

For others in a similar position – one foot at the edge of limbo and the other in paradise – the challenge might assume enervating proportions. Facing Bond again, Connery was doubtless concerned, but the well of his professional courage runs deep and he, more than many actors, was equipped for the gamble.

An iron will, a strong constitution and tenacity are Connery's principal attributes, according to his first acting tutor Robert Henderson – earned, not bestowed, in a jumbly life that led from Edinburgh's industrial heartland, through endless scummy lodging houses to London and the beguiling bright lights. These were the building blocks on which the original Bond success was founded and they have, it is fair to deduce, changed little in twenty years. But Connery is not, most agree, a presumptuous or lazy man. He disdains half-measures.

Facing Bond, Connery was quite gladly facing back – relying on his acquired expertise but, most significantly, exploring his capacities and strengths. Knocked from his heady perch, the canny kid was revived, finding muscle and meaning in a challenge that was figuratively, if not actually, as dangerous as shoe-skating on Edinburgh's frozen Union Canal as the fiercest winter thaws to an unsure spring.

In Bond, Connery was going home.

CHAPTER TWO

Fountainbridge, Fife
and a Feeling for Freedom

AULD REEKIE – old smoke – was the local's name for
Fountainbridge, an unprepossessing slab of industrial red
rock that lay in the valley fringing the south-western
slopes of Old Edinburgh. Then, in the twenties and thirties, Fountainbridge earned its scurrilous nickname, giving refuge to the factories and steam-driven businesses
the town proper did not want. Developed in the eight-
eenth century and expanded with the Industrial Revolution, Fountainbridge was an anomaly in a city which
prided itself in being professional-orientated, rather than
industrial, where even the railways are conscientiously
hidden away. High-living Edinburgh folk adverted to the
city's auspicious past – the links with Alan Ramsay,
Hume, Goldsmith, Sir Walter Scott and R. L. Stevenson;
but the hardy folk of Fountainbridge merely spat the black
dust of the district's innumerable chimneys, knuckled
down and coursed on with tough life. Underprivileged
they may have been, but they didn't – and with hindsight,
still don't – recognise that reality. For the dwellers of the
scattered residential blocks life had an isolated tribal close-
ness, a special sense of autonomy and was governed by
a rule-of-thumb morality. Auld Reekie was christened and
cursed with affection. Children of Fountainbridge were
Fountainbridgers forever.

Today the area which took its name from the main,
thirty-yards-wide thoroughfare is a saw-spined, forlorn
semi-wilderness, its pell-mell destruction checked by
Edinburgh's Housing Action Programme. But pointers to

the past stand stout and proud, and it is still easy to cross a busy cobbled street, through the close of a tenement, through dustbins and unchanged charred rubble – and imagine what it was like fifty-five years ago when Joe Connery took his 20-year-old bride across the threshold of number 176 Fountainbridge (now partly demolished) and set up home. The ground-floor wall of 176 behind which the Connerys lived when they first married still stands, and the view from the front window, were it not bricked up, remains as was: the sprawl of McEwans' Brewery, punctuated by the friendly face of the Fountain Bar, the Saturday night hot-spot. Down the road the rubber works that gave so much employment to the locals is gone and the Clanhouse Dancehall now sells fancy goods to wayward tourists and passers-through. But enough remains to draw Sean Connery back occasionally and to evoke affectionate, though sometimes oddly mixed, memories.

Joe Connery's settling in Fountainbridge in the twenties was a shrewd and necessary move, because the kind of work he needed, unskilled labouring, was most readily available in an area of concentrated industry. His father, remembered only as Baldy by grandsons Sean and Neil, was a giant of an Irishman – part-tinker – from County Wexford, who came to Scotland at the end of the last century, married an Edinburgh girl and found employment as an arithmetically unreliable bookie's runner. More often than not Joe totted the bookie's accounts. Neither Joe nor his father was the kind of man given to poetic whimsicality about remembering the past but Joe took some small rebel pride in his Irish ancestry. Had he delved into parish or civic records (something Neil has been threatening to do on behalf of himself and brother Sean for many years) he might have found an ancestral link with the prestigious Ó Conraoi or Mac Conraoi clans of County Galway, of which the most famous modern writer in the Irish language, Padraic Ó Conaire, is a descendant; though more probably he would have unearthed association with a quite separate sept, the Ó Conaires (specifically anglicised as Connery) of Munster. Smith's *History of County Waterford* records the O'Connerys as principal inhabitants of Waterford and environs around the end of the sixteenth century.

Joe was a simple, straight-from-the-shoulder man with a gravelly singing voice he chose to air loud and often. He liked beer first, whisky second and hard toil third and was engaged, and valued, by the North British Rubber Works as a £2-a-week labourer. The rubber mill had good working conditions and such small security afforded Joe the opportunity to contemplate marriage. He proposed to his first and life-long love, Euphemia (Effie) Maclean, an Edinburgh lass, and married her the same year. The ceremony and ensuing boozy, Christmassy celebrations on December 28th 1928 were attended by the roisterous Macleans and less outgoing Connerys in full numbers and, in the way of these affairs, a fine time was had by all. Joe took Effie home to a two-room Fountainbridge tenement with a lightless, damp-smelling hallway and outside toilet. He bought some sturdy ship's linoleum for the floor from the Forces Surplus Store round the corner in Grove Street and geared himself to carve out a comfortable life for a future growing family in the smoky tranquillity of factory-land. The encroaching Depression, recognised and gloomily discussed every night in the Grove or the Fountain Bar, didn't affect the young couple: Joe was 5' 8", 180 lbs of taut, bursting muscle, fit as a fiddle and work-hungry, like his father; they had a roof over their heads and rent for the landlord and, as soon as Effie got her hands on the rubber mill's paypack, the makings of a savings account. Physical stamina was Joe's forte, thriftiness Effie's. Together they made a formidable pair, close and resilient as the stained red brickwork of No. 176, and much admired by their neighbours in 'the stairs', as the tenements were known.

A neighbour from nearby Brandfield Street which boasted a different type of stair, but of identical proportions (12 to 14 families per house), remembers: 'The Connerys were poor for a time, that's to say they had no children. Big families were usual round Fountainbridge. It was the sort of place where the sounds of children, with

21

the paper-thin walls and all the rest, kept a fair pace with the noise of industry.'

But by Christmas '29 Effie was pregnant. Joe in his enthusiastic, responsible way took whatever overtime he could find, so much in fact that he was more often out of the stair than in, setting a home routine that was to stretch into the war years. On a muggy, late summer's day, August 25th 1930, with Joe standing by for once to mark the occasion with a whisky at the Fountain, Effie gave birth to a 10½ lb child whose name she had already decided upon: Thomas, later to become Sean.

Thomas Connery was a child of the Depression, arriving on the scene just as purse strings all over the country tightened, money vanished into mist and unemployment soared. Joe, like a thousand other unskilled workers in Fountainbridge, clung to his job tenaciously, accepted cut-backs where he had to and, for the first time, considered emergency contingency options of work outside Edinburgh, even abroad. But Effie, less practical perhaps but just as obdurate, was not about to give in. 'I had wonderful neighbours and good times in Fountainbridge,' she later declared, explaining pithily her reluctance to bolt for greener pastures.

In spite of Joe's energies and Effie's care with money, young Tommy's first awareness was of a grimly restricted world. The cramped flat consisted of a bedroom and a combined living-room-kitchen called in Scotland a butt-and-ben. An alcove off the living area housed the kitchen – a cast-iron coal fireplace with two side ovens and a top-plate, a cold-water stone sink with wooden drain 'bunker' and, above, a pulley arrangement screwed to the ceiling for drying clothes when inclement weather forbade the use of the outdoors drying green. Tommy slept in his parents' bedroom, in the bottom drawer of the wardrobe, a quite regular cot for newcomers. Later he graduated to the bed-settee in the butt-and-ben, a hunk of a kid at five with gypsy-black hair and piercing chocolate eyes. Even then he was, as his mother recalled, 'different from Neil, who came along much later – impulsive, independent, ambitious.' He had Joe's restless energy, a flair for games and a passion for comic strips which quickly led, his friend John Brady remembers, to 'an interest in all kinds of reading matter'. At five he was quite ready for the strictly-disciplined primary school that was his destiny, but more than a little dismayed too at leaving the full freedom of the streets. His playing world was bordered east and west by factories, north and south by a rough-hewn recreation ground and the basins of the Grand Union Canal. The canal was officially out of bounds to very young minors, but Tommy was never deterred by threats of authority. He fished for tiddlers with the older kids, using the end of one of his mother's old stockings, and boated on the lower basin at some risk. Altogether a safer proposition and far more significant in his young life, was the playground behind his stair, popularly called 'the biggie'. Here, with John Brady, Michael O'Sullivan and others he discovered the challenge of soccer for the first time, bruising toes, scuffing elbows and scoring the odd bleeding nose. 'He was football wild from very early,' says Brady. 'Not especially good,' says another friend of the period, 'more useful.'

Tollcross Primary School, an imposing Georgian building that even today exudes a finger-wagging earnestness, swallowed up most of the 5 to 11-year-olds from Fountainbridge and attempted to displace that endemic braggart street-wisdom with academic ABC's. Here, surprisingly, young Connery was somewhat out-of-place. By five he could read and write and was proficient at mental arithmetic, a knack handed down from Joe. He was in trouble often for totting sums too fast, or lapsing to loud-mouthed boredom when half the class was fumbling over A-is-for-apple. Effie scolded him in the evenings, just as she did every other weekend when he slunk off adventurously to the canal or tackled shins relentlessly in the biggie, but Joe, fighting for family survival as job lay-offs threatened every factory in the area, was seldom round long enough to observe or object.

'My background was harsh,' Connery has said. 'We were poor, but I never knew how poor till years after.' It was impossible for a youngster to be objective about the situation but Tommy intuitively sensed Joe's deepening inability to cope, despite Effie's efforts. The birth of Neil in 1938 when the home financial situation was at its worst complicated matters not a little. So at nine Tommy decided, fully on his own account, to stop off at 'the store' – St Cuthbert's Dairy Stables in Grove Street – on his way home from school and ask for a job. He was precocious, alert and willing and, in spite of the jobs pinch, a place was found for him on a delivery dray. Thus began an eight year on-off spell with St Cuthbert's. The early days, for sure, were the most strenuous. 'I was up at dawn,' Connery recollects, 'then through a milk round before school.' There followed the long, dull school day then, after a while – an almost unbelievable self-inflicted punishment for a sporty, freedom-loving boy – an evening shift as a butcher's helper. Effie, naturally, was proud of him. 'With two jobs he was bringing me home £3 a week,' she glowed, 'and that was before the war. He gave me every penny he earned and I banked savings for him.'

The main reason Tommy chose the milk round rested, truthfully, in a love for horses. 'He was horse daft in those days,' Effie recalled for the Scottish *Sunday Express* in 1964. 'Always taking my dusters to rub down the milk horse. And he loved driving the cart.' Connery's own memories broadly concur but over the years in varied interviews a barb of deeper insight has revealed itself. He told *Playboy* magazine: 'One's parents left one free to make one's own way. When I was nine my mother caught me smoking and she said, "Don't let your father find out, because if he does he'll beat you so hard he'll break your bottom." From the time I started working I always paid my share of the rent, and the attitude at home was the prevalent one in Scotland – you make your own bed and so you have to lie on it. I didn't ask for advice and I didn't get it. I had to make it on my own or not at all.' The implication, borne out in later interviews, was that Tommy was made aware early on that once he could stand, talk and read the duty of taking care of himself and his own life was fully in his own hands. There was only so much Joe could provide – good example and a relatively stable home –

after that Tommy had to find his own niche, and pay his way.

For a short time, for reasons unrecorded and unknown to Neil, Tommy transferred to Bruntsfield Primary School. Finally, at Tollcross, he sat the customary qualifying examination and was passed out. By now the war in Europe was raging, rationing was on and Joe was pursuing the tack he always guessed lay before him – working for Rolls-Royce in Glasgow, travelling home at weekends only. Tommy seems to have taken ominous warning from his father's experience and clenched his hold on his part-time jobs even though the obligatory two-year course of secondary education now lay before him. A contemporary of that time, Craigie Veitch, remembers facing the prospect of second-level, career-orientated education: 'Fountainbridge children had two main avenues open to them. Those who had the aptitude, or won scholarships as a result of their qualifying exams, went to Boroughmuir School. Boroughmuir had commercial ends in mind, and that's where people learnt languages, French and Italian, or economics. The second choice, the second best for many, was Darroch, a school that gave you a good basic technical education, where you learnt science and metalwork and craft. In some ways, I suppose, the measure of a man's learning capacity was which school he ended up in. Sean, of course, ended up – with me – at Darroch.'

Connery entered Darroch Secondary determined, by his own account, to fail. What is more likely, in perspective, is that his exhausting extra-curricular activities allowed him no chance to succeed. At any rate, John Brady says, he proved himself 'a fair scholar.' Craigie Veitch painted a compelling picture in an article he published in the Edinburgh *Evening News*:

A gaunt, grey building, Darroch was staffed by no-nonsense teachers with strong right arms, the better to belt you with, and attended by plus-12 girls in print dresses and rough-and-ready boys whose school uniform was a woolly pullover and short trousers with a shirt tail peeping through, topped off in winter with a balaclava helmet. Pop

Hendry, our English teacher, always insisted that the well-rounded man must be accurate in his spelling and he kept to hand a largish Chambers Dictionary which he would bounce on the head of any boy thick enough to think that seize was sieze. . .

We were versed in poetry too, but I cannot recall Connery ever being called to the front of the class to recite lines from three epic poems which happened to be in vogue in the Forties: *Splendour Falls on Castle Walls . . . A Wet Sheet and a Flowing Sea . . .* and something about a slave having a dream with his matted hair buried in sand. . .

There was nothing of the long-haired poet about schoolboy Connery. He was big and he was as hard as nails in an easy-going way and anyone at school who messed him about got a thick ear and a black eye; one torrid encounter, Connery v. Anderson, going the best part of 12 bloody rounds in the playground before the janitor and two teachers managed to break it up.

Though Neil asserts Tommy was inclined to be 'over-sensitive' in some regards, it is apparent he was also quite tough and ready for whatever trouble came his way – a by-product no doubt of his already well-developed physique and the fit agility forced on him by early-morning rising and, now, an evening newspaper round. Neil remembers Tommy had little sense of his own strength. He had, too, a precocious talent for melodrama. Once, unthinkingly, he squeezed the fancy glass handle of his parents' bedroom door so fiercely that it shattered in his grip. In shock, and a shade of black humour perhaps, Tommy danced round the room, screaming so shrilly that Joe was convinced he was clowning. When he calmed down and everyone saw the blood pouring from his hand, they were at last stirred to first-aid action. 'They had quite a job digging all the glass splinters out of him,' Neil says. Later there was a sledging accident in the snows of a particularly bad winter. Tommy hammered up a makeshift contraption in the walled back drying green and christened it 'The Coffin' in his typical wryly sardonic way. He crossed Tollcross to the Meadows, a huge public park half a mile from 176. The park was full of snowcrazed kids playing recklessly safe but Tommy wanted to test real risk. He found the steepest slope, padded up, mounted his rickety sledge and hurtled down. Flushed with success and the admiration of the weak-willed, he tried again. This time the inevitable mischance befell him. The sledge went out of control and thundered into a tree. Tommy met the bole head first, but recovered enough to fling the sledge on his back and stagger home. At first Effie noticed nothing wrong and raged at the boy for being late for tea. Then his pallor and unusual quietness took her attention. He claimed he was fine – fully cool – but when he went to the sink to wash up she noticed the blood spilling down the back of his neck. The injury in his skull, Neil says, was 'huge'. Joe was in Glasgow at the time, so Effie called on her next door neighbour for help. The neighbour ran to a telephone for an ambulance and Tommy, wide-eyed and stoical – underplaying his obvious condition dramatically – was rushed off to hospital. Thirty-two stitches in a jagged wound was Connery's reward for his casual daring. 'He was five days in hospital, ten days convalescent after that – and a day or two after he came home he was away again to the Meadows with that sledge,' Neil grins.

Whatever histrionic facility Connery developed during his early teens found plenty to feed on in Fountainbridge. As the spreading war effort injected life back into the factories that had been foundering, vacated stairs filled up again, dormant businesses awoke to churn out dirt, smoke and rowdy men. A neighbour who lived off Freer Street, down the road from the Connerys, says: 'Everything there was dominated by the smell, such a mixed blend. You had the sweetie factory, MacKay's, just fifty yards up from the Connerys, gushing out a sickly stuff; then the acrid rubber smell, then the yeasty smell from the brewery opposite . . . at times it was overpowering. Especially to newcomers. But people flocked in, looking for work. The men's lodging house in Grove Street did great business . . . and the bars did a bit too. There was plenty of drama, what with Saturday night rowing and all the rest.' Wherever immigrant workers – most Irish, some

English – came to swell the slums, trickster troubadors followed, begging for scraps. A noisy busker from no-where, weighed down with instruments he could barely coordinate was a favourite with the stair children. He would park outside the men's lodging house or Sammy's Ice Cream Parlour, right next door to 176, and rattle off free rubbish. A crooning drifter called, inevitably, 'Bing' was another Fountainbridge favourite. His repertoire in-cluded 'South of the Border down Texaco Way'. Bing's inability to remember five lines of any song, combined with his entrancing habit of muffling one ear, closing his eyes and singing into a bean can, inspired the children especially with pure joy. Asa Wass, a wizened Jew with a huckster shop of sorts in a close beside Freer Street, was a kind of children's – and adults' – hero. By dint of turning unneeded clothing and ornaments into hard cash, Asa won Fountainbridge's devotion. Asa was gruff but good with children and, on a few occasions, Tommy was des-patched with the booties of spring cleaning to make a deal. Sixpence for a cast-off jersey of Joe's was fair money and Tommy had exactly the kind of hulking inscrutability to clinch six when fivepence halfpenny might be more to Asa's thinking. Tommy was, by all accounts, a popular choice to be sent on bargaining errands.

Outside school, work and the distractions of Fountain-bridge drifters, Tommy's main and increasingly important interest was football. In an overpopulated district where space was at a premium, it was the most natural thing in the world that games which could comfortably accom-modate two twenty-man sides, with a ref thrown in, would reign paramount. Connery had the advantage of being genuinely, well, capable. He was also, apparently, sensible enough to recognise the advantages of the game's huge popularity. 'We didn't carry coshes or bicycle chains or knives,' he points out keenly, 'we spent all our energy on football. I was football mad. That's why I left school when I was thirteen, because they played rugger at the grammar school. I set out to fail the qualifying examina-tion, and I made it.'

There are varying stories about the abrupt conclusion

of Connery's scholastic stretch. The precise facts, as Craigie Veitch said, went 'down with the ship'. No school
rolls or records of Darroch for the period survive, probably
mercifully. The lingering, symbolically significant memory
of those who served with Connery in that unpretentious
throng is of morning assembly in the big hall. *Hail Darroch!*
was the school song, drilled out pitilessly every morning
at nine sharp. One line rang, 'Darroch ways are honest
ways' (ironic, Veitch suggests, because quite a few of their
numbers were residing in Borstal at the time). Connery
aired his lungs with enthusiasm on that song. 'He was
nothing as a scholar,' another Darroch boy claims, 'but he
was straight as the day's long.'

Survival, with the necessary hard work it entailed, was,
it seems, Tommy Connery's preoccupation. Schooling, he
judged, offered him no good rung on any worthwhile
ladder. Fitness and football on the other hand offered
benefits – if not in the direction of self-improvement and
success, then at least in terms of some fun.

Fun and freedom for Tommy were largely connected
with life away from Fountainbridge. In this, compara-
tively, he was privileged. Neil and Helen Maclean, the
grandparents, were in their sixties; worldwise, clever,
fun-loving people, utterly at ease with children and passionate in particular about their grandsons. Grandfather
Neil was a plasterer who rose to public works foreman
before retiring to a peaceful house in Gorgie, Edinburgh.
An open-air fanatic, Gorgie satisfied his needs only for a
short time. Upping roots, the Macleans moved to a country cottage north of Kirkcaldy, Fife, where they bred pigs
and kept chickens. It was to here, on summer holidays
during and after the war, the Connery youngsters came
and Tommy found a slice of heaven somewhat larger than
the biggie. The shock of pleasure he experienced on first
encountering 'wild' farm animals and wide open skies
would, Neil hints, have been worth witnessing. 'There
was no running water and we washed at the spring. First
thing each morning granny would give us a pitcher and
Sean and I would go down the road to the farm for milk
still fresh and warm from the cow. . . There was a pond

where we fished for tadpoles, newts and frogs . . . and a huge Clydesdale horse on the farm, a real whopper.' In contrast to jam-packed, airless Fountainbridge the country life idyll took on magical aspects. Here were the luxuries of real space and free time. There was room to kick a ball crazily, with no concern for close-ranked neighbours' windows, and time to idle, time to think. For Tommy, temporarily relieved of the responsibilities of wage-earning, the chance to play kid again was precious. In Fife he discovered things about himself that had been buried under the rush to grow up. He found he liked his own company, liked to indulge his fantasies about being a cowboy riding the range. The big Clydesdale horse came in useful, far better, *wilder*, than anything back at St Cuthbert's. It was possible to actually mount the Clydesdale and romp over prairie-like meadows – with never a fear of admonition. Day in, day out, almost as if freedom had no boundaries.

Neil Maclean was an inspiration too. He was big, tough, whisky-loving, a Scottish John Wayne who could lift the kitchen table single-handed and down raw eggs for breakfast without the blink of an eye. His purpose, in a nutshell, was to get the best out of life by living brave and uncompromisingly. Tommy spun boyish fantasies around him, and cherished them into adulthood. As late as 1963 he was blustering about 'this 86 year-old grandfather who drinks a bottle of Scotch a day, and he's in great shape because he always eats with it'. Neil Maclean's recipe for a long life, Connery claimed, centred on cold food, and plenty of alcohol. In a newspaper interview in 1964 the old man laughingly dismissed his grandson's remarks. Exercise, he insisted, was the secret of a healthy long life. Neil Connery remembers his grandfather's dying request: for 'a drop of the hard stuff'. Neil's greatest regret is that the request was never fulfilled; having checked with nursing staff at the Edinburgh Infirmary where the old man lay dying – at the age of 93 – Neil himself undertook to bring the whisky; by the time he arrived with the half-full bottle from behind the dresser in his grandfather's room, the old man was dead.

Most important of all, Fife threw fresh light on life in Fountainbridge. It represented the other, unexpected, side of the coin. An attainable alternative, a sweeter, cleaner life. All right, one might have to work fifty-odd years to achieve this fulfilling freedom. But it was remotely possible, Tommy supposed, that such freedom and retirement did not necessarily go hand-in-hand. Some way, some time, there might be a shortcut to Fife.

Tommy Connery, the slum kid, just might not be a Fountainbridger forever.

CHAPTER THREE

'It's as well he made it as an actor – he'd no' have made it as a milkman. . .'

DURING THE Second World War British cinema-going thrived. British film-making, which had hiccupped with the requisitioning of thirteen out of twenty-two studios and the call-up of two-thirds of its technicians, started an upswing. J. Arthur Rank, the future hero of the industry, started his meteoric rise in 1942 with his first major film, the morally starchy *The Great Mr Handel*, and within two years the dam had burst and production of entertainments as opposed to morale-boosting documentaries was flowing again. Annual audience attendances were steadily moving towards their 1946 all-time high of 1635 million. Though restrictions continued – film stock was in short supply, individual theatres played to limited hours, etc – an estimated 30 million cinema-goers were regularly entertained in some 5000 cinemas. In 1944 in Edinburgh, as across the country, they flocked to see Pressburger and Powell's cheeky *The Life and Death of Colonel Blimp*, Carol Reed's *The Way Ahead* and, among the swarm of irresistible Hollywood imports Billy Wilder's *Double Indemnity*.

Tommy Connery's main local cinema was called, romantically, the Blue Halls. It stood on the northern border of Fountainbridge and was known to the slum kids as the gaff. 'It was,' an old Fountainbridge boy recalls, 'everything flea-pits are cracked up to be.' The place was constantly the butt of spiky jokes, few requiring imaginative exaggeration. The standard blithe insult, well and truly meant, ran: you go to the gaff with a cardigan and come out with a jumper – jumpers being fleas. Tommy was not, perhaps, as movie-addicted as his father, but he liked the rainy Saturday afternoon at the gaff, watching a good Hitchcock – or maybe Ralph Richardson in Brian Desmond Hurst's *On the Night of the Fire*, a thriller. Admission often only cost a jam-jar or two but by the time Tommy was in charge of baby brother Neil the price had risen to 2d each. Both brothers enjoyed the serial adventures of *Flash Gordon* but Tommy, rich with his memories of Fife and his love for the old milk cart dobbins, had a particular fondness for westerns. Tough men living gritty, heel-kicking lives on the range – men like grandfather Neil – appealed to him. When he first breached the film business in the late fifties Connery expressed his desire to make westerns. He did eventually make the notable British western *Shalako* (1968) – a not altogether happy experience – but Neil for one is surprised that he has not tackled more. 'He never lost that early craze for westerns, which was tied up with his love for horses,' Neil says.

With Darroch ingloriously behind him, horses were playing a much larger part in Connery's life. Milk delivery work for the store became his full time occupation, horses a near obsession. For a time he was helper on Danny Fraser's dray – Connery fourteen, Fraser the senior at fifteen – then he was assigned his own route, the rounds of Cramond and Davidson's Mains, and his own cart. His horse was Tich, smallest of the several score at the store but fawned upon like none other. The restlessness that was to mark the later part of his teens might have been more evident now had it not been for the fact that Joe was out of work, having smashed a wrist and crushed his nose in a machinery accident in Glasgow. Effie was at work, charring in 'the rich houses quite a bit away from Fountainbridge', in John Brady's words, earning thirty shillings a week, but not managing to make ends meet. The pressure of supplementing the income to keep the family together fell squarely on young Tommy. He laboured like a Trojan during this time, handing £2. 10s to Effie every Thursday night, but still finding means, through his newspaper round, to maintain a personal Post Office

Savings account, building on the shillings Effie had banked for him during his schooldays.

The fashionable Fountainbridge vision of a working man's lot was the common one: a man simply works to live. Tommy Connery was unusual in that a part of his psyche could not accept that standard. Denied the perpetual bliss of Fife, his independent spirit demanded recompense. One sweated *to gain*, he decided. So, keeping the family was accepted for the trial it was – but conditionally. A hundred per cent work effort would be augmented by another ten, and in the end Tommy would walk away from his chores with a swag that would justify the effort. These 'spoils of war' were calculatedly decided upon, and in due course won. One Christmas, Neil remembers, Tommy canvassed for and earned the vast sum of £16 in tips. By the time he was sixteen, with Joe cautiously back to work after an eighteen-month lay-off – this time employed as van driver for Duncan's Removals of Gilmore Place – he had £75 to his name in the Post Office account. The noose of responsibility no longer tight round his throat, Connery mulled over the practical value of his wealth. £75 wouldn't buy him a smallholding in Fife or a horse and a stable of his own, but it might open a door out of Fountainbridge.

'What do you want to buy, son?' Joe asked as they faced each other across the dim-lit table in the butt-and-ben, young Connery poring over the yellowed savings booklet.

'A motor bike.'

'You're *not* getting a bike. Forget that.' Joe was adamant: he was suspicious, mistakenly, of Tommy's motives. Fountainbridge was full of pubescent punks, gangs like the Valdors, with their rust-rotted high-power bikes and tight-skirted tarts. Teenage warfare was rare, but from time to time it spilled in from tougher areas. On top of that, Joe was concerned about road accident risk, because of his own bitter experience. Tommy, he judged, was developing too fast. He was too big for his age, too bold, the bread-earner too early. It is possible, for that short time, Joe felt stifled by his elder son's precocity. At any rate, in Effie's words, he put down his foot and 'that was

34

that. No arguments. In those days you could tell a young-ster what to do.'

Tommy didn't brood too long over this impasse. He resumed his milk round, ambled down to the gaff and chewed it over. Within a couple of days he had resolved the matter to his own quirky liking: out of the blue a fine secondhand piano, all of £56. 10s worth, was delivered to 176. The neighbours were impressed and so was Effie, but Joe was nonplussed. Nobody in the stair could play the damned piano, least of all Tommy. 'I'll get lessons,' Tommy reassured them – but the likelihood of his finding time for study, everyone knew, was next to nonexistent. As it was, he was spending no more than an hour before every bedtime in the stair: from dawn till 3 in the after-noon was taken up with the milk round, early evening went on the newspaper deliveries, later in the evenings it was either back to the store to brush up Tich or across to the Meadows at Tollcross for properly organized foot-ball with Grove Vale Juveniles. Joe wanted the space-cramping piano to be removed at first, but Tommy in his cunning, obstinate way, resisted. *He* wanted some tangi-ble evidence of his cruelly strenuous work, some repre-sentative image that reached beyond grim monotone Fountainbridge. The piano idea, a friend today guesses, probably rose out of some saga of swish life Connery saw at the Blue Halls. Eventually Joe was appeased by Tom-my's snatches of seriousness. Every so often, just when family patience began to run out, Tommy would sit by the gleaming monstrosity and bash out a one-fingered *Bluebells of Scotland* or *Annie Laurie*. Effie was transported to ecstasy and Joe's savage breast, intermittently at least, was soothed. Never before, one suspects, was a bad piano played with such staggeringly sardonic – and brave – irony.

Though Connery had, in his own words, 'no sense of the future then', by early 1947 it was apparent to his friends that he would quit Fountainbridge within a short time. Among casual acquaintances there were boys who had worked as merchant navymen and others who had served with the Forces and, secretly, Connery had already decided his way out: he would not settle for half-measures – what had Glasgow given Joe but a few shillings accident compensation and a one-way ticket home? – instead he would cross the Firth of Forth, find a ship and sail abroad. It might seem fitting, in view of his later artistic development, to see this decision in terms of romantic idealism – the search for an easy perennial Fife – but earthier considerations weighed heavily too. As he neared seventeen and matured, the unacceptable aspects of Fountainbridge life became clearly identifiable to him. He wanted to run but 'it wasn't because of an unhappy home life. Quite the reverse. I suppose I felt that a hard job like my father's, or the milk round . . . would never let me use body and mind to the full. And I think anything less is a waste of a human being.'

The realities of the Connerys' poverty were suddenly manifest. Even in the face of hard work, minor luxuries were unknown. The family diet was as basic as could be: porridge, bread and potatoes, milk, Irish stews. Cakes were unknown, clothes almost always second-hand. In order to acquire money for football boots, or new laces for that matter, one had to stretch a twelve-hour working day to fourteen, thereby forging the old vicious circle: if one must toil so hard for the smallest freedoms – where lay everyman's due, the relaxed fulfilment of outgoing pleasures? At sixteen, for example, Tommy Connery was a big local hit with the girls – 'he did better than most of us, without trying', says John Brady – but the pressures on his time afforded him no more than a night a week 'scouting for talent'. The worst part of being poor and reaching teen age, Connery claims, was that: 'Life was completely governed by economics. You didn't leave the light on when you didn't actually need it because it cost money. You had to count up tram fares. You couldn't have a bath when you felt like it – there was the price of a plunge at the public baths to think of. I wanted to do something with my life. I wanted to have pride in it, feel the joy of it. There was far too little joy about.'

Effie herself was slightly restless in the stair now, speculating inwardly about the fortunes of those who had left during the ebb of the Depression and were, reputedly, finding all they dreamt of in less fettered environments. She began tossing round progressive ideas for Tommy, suggesting Edinburgh jobs – jobs beyond Fountainbridge – with better prospects. But Tommy's stock answer even to his mother whom, in his genuine devotion he hated to disappoint, was: 'Don't put me to a trade. Give me a chance to find out what I want.'

The milk round was a stopgap though the gruff and flinty Mr Marshall, the store's manager, would not have appreciated the knowledge of that. The beloved Tich was still Connery's bond with the store. Highlight of the year was entering Tich for the 'Best Horse & Cart' competition at the stables. Connery spent hours polishing the brass-work of the harness and plaiting tail and mane. For his troubles he received an embossed *Highly Commended* card, treasured and displayed in the stairs and at the Meadows till it fell apart.

Not everyone remembers Connery the milkman as an asset to the store. Today, as a division of Scottish Co-Op Dairies, St Cuthbert's stables have altered little in character or appearance. Where once there was 'near a hundred' horses for the carts, now there are seventeen. But a number of old faces from the forties remain. One roundsman, Jimmy, who has worked Rose-street, Silverknowes, Craigmillar and Corstorphine for as long as he can recall, knew Connery as a fitfully enthusiastic worker, not always 'using his brain'. An incident with a fully-laden dray in the heart of the city lingers with Jimmy. Connery had just commenced his round when, in a busy street, the bridle bit broke, rendering the harness control on the horse useless. Connery panicked and instead of improvising or summoning aid from passers-by he abandoned the cart and walked back to the store. Jimmy was appalled when he was informed that a full cart and lone horse had been deserted. Connery stood before him, helpless, hands in pockets, mouth agape. Jimmy was ordered to retrieve the dray immediately, and went running. Fortunately most of the contents of the crates were still intact. Looking back with a wry, humourless grin Jimmy reflects,

'It's as well he made it as an actor – he'd no' have made it as a milkman.'

John Brady was not surprised when the end of the dairy job loomed. 'Tommy *always* gave the impression he'd better things in store. I was serving my time as a painter-decorator. But Tommy had something extra, and he was kind of bursting with drive.' Excess energy was still mainly worked off with Grove Vale Juveniles or, later, Oxgangs Rovers. Tommy's style was improving all the time. He was strong and deceptively fast on his feet, an ideal forward player. He smoked a bit, drank a bit but was, says Brady, 'never the boozy type. Tommy's whole image was outdoorsy.' 'He ran everywhere,' says another friend, 'giving you the impression Fountainbridge was a training track, and he was limbering to get out.'

When finally he made the decisive move Connery did so in a characteristic gust of inflexible wilfulness – alone. He took a tram across the firth then made his way on foot to HMS Lochinvar at the naval shore base of South Queensferry and there filled out the recruitment forms. He signed for seven years active service, and a further five in the Volunteer Reserve. Returning home, he surprised his friends and this time shocked not Joe, but Effie. According to Neil, Effie was 'upset' by the suddenness of her son's action. Joe resigned himself quickly: the Forces kept a lad out of trouble; the navy was an honourable job, with adequate pay – not as good perhaps as the post office, where all the shrewdest lads tied down lifelong, pension-safe posts, but quite acceptable from every angle. Conceivably too, Joe was relieved that his biggest boy was properly and safely out of the way: now there would be more room in 176, the butt-and-ben need only house Neil; Joe would be the sole 'man about the house' again, his views unchallenged by wit or wiles. Effie's point of view was probably different. Tommy's departure spelt a smaller house purse, less financial input, less to save.

Connery sees his rush to the navy as an elementary case of escapism – and a mistake. The negative aspects of Fountainbridge were too great, he says, his ever-growing responsibilities unbearable. 'It was that kind of condition-

38

ing that led me to think, "Wow – the navy – abroad – China!" ' As it happened, he never saw China, indeed rarely roamed far from British coastal waters. Butlaw Camp, next door to Lochinvar, was his first unexciting port of call, where he began training. In rapid, undramatic succession he was trainee with a gunnery school, boy seaman member of an anti-aircraft squadron then able seaman assigned, Neil remembers, to HMS *Formidable* out of Portsmouth. From the start Connery was neither a very active nor interested seaman. Neil cannot recollect any postcards home from exotic ports, nor do his Fountainbridge mates recall much enthusing during the shore leaves. One casual friend says, 'He made no big deal about his uniform or anything like that and anyway, after the war there were uniforms galore in Fountainbridge. The Clanhouse Dancehall (next door to St Cuthbert's) was virtually a Forces' dancehall. . . Tommy gave the general impression that the navy was a dull job best not talked about.'

Portsmouth had its moments, though. With his wiry iron build Connery was nominated for and elected onto the navy boxing team. He fought a few battles, enjoyed the release of pent-up energies and earned a new muscle or two to match the bruises. He also awarded himself the basic naval honour – twin tattoos inked on his right forearm in a dockside dive. Both bellowed the mindless, conceited chauvinism of the young – *Scotland Forever* and *Mum & Dad* – yet hints of a sensitivity in his outlook at this time suggest a possible truer feeling.

Inside the space of a year rumbling stomach cramps became chronic localised duodenal discomfort. He was sent to see the M.O. and, after tests, hospitalized. The diagnosis was ulcers, the prognosis fine – provided stress and the regular mess diet was avoided. In a word, the M.O. was giving able-seaman Connery, aged 19, the passport to a premature pension.

Though he had been a Sea Cadet in his early teens, Connery is quite emphatic about his unsuitability for navy life. Within months of enlisting, he claims, he realized sourly he 'didn't have the equipment for the task. No scholastic training as such'. The ulcers, he believes, developed from 'the growing knowledge that the seafaring life wasn't all that one had fantasised it to be. I was a boy seaman, and there was an ordinary seaman above me, and if you reached his status there was a naval seaman and beyond that a leading seaman, and then a petty officer and a chief petty officer – and I was aware that I had not done enough to make this kind of progress.' The dilemma, this conflict between the dream of manly escape and the reality, caused the anxiety which led to nervous ulcers. Connery also by his own account resisted the navy's paternalist authority. For a time, he said, he had been 'conscious of keeping myself emotionally in check, never permitting an outburst'. The end result of such stringent emotional control put him in hospital for eight weeks (after which time the ulcers had, apparently, gone away) and back onto civvy street less than three years after he had signed up.

Back in Edinburgh he celebrated his discharge – and his 6s. 8d weekly disability pension – with a drink with friends at the Fountain Bar. John Brady says that he looked fine on discharge. Another acquaintance hints he looked too fine and mentions he was also 'a resourceful chappie'. The inference might be that, like so many other immature dreamers who sign their lives away to the colours and reserves, Connery's disillusionment inspired the ruse of an ulcer. But against this one must consider the fussiness and intelligence of Forces' medical personnel, and indeed the fact that ulcers seem to run in the Connery family. Both Joe and Neil suffered stomach complaints. And the actor Ian Bannen reckons Sean never really shook off that 'ulcer-ish uptightness'. Bannen observes Connery today in company of 'chit-chatting women or boring people' at parties – 'You can sense it flaring, this ulcer thing. Sean tightens up and you see it in his face. You just know he wants to be elsewhere.'

Elsewhere in 1949 was nowhere. Whatever the exact circumstances of his release from the navy it is evident that the man who returned to the stair was considerably different in temperament from the boy who left. Outwardly, to street pals like Michael O'Sullivan and Brady, he was the same humorous, tearaway Tommy, but privately he was, very seriously, at war with himself. No matter which way one interpreted his service record it was, in his eyes, a catalogue of failure. He had seen little travel, achieved nothing in rank and, despite his brawn, ended up with an invalid's discharge chit. He had not made any close friends and his options in terms of places to run to were nil. With a face of bravado that barely concealed wounded self-esteem, he reluctantly moved back into the butt-and-ben, squeezing back into Joe's territory and taking a shakedown bed opposite's Neil's settee. Effie did not need to hear the gossip along the stairs; she knew Tommy was desperately unhappy about his return. The navy had certainly helped hatch him into manhood, but the maturer Tommy was difficult, sharp-tongued and uneasy as a cornered cat. Joe was working on long-distance lorry runs, usually absent from the house from nine in the morning till nine at night, but the strain of cramped living and the heart-sickening gloom of near-poverty were unchanged. Without much fore-planning, Tommy decided to go back to work – tackling any job he could get, except the milk round; it was essential he retained some dignity, some sense of having *moved on.*

Effie was quick to inquire after and suggest jobs, but Tommy had decided a course in his own mind. He wanted breathing space, time to find a direction and work that would not commit him to a Fountainbridge existence. 'Give me room,' he implored. 'I'm going to keep on going from job to job till I find the right one – and the right money. I'm not going to be like Dad and work for sweeties all my life.'

By Christmas he had torn up his medical diet card and flung himself into a routine of physically gruelling, pointless, but reasonably well-paying jobs. He was a coal-delivery man for three weeks, a steelworker for eight, a corporation road worker, an any-hours odd-job man. There was, friends suggest, almost an element of self-humiliation about the fury of effort Connery applied to some of these jobs; there was, too, his usual contemptuous wryness; the navy debacle had not suppressed all his old spirit. 'Money was all that really concerned him,' a labourer acquaintance says. 'He didn't give two hoots about quality of work or anything else. He just wanted cash to splash on girls, to *do things* with.' His 20 per cent disability rating didn't slow him down. He worked plenty of overtime, netting a princely £10–£11 per week, 'splashing' on beer at the Fountain and, now, farther afield, up the glamorous West End, on girls. Navy life had taught him the facts of love and with his Latin louche looks he had no trouble pulling the girls he wanted. 'He had no strict preferences in girls,' says Brady laughingly, 'Tommy went for all women.'

The casual relationships with the opposite sex did not provide enough distraction though and, in his own words, Connery found himself 'dissatisfied with everything' within a year. Then, out of the blue, the British Legion came to the rescue. Founded in 1921 to lend assistance to ex-servicemen, the Legion was especially active in schemes to help the young disabled. Qualifying with his minor 'disability', Connery was granted a scholarship to a trade training course. 'You could become a tailor or a barber or a plasterer or a plumber,' Connery says, 'and I chose to be a French polisher. The whole training school practised on one another. You had to go and let some of them cut your hair, and others make suits for you.' Connery polished the ramshackle furniture of tenement Edinburgh, a lusty, energy-consuming task, before being landed in the Craighouse Gardens cabinet works of Jack Vinestock in the summer of 1951. He was taken on at £7 a week – a sizeable drop in earnings – but then, to Effie's thinking, he was learning a worthwhile trade. His hours were 8 till 5.30, five days a week, and the working conditions good. 'There was a staff of about sixty then,' Jack Jr., son of the company's founder, recounts, 'and a jolly atmosphere. We hadn't been allowed to manufacture household furniture during the war, of course, and by '51 the rush on utility stuff was finished. People were going in for a better grade of contemporary designs. We prided ourselves and worked to a high standard, and Tommy was an assistant, doing everything from dressers to ward-robes to coffins. He was a lively fellow who was tremen-dously popular with many of the workforce, but there wasn't a lot of time for fun-making because we were working fast and under some pressure.' Vinestock adds that he was 'very physical, and he laughed a lot . . . but he wasn't really a French polisher, he had no talent for it.' Co-workers William Strain and Johnny Wallis found him to be a relentless prankster and, as Wallis recalls, 'wild'.

Earlier it was easy to interpret Connery's unstoppable energy and wit as carefree wildness but now it was the open manifestation of his resentment at the trap that was Fountainbridge and his failure in the navy. He was never the most candid of people, and some of his friends found him at this stage unfathomable. He talked idly about great ambitions – intentions to travel the world, to go to Glas-gow, even to London. But his future, it was clear to Wallis and others, was entirely shapeless. One day it was specu-lation about the high life down south, the next he was railing against Vinestock wages and planning a resump-tion of road labour work.

Then John Hogg, an experienced cabinet-maker at the works, posed an idea which caught Connery's interest. It was coming near Christmas and the King's Theatre in Leven Street, that hallowed bastion of upper-crust enter-tainment, needed backstage help for the busy season. Hogg, now deceased, worked nights as a dresser and, naturally, enjoyed the pocketmoney as much as the smell of the greasepaint. As they sweated side-by-side over a high-gloss finish on a table bound for a rich man's home, Hogg told Connery about the easy money world of the theatre. He was, he said, quite sure he could secure for Connery the job as dresser-assistant. All that was necess-ary was an introduction to the stage manager. Connery had never been in a theatre in his life but the next evening after work he went along with Hogg to the King's and spoke to the manager. A few nights later he was back-stage, an employee, part of the theatrical group, looking after wardrobe and sets.

43

He enjoyed the atmosphere and the money in equal measure and for the few weeks of his engagement his wildness and recalcitrance were, in part anyway, tamed. Here at last he had found blood brothers, respected bohemians who lived by their wits, roamed endlessly, freely, and were, incredibly, related to the stout-hearted riders of the gaff range.

CHAPTER FOUR

A Scottish Arnold Schwarzenegger in South Pacific

'I DON'T KNOW when I first envisioned myself as a sort of muscle-boy, a Scottish Arnold Schwarzenegger, but it must have been in my mid-teens. Teenagers are very conscious of their bodies anyway, and the rugged jobs I'd held helped build up those muscles. . .'

Despite his well-moulded height – 6' 2" at eighteen – and beefy shoulders Tommy was, by Neil's reckoning, 'skinny' when he came out of the navy. He was also, after a period of readjustment to the tenement cage, socially hyperactive and aggressively girl-hungry. As a prominent football player he enjoyed the fan following for Fet-Lor Amateurs, the boys' club team sponsored by the wealthy patrons and former pupils of Fettes College and Loretto Public School in the old part of the city. In 1950 Fet-Lor's victory in a newspaper cup competition won him a medal and, more valuably, the adulation of a handful of free 'n' easy girl supporters. Later, having demonstrated a definite burgeoning flair that was at last being applauded as talent, he was voted into Bonnyrigg Rose, the junior league mining village team. Once again his speed and strength were noted, this time arousing the interest of the celebrated East Fife. Fife sent scouts to watch Connery play and offered him a £25 signing fee which he declined but which, friends surmise, jolted him into thinking about professional football as a possible escape route from Vinestock and the grind. 'The football business was always in the background,' John Brady says. 'Tommy was showing constant improvement as he got fitter and event-

45

ually Celtic gave him a trial. But something held him back, he didn't seem to want to latch to it as a career.'

By his own admission Connery turned seriously towards body-building 'to look good and get the girls'. 'Jimmy Laurie was the man he idolized,' says a Fet-Lor team mate. 'At the end of the Meadows there was a tin-shed place called the Dunedin Amateur Weight-Lifting Club and Jimmy was the star member. Jimmy himself was only 5' 6½", but he was built powerfully and he became a Mr Scotland. Jimmy became Tommy's coach and friend. He saw great potential in Tommy's independent determination.' Entrance to the club cost Connery 15s., and he wasn't about to throw that fortune away lightly. Once promised to Laurie's back-breaking course, he settled to a 3-night-a-week unshakable schedule, interrupting football training, girl-hunting and Vinestock overtime.

The records and accounts of Craighouse Cabinet Works were destroyed in the early eighties but a pervasive suspicion suggests that Connery got the sack. Vinestock is foggy about the details but Wallis, who had been called up for national service late in '51, says he would not have been surprised. Either way, Connery left Vinestock's in the spring of '52, took a 1d. tram ride down Princess Street and offered himself as a lifeguard at the huge Portobello pool, one of the largest salt water pools in Britain, just as the season started. A strong swimmer since Joe taught him at the Dalry Baths when he was five, Connery was a sound and conscientious guard, only ever distracted by the flattering attention of corset-suited sylphs. His physique, thanks to the dumb-bells and chest-expanders he had brought home to the stair, had improved massively. That hot summer, his friends swear, Connery caught 'more birds than any man deserves'.

Popularity at Bonnyrigg, Portobello pool, afternoon picnics at Gullane Beach, the dips and swells of complaisant girls seduced by a sailor's yarns and the ripple of tanned muscle. . . After countless years of grey clouds the silver lining was sparkling through. Those halcyon days reaped all sorts of unexpected bonuses. At the Dunedin club a former Mr Scotland, Archie Brennan, was encouraging Connery to take up competitive weight-lifting and model work; like Laurie, he believed Connery's fortune lay in his strength and swarthy looks. The navy pension-payers were offering a fat once-and-for-all settlement of £90 – taken, and spent on (at last, and without Joe's objection) a motorcycle. There was even a chance to earn good money, part-time, for doing . . . nothing. At the Edinburgh College of Art, posing only in a pouch g-string, Connery bagged 6s. 8d an hour, standing on a dais ('The girls always wanted to sketch me up close, it was embarrassing') and reclining on a bare-wood couch that had probably found its way from Vinestock's. Norfolk-based artist Martin MacKeown, now moderately successful, once studied at the college and cherishes hazy memories of the casual model. 'I can remember that I felt very sorry for him. He had a dead end job with no future while I was busy working to become a Great Artist. Well, look how wrong one can be. . .'

Best bonus of all, stumbled upon like everything else in a headlong venture to rebuild ego and find purpose to life, was a chance in the autumn to return to the stage – this time flexing muscles *in front of* the props. An advertisement in the Edinburgh *Evening News* attracted Connery to the poorly-paid vacancies of background 'spear-carriers' for the touring play *The Glorious Years*, due at the Empire Theatre in Nicolson Street (now gone) for a five-week run. Anna Neagle, first lady of British films who had hit starry heights with such bracing potboilers as *Nurse Edith Cavell* (1939) and *Piccadilly Incident* (1946), was the star, the production had been a major West End success and there was every reason to believe it would break records at the Empire. Connery applied for and got the job as a guardsman in a crowd scene, solely because of his height. The show was a hit – not that that affected Connery's career, or his pocket. Crowd parts do not exactly establish good or bad performers. But Connery got a kick out of roughing it with the other actors, and enjoyed the excitement of the make-believe, the audience expectation and the applause more than anything he had yet done. Overriding everything, of course, was the accepted transience of the whole thing – an aspect that brought back the joys of the King's at Christmas and impressed itself now very strongly on Connery. Here in the theatre there was no need to pretend allegiance in perpetuity. One accepted that the make-believe was part-time, tomorrow was another day, another problem perhaps but – most precious to so many actors – another town. Actors, it seemed to Connery, were imprisoned only by their temporary fantasy lives. Their nights were busy but their days were free, and their futures fantastically mysterious. For once in his museful analysis of a job's potential, money didn't come into it. The theatre was, simply, curious fun.

No efforts were made to persuade friends or lovers along to the Empire to watch the brief moments of public glory. 'To me it was just another of his casual jobs,' Brady says, 'he didn't talk about it any more than he talked about life-saving at the pool. It just happened, and a few weeks later it was over. Tommy was back playing billiards at the Lothian Hall, back exercising at his club.'

The kind of restless, moody stirrings that foretold his escape to the Royal Navy were not now evident, even though his days in Edinburgh were numbered. On the face of it he appeared to be contenting himself with a new weekly ritual divided between French polishing (the Portobello pool had closed for the season), working-out at the club, a bit of modelling and Saturday nights at the Palais de Danse, Fountainbridge's main dancehall. For a short time he was a bouncer at the hall, and for a long time the regular boyfriend of Isa Farmer, a well-brought-up girl from the Grass Market, behind Edinburgh Castle. Isa, a tiny dark-haired good-looker, was the only girl Connery ever took home to Effie, and there was serious talk of marriage but, because of the competition at the Palais and Connery's fast-roving eye, the affair petered out. 'The Palais de Danse was mecca at the weekends,' says Craigie Veitch. 'It had the finest, biggest floor in Scotland and regularly took upwards of two thousand people. On Friday and Saturday nights there was this tremendous, electric atmosphere – like everyone had struggled through

48

another hard week in the smoke and were now out to make the best of hard-earned money. Connery had developed into a fine hunk of a fellow, all shoulders, and he had this notable, trendy style of dress. He appeared to be doing well. He was making money and spending it on nifty clothes. The average get-up then was pretty awful – hacking jackets and what have you. Connery – or "Big Tam", as he was known by then – wore classy semi-drapes, slim-fitting single-button suits, and shiny shoes. He was an eye-catcher, and he had no shortage of dance partners, that's for certain.' His appetite for ever-changing partners – a blonde this week, a redhead next – was, others suggest, insatiable. But he carried on his affairs with discretion and a dignity that bordered on the freak in Fountainbridge terms. There were the gropings in alleys behind the sweetie factory and all the rest, of course, but he was not averse to meeting an elegant lady at Binn's Corner beneath the famous store clock, and taking her for a decent meal in reasonable surroundings, up in the posh West End.

'Money was no problem,' Brady says, 'because Tommy always found a way to boost his pocket. Around this time he was biking down to Vince Studios in Manchester – they published photo-magazines for musclemen. Tommy did modelling for them, and earned quite a bit. He'd drive down, do a session, then motor back the same day.' Next morning he'd be back in some small-time furniture-restorers, scrubbing away with sandpaper and oils, topping up his week's earnings. At home, the pressure of contributing heavily to the family purse was reduced. By now the family was living on the second floor, with a little more room in a broader butt-and-ben and Joe was finding overtime easier to cope with. Neil too was working, having graduated satisfactorily from Darroch. He was assistant to a plasterer, resolved to following the hero-grandfather Maclean after whom he had been named (Neil's full name is Neil Maclean Connery) into fulltime plastering.

With two happy and successful years behind him of recovery from the navy failure, Connery found himself in the winter of '52 primed for a change. *All* the uncompromising pluckiness that had been knocked from him during the first flight from Fountainbridge had returned. He felt good, looked good, had trustworthy friends in Jimmy Laurie, John Brady and others. Now more than ever he was ruthless about excising from his life anything that he disliked. A spell polishing for a coffin-maker depressed him. 'The boss was a remarkable man. He knew everyone and as soon as he heard that anyone was ill he would nip around and look them over as they lay weakly in bed. With his eye he measured them for the coffin. Then he'd come back and get us to make a coffin. Sometimes they cheated him and lived.' Connery 'retired' from coffin-making and took a heartier job, something more akin to Vinestock's, which he had enjoyed. He went to work in the printing-press room of the Edinburgh *Evening News*, becoming a greasy-faced, cloth-capped machine help – but winning Effie's beaming admiration. 'My lad works on the *News*.' The declaration had a fine, north-of-Fountainbridge ring to it, an apparent respectability to match the Post Office as a career. In her tirelessly optimistic mother-hen way Effie might have hoped the *News* would be the turning point in Tommy's life. There were plenty of cases of assiduous workers who built up from careers in the machine room to become reception, sales or editorial staff. Craigie Veitch himself worked up to sports editorial. But Connery, his new work mates learnt from the start, had no intention of pinning his colours to the *News* mast indefinitely. His staple conversational favourite, when the drone of the presses abated and seriousness crept into the chatter, was emigration.

It was Jimmy Laurie's initial practicality and not some pipe dream of promise that led Connery away from Fountainbridge for the second – and final – time. Laurie was many years Connery's senior but he shared much in common with his protégé. He was intelligent, ambitious beyond Fountainbridge, dedicated to fitness, and possessed a discerning eye. 'Jimmy Laurie wanted Tommy to try his luck in competition,' Brady says. 'Tommy was Dunedin's new star pupil, no question. When it came to discipline in training no one was like Tommy. And the training wasn't confined to the club.' As Connery saw the dividends of following Laurie's advice – at very least the value of rippling biceps when trying to impress the birds – he extended his work-outs. Ray Ellington, the popular bandleader, was another fitness fanatic. Every Traders' Holiday, when industry enjoyed its fortnight's summer let-off, Ellington's band graced the Palais stage. Tommy, who had always been popular and friendly with the management (which led to his bouncer's job), hit it off with the mercurial Ellington. Together, after Ellington's shows, the pair practised backstage. 'It was almost funny to see them, chalk and cheese, very dissimilar fellows but both obsessed by "toning up". Ellington brought equipment with him, and they shared the dumb-bells and weights.'

Connery had purchased a track suit too and ran regularly round the Meadows, regardless of weather conditions. Connery was 22, and Dunedin judged him to be near his athletic peak. After training one Friday Laurie put a proposal to Connery: each year a variety of 'body-beautiful' contests took place in London, most open to all comers from recognized health and fitness clubs; many were valueless indulgent exercises but one or two carried prestige; the Mr Universe contest, Laurie believed, meant something – contenders always received some press attention and winners took away more than gold medals. Connery, Laurie said, was ripe for a try. In his junior category he would romp home. The title would bring acclaim to the Dunedin Club and the ground-plan of a new, more meaningful career to Connery.

At first the suggestion seemed too preposterous to consider. Connery had met plenty of professional muscle-men, and most fitted quite a different physical mould: they were squat, 5' 10"ish, bull-necked and thick-fisted. In contrast, he had a lithe sinewy frame which, in the words of a girl friend, befitted 'a champion swimmer'. But Laurie's proposal was well timed. Connery *was* seriously contemplating emigration – or at any rate some major redesign of lifestyle. Most of his friends on the *News* and elsewhere still lived at home, cherishing ambitions perhaps, but wistfully, immaturely; Connery considered it mildly shameful that, in their twenties, these clever young men were still dependent on a family roof.

He mulled over Laurie's suggestion for a few days, then agreed. Excited, the pair revised the training schedules and set about making the arrangements for London.

Effie was unmoved. She saw the London venture as a bit of 'a joke', the natural extension of the boyish daftness of playing lifeguard at the baths or on Portobello beach. Jimmy Laurie anyway was sensible and reliable: he wouldn't lead Tommy into anything reckless. Neil scarcely turned a hair and Joe wasn't even present – he was away on a long-haul furniture run – when Tommy packed his solitary bag and left with Laurie for London. They planned to stay for a few weeks taking a bedsit, for convenience, in Chelsea.

The Mr Universe contest at the rundown Scala Theatre in West London was a near comic disappointment for Laurie and Connery. Laurie, according to friends, entered the competition too, but failed to win any placing. Connery was more fortunate. In his category he was third, winning a bronze. Laurie's disgust and embarrassment at the magnitude of their (relative) abject failure was mirrored by Connery. Years later he recalled bitterly, 'I did no good at all. The Americans always won those things. They were much bigger and everybody was impressed by the size of them. It was quite a disillusionment for me to meet them, because at the club I went to . . . we were all very health and strength conscious, and we used to run and swim and do many other things. But all the American and the London fellas seemed to be solely intent on acquiring inches and bulk. I was absolutely shattered to discover that somebody wouldn't run for a bus because he might lose some of his bulk. . . Just to be a bulky physique would be boring to me. Not to run, not to play football, not to swim – a cul-de-sac.' So Connery's gut response, the keenly honed sense of instinct that would serve him so well in his future career, had been right first time: he was *not* champion class in the unimaginatively standardized body-building stakes. Neither, he discovered, did he want to be. The fuss and 'glamour' of the occasion was fine, comfortably reminiscent of the Empire stage, but the passive meat-market mentality of so many of the contenders left him cold. Since he had settled down after the navy stir, Connery had developed and displayed a special fondness for a particular kind of casual acquaintance. He wasn't exactly your average star-struck stage door Johnny but, a close friend observes, 'he made no bones about the types he liked. Theatrical-type people, the nomads, the slightly way-out, if you like, appealed to him.' The friend vividly recalls Connery raising eyebrows back home by strutting into a popular uptown young people's meeting place, The West End Café, with a coloured girl on his arm. 'Her name was Maxine Daniels and she was a top singer up north at the time. She'd been appearing at the Empire and was, we reckoned, right outside our league. I suppose you could say there were conventions about the kind of people one socialized with – but Tommy didn't bother about them. And it wasn't only Maxine. He kept other acquaintanceships going with theatre people – not, we thought, for any special purpose, mind. Among his mates the general feeling was that Tommy, or Tammy as we still knew him, had a power of attraction that enabled him to make a better 'class' of friend. Glamorous women especially were drawn to him, theatrical women. And of course he enjoyed their attention.'

By extraordinary chance, the theatre offered itself to Connery again just as he and Laurie were running out of cash and readying themselves for a home journey. They had kicked around London for a couple of weeks, drowning their disappointment in good brown ale, taking in the sights. For Connery the pace was alien, the landscape familiar. Never a slouch, he was attracted to blustery Piccadilly and Charing Cross, the urgency of the crowds, the din of through-going important traffic. Nothing he had seen in the navy compared with London at full charge, seen from the inside. Here was the true, fantastic cosmopolis, of which the stage was a vibrant microcosm. Part of him wanted to stay, but the impracticable aspect of merely lingering on affronted his basically responsible nature. Back in Edinburgh the *News* was waiting for him – a job he bragged to friends as his 'best yet', albeit one that partially stifled him. The press attention Dunedin believed Connery might win had not happened but, at the very last minute, London yielded its real reward. Stanley Howlett, one of the Mr Universe entrants, detailed for Connery the side benefits of *his* weight-training: London's countless theatres were always looking for muscular, fair-looking fellows to heft svelte nymphs round or, at worst, shift props. Connery perked immediately: he had experience on both sides of the theatrical backcloth. The men got talking, got friendly. Howlett was currently one of the navy back-boys chanting Rogers and Hammerstein every night in the marathon classic *South Pacific*. 'Why not try it?' Howlett put forward. 'The show is winding down its West End run before going on tour, and they're looking for cast replacements. You have experience.'

'But I can't sing, or dance.'

'You've been in the navy,' Howlett chuckled.

Connery and Laurie bulldozed into the auditions for chorus parts at the Theatre Royal, Drury Lane. If there was hesitation in Connery about the negative factors of a long engagement in a London-and-touring job it centred only on losing out with Bonnyrigg Rose football team. Otherwise, Connery auditioned because, quite passionately, he wanted the job. Jerome White was the producer who oversaw the auditions, assessing in an afternoon some twenty-five hopefuls. Connery impressed him with a slick combination of toughness, conversational circumspection and shining self-confidence. 'Are you an actor?' the casting director boomed. Connery nodded from the splendidly ornate stage. 'And you sing?' Again Connery nodded. 'I've done plenty of rep in Scotland,' he lied boldly. 'Singing, dancing, you name it.' When it came to reading a test line or two of dialogue, Neil says, Connery's nerviness got the better of him. He dropped the pages of his script and heard the director call him clumsy. Enraged, Connery flung the script aside. He pounded towards the wings but was stopped in his tracks by White recalling him politely. 'Read again, please.' Connery composed himself, remembered the Empire, relaxed and rendered a half-dozen American-accented lines. 'I did the best I could,' says Connery. 'I more or less mouthed one of the songs from the show and did a few fancy steps that were a hangover from my ballroom dancing . . . not bad, I concluded as I left the stage, but obviously not professional enough for their demands.' Before dismissing him, White asked Connery a few questions about his physique and background.

Most aspirant hoofers and singers retired in shaky-kneed deference after this final exchange but Connery stalked forward and called over the footlights, 'What's the wage?'

Not at all amused, White barked back, 'It doesn't concern me.'

Po-faced, Connery retorted, 'But it concerns me.'

A whisper of concerned discussion ran through the production group in the stalls long after Connery's exit. But the consensus weighed in favour of his ability to reverse disaster. Two days after the audition a phone call came to the Chelsea bedsit informing Connery, 'OK, you got the part. You're in.' £12 per week was offered, and accepted. Laurie, unfortunately, had failed but they went out to celebrate anyway, then made a lightning trip back to Edinburgh to break the news. 'His phenomenal self-confidence was *the* quality,' a neighbour from 176 remembers. 'It was nothing ordinary. Maybe it stemmed from the girls who threw themselves at him, maybe that boosted him. But you got the impression he could choose or do *anything*.' Back at 176 Effie smiled to herself when Tommy expounded the significance of 'the break'. £12 a week for working a few hours nightly was money for jam! He would have his days off to do with as he pleased; he would read, educate himself, maybe get some useful part-time work. After London there would be a tour. There was even the possibility of further, better paid stage work. Howlett had stories. . . In her heart Effie knew Tommy was merely trying to sugar the pill: the simple truth was, he was done with Auld Reekie.

Neil vividly remembers Tommy's excitement on his return from London. Others shrug their shoulders: Big Tam liked money before anything, the chorus work was just rich light labour – sweetened by the ticket to a more permanent London. Connery himself surveys that first crucial toehold on an acting life with some self-mockery. Just before the triumphant Drury Lane run ended he joined the company but 'the whole idea of travelling round the country was what appealed to me. I didn't seriously consider myself as an actor . . . it all seemed like a giggle.'

If it started as a giggle, the humour died quickly. Jerry White was a man of great wit and generosity, but he was running in the shadow of fellow-countryman Joshua Logan who had hiked *South Pacific* to Broadway success, and he was determined to keep the quality comparison. For him the upcoming tour would be arduous and trying: there was no room for lazy amateurs or star-struck 'boys'. White needed to be surrounded by committed perfectionists.

After a short time Connery realized that *South Pacific* trundled forward by grace of its wonderfully conceived construction (a discovery, this: entertainments didn't just happen – they were lovingly sculpted), and authoritarian rule. The strict authority of the navy had not suited young Connery. White's methods did.

Back at the machine room of the Edinburgh *Evening News* there were those who patiently believed Big Tam would get his picture in the paper, earn a bob or two, and be back begging off the personnel manager by Christmas next year.

CHAPTER FIVE

Love in the Sticks

A CONVERSATION ABOUT Ibsen transformed Connery the odd-job man to Connery the actor. Robert Henderson, the American actor-director, remembers the occasion well:

'*South Pacific* was a quarter way through its long and extraordinarily successful tour. We'd just done Scotland and we were then in the middle of nine weeks at the Opera House in Manchester. Sean and I were in the same lodging house a bit away from the theatre and it just happened we walked home together one night. We were chatting and I mentioned Ibsen and Sean said, "Who's he?" So I told him – he's this famous modern dramatist, and all the rest. And I suggested he read a few of Ibsen's plays, thinking of course I'd hear nothing about it again. Those musclemen, you see, weren't employed for their brains. In the strict sense it wasn't chorus boys the show's management wanted, just capable big fellows for the "Dames" routine.'

The plays Henderson loaned Connery were *The Wild Duck*, *When We Dead Awake* and the classic *Hedda Gabler*. Connery read them, obviously with some difficulty here and there, but surprised Henderson by returning to discuss them intelligently. A voracious student of all theatre but (by his own admission) with no particular eye for new talent, Henderson was flattered and intrigued by the burst of avid interest displayed by the chatty 'muscleman'. Connery, in turn, was grateful for a sympathetic ear, most of all someone who was rooted in the milieu and knew his p's and q's. A considerable part of Connery's problem in comfortably settling into the show was his accent. 'In the beginning very few of the cast would speak to me,' he

57

said. 'For some reason they thought I was Polish!' The accent certainly jarred with Henderson – 'very awkward,' Henderson describes. 'I urged him to get rid of it, and he did soften it down.'

Edinburgh friends claim Connery has consciously preserved his rolling dialectal accent. 'There's a scene in *You Only Live Twice*,' an old neighbour says, 'where Sean and the girl (Mie Hama as Kissy) are about to climb the volcano slope. "We must get *up* there," Sean says. That small sentence, the stress on the demonstrative "up" – that's pure Fountainbridge. Get a Glaswegian, anyone, to say that and it'll be totally different. No doubts, Sean kept on being a Fountainbridger in that regard.' The director John Boorman recalls a dinner party where Connery was queried about his brogue – playing an Arab – in *The Wind and the Lion*. 'Sean's a wonderful mimic, but his response then was "If I didn't play in my normal voice I wouldn't know who the fuck I was." '

Speaking with Henderson today it is easy to imagine how Connery's enthusiasm was fired. Now 77, he still invests his every word with the love of theatre. He came to London in '47 to direct, graduated to musicals and won attention for fine performances in *Damn Yankees* and *West Side Story* in the late fifties and sixties. He is married to the celebrated character actress Estelle Winwood (who starred with Connery in *Darby O'Gill and the Little People*), and has the fondest memories of Connery, the chap who 'had Romany blood in him, he must have. The features, the eyes – it's there all right.' If Connery's matinée-idol features won over successive future talent scouts, his 'divine curiosity' captured Henderson's interest. 'It was quite remarkable. After Ibsen he wanted to know more and more, and he seemed deadly serious about it. So, with a twinkle in my eye I listed for him six books that were worth studying.' There was Proust's *Remembrances of Things Past*, *War and Peace*, James Joyce's *Ulysses* and *Finnegans Wake*, the Bernard Shaw-Ellen Terry letters and Thomas Wolfe's *Look Homeward, Angel*. Henderson considered the books 'a dry choice, but they led to endless channels that have been explored in the theatre. I wondered would he pursue them.'

Quite apart from Henderson's contribution, Connery was already showing signs of progress in his new job though, objectively, such progress probably had more to do with energy than ambition in career terms. On the tour's first visit to the King's Theatre in Edinburgh Connery was still hand-springing with 'the guys', blaring *There is Nothing Like a Dame!*, but he was understudying two reasonably important parts and his salary was up to £14. 10s. When Neil saw him during the first tour visit he found him to be 'as happy as I'd ever known him', and eager to prove his worth to the show. A fellow actor on the tour comments, 'It was jokey at the start and then, very quickly, he wanted to do well. He had a bit of a chip on his shoulder to my thinking and figured he could do as well as anyone out front. Early on I knew he'd stick with it, and try for a proper part.'

Among the men his own age – those who did not mistake him for a Pole – Connery was popular, though considered 'bloody independent'. He was a star player at the weekend poker sessions in damp-scarred lodging houses, cherished centre-forward with the cast football team and hoarder of rare Scottish jokes. His allegiances, it seems, were confused. 'He loved Scotland, sure,' one player says, 'but you get the impression he never wanted to live there again.' Most old Fountainbridge cronies lost touch around this time. 'He changed,' one recalls. 'In London there had been a blow-up with Jimmy Laurie. Something boyish and crazy. Let's say Tommy was a grafter and Jimmy got fed up with London work. So the flat they shared came unstuck, and Tommy hit the road. After that Tommy didn't want to look back, he just wanted to get himself on.'

Jerry White, Robert Henderson and the rest knew Connery only as Sean. The origin of the name-change reaches back to childhood. Connery had a primary school friend nicknamed 'Shane' and it is likely George Stevens's Oscar-winning film starring Alan Ladd, released in 1953 at about the time Connery restyled himself for Drury

Lane, influenced the final choice of a new name for a new career. Connery saw and admired the movie *Shane*, which, in the character of its lone-protector western hero, had much in common with Connery's cowboy *Shalako*.

Meanwhile, Connery's mode of transport was by 3 horse-power motorcycle, a post-war relic that reliably took him from town to town in the tracks of the tour party. The bike gave him a charge of power and freedom he enjoyed, and the chance to go for country spins, where he could flee alone to the great outdoors beyond the Manchester Opera House and contemplate *War and Peace*. Henderson's speculation about young Connery's earnestness came to an abrupt stop just a week after the 'dry book list' had been proposed. Connery was devouring Tolstoy and Proust – 'on loan from the library of course; he's Scottish, what else would you expect?' – with the help of a hefty dictionary.

Henderson's key snatch of advice came, coincidentally, on the eve of a momentous occurrence in Connery's football life. 'He looked basically like a lorry driver to me,' Henderson says. 'So I told him, "Tolstoy will lead you on to Dostoevsky and Stanislavsky and so on. Now I don't know a lot about these things but I have a feeling you could be a big star. I don't know about Britain, but you could be something in the States. Now, if you can talk Dostoevsky and look like a truck driver you've got it made. Speak one thing, look another. That's the essence of an artist." And Sean said, "yes, yes", like he meant it, as though he'd discovered gold.'

Next day Connery was on the football field, leading the *South Pacific* crew against a local junior team. Among the onlookers was Manchester United's manager and architect supreme, Matt Busby. The match was a raging, close-fought affair, with the *Pacific* team clutching victory in the last minutes. Busby was exhilarated, excited particularly by the aggressive determination of forward Connery. After the game in the changing shed he took Connery aside and offered him a place at Old Trafford. Connery asked for time to consider: he was stunned by the unexpected breakthrough and fully aware of its value. Fellow actors enviously patted his shoulder, sure in their hearts he would drop from the tour. That night, back at the lodging house after the show, Connery knocked on Henderson's door and explained Busby's offer. 'Don't take it,' Henderson advised, 'remember what we discussed. If you can take Tolstoy, and *take your time*, you'll make it in movies.'

Connery slept on it, and decided to decline. He rang United with the news and defiantly spread the word around the cast. When Jerry White heard he was appalled. Backstage at the Opera House he confronted Henderson, red-faced. 'Do you know what you've done?' he ranted. 'You've built up the kid's hopes with this talk about movie success. United were offering him something positive, the chance to earn bloody good money for a couple of years. In this business, he has no guarantees. He's a nobody, he might always be a nobody.'

Henderson was apologetic but showed no remorse. 'In the space of a few weeks,' he says, 'Sean proved his worth to me. Lots of young actors are dead keen to become a star. Lots of young actors are also dead lazy. Sean had a real insatiable desire to learn the business. Later, when people looked at the cool urbanity of Bond and the huge success they said, wow, that was easy for him. But, by God, it was sweat and tears all the way. I know. I saw it from the start.'

On stage Henderson, along with other major characters in the cast like Millicent Martin and Michael Medwin, were taken with Connery's calm aplomb. 'He had his qualms in daily life,' a fellow actor states, but once on stage, in Henderson's words, 'he hadn't a nerve in his body.' In many unscheduled incidents along the two-year run, Connery distinguished himself with sheer neck, often demonstrating that incompliant reluctance to accept the word 'failure'. Michael Medwin recalls the simulated night-time bomb attack sequence, where black-clad bit-part actors pranced on an unlit stage, invisible to the audience, but flashing flare lamps that burnt briefly bright, like ground gunfire, while in the background sound effects duplicated a noisy raid. On one occasion Connery, draped in black, leapt out to the wrong cue, slap in the middle of a tame, gentle scene. For a frantic second he hopped round, arms swirling with the flare torches, like some maniac on the loose. A gasp of shock rose from the audience. In mid-stride Connery realized, in sudden horrific silence, that his timing was wrong: he belonged backstage at the poker table, not here. He froze, dropped his torches by his side, grinned wide and ambled off. The audience breathed easy, and the show rumbled on.

About a year out on the tour, at the Brighton Hippodrome, Connery at last got elected onto the printed programme, taking over the part of Lieutenant Buzz Adams, originally created on the West End stage by Larry Hagman, later J.R. of *Dallas*, the record-breaking television show. A small-time Australian actor had been holding the part and when he quit Henderson led the group of principals in a deputation to demand Connery's promotion. Connery had been popular, now he had their respect: all the major actors in the production felt he had the strengths for a regular speaking part. Jerry White needed little persuasion. Connery became Lt. Adams and assumed responsibility for his first true acting scene. 'It wasn't a very big slice,' Henderson says, 'but it was important. I was playing Captain Brackett and Adams was to come to my hut and tell me about the marine landing on the Japanese islands. It was quite intense, I suppose, and Sean delivered it beautifully. From the first night he was flawless, not a bit scared by the onus of a speech.'

Connery's strength was Henderson's tutorage, most agree. The speak-one-thing-look-another trick became the staple of Connery's acting philosophy, utilized for the first time with Buzz Adams and never abandoned. Almost thirty years after *South Pacific* Fred Zinnemann pinpointed for me the 'special qualification' that made Connery right for the part of Douglas, the love-lorn mountaineer in *Five Days One Summer*: 'I wanted a man who could convey profound sensitivity, yet who could look capable of, and indeed partake in, the very physical feats required of him.' There was no comparison, Zinnemann made clear, with his other favourite hero, Gary

62

Cooper, who stylized the compassionate hero, though with some exotic magic.

'I was twenty-five years Sean's senior,' Henderson says, 'so I guess he regarded me as some sort of father figure on the road to a new life.' He hastens to add: 'But don't let anyone kid you. I didn't *discover* Sean. The gifts he had were there, I just encouraged him to let them show.'

Two women figured large in Connery's touring life: one he loved, the other adored him and, like Henderson, was convinced he was a budding international talent.

Carol Sopel, a gorgeous, gentle-souled young actress joined the company in the middle of the tour to take over the part of the Polynesian girl whose jolly number 'Happy Talk' was, from town to town, a show-stopper. Tsin Yu, the Eurasian actress, had held the role till then, but Carol's serene ingénue was imbued with near genius. A punctilious and charmingly serious actress, Carol was also 'great fun, and a favourite among the cast very quickly'. Her experience wasn't wide, but she was eager to cultivate the flair she had and, in that, found a soul-mate in Sean Connery. Connery fell in love with Carol in a matter of days and, though Robert Henderson stresses he involved himself hardly at all in Connery's private life, he was close enough to observe that, 'Sean felt deeply, deeply for Carol. They were the closest of friends.' Naturally the relationship intensified as the tour progressed, and Connery spent more and more of his free time with Carol. By now, to Henderson and Carol at least, he had confided his certain resolve to apply himself to an actor's life, for better or worse. At night in his lodgings he read into the small hours. By day he studied with the aid of a portable tape-recorder, practising speeches from Ibsen and Shaw, working on his accent. Whenever the tour hit a big town Connery and Carol went to 'anything else that was playing at the matinées. All the local reps in whatever plays they were doing.' Connery assimilated material very fast, displaying 'the quality of a sponge' – as though the cultural desert of Fountainbridge had wrung him and he needed to absorb nourishment quickly. Carol kept the pace and though Connery was – and is, according to

Honor Blackman and others – 'first and foremost a man's man', for several months through 1954–55 the couple became almost inseparable.

Eventually the subject of home-making reared its head, and Connery hinted to several members of the cast his intention to wed Carol. 'He wanted to marry her,' says one, 'of that there's no doubt. And as they grew closer eventual marriage became, we thought, inevitable. It was just a question of where and when.' Temperamentally, careerwise, in every way, Carol and Connery suited each other – but the cloud that darkened their lives from the day they first met finally descended and took the shape of the dreaded insurmountable hitch. Carol was Jewish, and her parents conservative and honour-bound. They might have liked their daughter's devoted inamorato, but tradition would not permit them even to consider allowing wedlock. Carol wrangled and begged but in the end conceded to her parents' wishes. Almost as suddenly as it had begun, the love affair with Carol was over. Connery was shattered, his closer male friends on the cast truly surprised. One actor says, 'They were compatible, they didn't ever argue, but when the break-up came it was blunt and final.' The conscience-searching agonies of the parents and Carol's wrench upset Connery greatly. When he visited Henderson to explain that Carol had broken it off he wept. 'You can't imagine it, I know,' says a colleague, 'but it was terribly sad to see this tough guy we've all come to see as ruthless James Bond so heartbroken.'

Consolation of a sort came from another girl Connery became friendly with during *Pacific* – Julie Hamilton, step-daughter of Labour Party leader Michael Foot. Julie was a 'Fleet-Streeter', a freelance photographer who often worked for the *Daily Mail* and whose favoured patch was theatreland. On a job assignment at the musical she met Connery and fell for him. 'Nice girl,' Ian Bannen says, 'but not a great photographer. She photographed me at the Old Vic in *The Iceman Cometh* . . . but for some damned reason it was always out of focus. I began to wonder was her eyesight impaired.' (Julie became romantically involved with Bannen after her break-up with Connery.)

Julie found Connery's striving, self-improvement obsession inescapably magnetic. She was young but well educated and impressively versed in the history of theatre. Connery's quest for knowledge, intensified somewhat as a compensatory measure after the break-up with Carol, led him to anyone who was prepared to share expertise and experience. In character Julie was Carol's absolute opposite – she was witty, fast-tongued, pushy – but Connery started to date her, and for a long while they got on famously. 'It was quite simple,' says Henderson, 'Julie wanted to help Sean's career.' Sean, for his part, wanted all the help he could get. With *South Pacific* nearing the end of almost a two-year tour, Connery recognized the watershed he was approaching. He could look back on a bumpy period of his life which had marked him emotionally, given him a real education, real fun and, above all, unscrambled his needs. The joys of the childhood freedom he cherished in Fife were distilled and crystallized in an acting life.

On the second tour visit to Edinburgh Effie had greeted a rowdy, happy bunch from the cast at 176: Tommy had brought them home to show them off, indifferent to whatever any thespian 'nob' thought of the rundown stair. Effie knew then Tommy had chosen a definite career at last. Even Joe learnt to encourage what to him appeared a wayward and distinctly odd profession. Tommy was truly, consistently happy, that was all that mattered. The one wee doubt for Effie, as for Tommy of course, was the future.

South Pacific ended in Dublin at the Gaiety Theatre and Connery toasted his success in a Liffeyside pub. In all he had understudied five parts, succeeded snugly with Buzz Adams and advanced further than any other 'muscleman'. He had a few pounds in the bank, and the loving support of Julie Hamilton. But the future, in work opportunity terms, was a colossal question mark. Henderson said goodbye to Connery to go on to *Damn Yankees* at the Coliseum. 'It looked like it was going to be lean for him, but he was decided to stay at it. We promised to keep in touch and I wished him luck.'

Back in London and out of work Connery moved into a one-room basement flat at 12 Shalcomb Street, off the King's Road – arranged by Henderson almost as a reward, friends say, for upholding the acting commitment. He signed on at Westminster Labour Exchange (£6 per week unemployment benefit) and, with Julie's prompting, commenced elocution lessons. Neil reckons his weekly outgoings were about £10 – so he was feeling the economic pinch within a matter of weeks. Various steps were taken to counter the crisis: his motorcycle was swapped for a lady's pedal-cycle, second-hand, costing £2; nightly entertainments – the odd booze-up, the cinema – were stopped; even daily food was rationed. Henderson remembers Connery keeping a pot on the stove 'day and night. It was a combination of porridge and stew . . . and I never touched it.'

Connery toured the major agents' offices, brashly proclaiming his talents – but achieved nothing. He tried the theatres, without luck, and came close to despairing when money ran dangerously low. Consolation came from other ex-*Pacific* out-of-workers and from Julie; the tireless voice of encouragement from phone calls to Henderson. 'He never let any of us know if anything was wrong,' Neil wrote later in the Scottish *Sunday Express*. 'Even when he was ill and in bed for something like three weeks with a soaring temperature we knew nothing about it until months afterwards. And only then because one of his friends happened to mention it.'

Just when the lowest ebb was reached and the situation seemed untenable, Henderson swooped back to the rescue. Assigned as director to 'that exquisite Agatha Christie play' *Witness for the Prosecution*, at the Kew Theatre, Henderson phoned Connery and offered him the very minor (non-speaking) court usher part. Connery jumped at the £6-weekly fee, and stayed on the dole. Any murmuring doubts that lingered in Henderson's head about Connery's maturity for 'major' stage playing were silenced by an incidental event which almost escaped the director's notice. Rehearsals were fine, the unstarry cast competent. Connery's part involved nothing more than shifting documents of evidence from one side of the stage to the other. Then the first night came. 'Sean was your average usher,' Henderson recalls, 'wearing this full black cloak. My concentration was on the main players obviously but then it was brought to my attention that Sean's movement across the stage was, well, too eye-catching. He had this way of walking, a great, elaborate stride that swished the cloak all over the place. . . It looked absolutely great, *he* looked great – but after a performance or two I had to take the cloak off him. He was just diverting attention too much. It was all in that *walk*.' (Five years later Harry Saltzman was to claim his main reason for alotting the Bond role to Connery was the actor's walk; Cubby Broccoli later said, 'Only one other actor moves like him, and that's Albert Finney.')

At Kew over a patchy period – 'I was out of work for seven months' – Connery found further parts in the popular plays *Point of Departure* and *A Witch in Time*. The fruits of the elocution training are arguable, but everyone who encountered Connery around this time recollects what Henderson calls 'his beautifully perfect figure'. Ian Bannen's very first meeting with Connery was in the foyer of the Kew Theatre. 'I was appearing in an Anouilh play and Sean was waiting to see the director, hoping to land a part. My memory of him is as a towering, huge fellow with hair everywhere – all over his cheeks, huge eyebrows like a squirrel's tail, the lot. He looked formidable, like some sort of gangster. I felt I wouldn't have liked to meet him down some alley.'

The director Lewis Gilbert, who directed Connery's wife-to-be Diane Cilento in *The Admirable Crichton* (1957) and was later to reshape the Bond series with *You Only Live Twice* (1967), recalls early meetings with the struggling actor: 'I can't say there was anything striking about him, no sense that he would one day be a superstar. But he was good-looking, and he had a build that made you look twice.' Michael Caine who became friendly with Connery in the late fifties puts a different perspective on Gilbert's comments: 'In my eye, Sean had it from the word go. You must remember that Lewis was viewing him then from a different level. Lewis was working with established great stars, people like Kenny More and Virginia McKenna. He was very successful and operating on a different plane from most of us. It's significant that he took any note of Sean. Sean, to me, had charisma. He looked great, had a great line in chat and, well, look at the way he was built!'

An abhorrence of idleness and a sustained burst of job-hunting in the middle of 1956 broke the ice with decent, if secondary, speaking roles on stage – and paved the path for a first, lukewarm incursion into television. Part-time rep work at Kew led to offers to appear at Oxford as Pentheus opposite Yvonne Mitchell's Agave in *The Bacchae*, and with Jill Bennett in Eugene O'Neill's *Anna Christie*, a play which, in its revival on television some 12 months later, was to assume a special significance in Connery's life. TV parts were found in *The Condemned* and *Epitaph* at the BBC, and as a smalltime hood (serving Bannen's fantasy fears) in an episode of *Dixon of Dock Green*. A BBC floor assistant recalls Connery's 'awe' when rehearsing this early live TV but the pleasant surprise was a singular adroit gracefulness of movement that had him zipping round cluttered sets in no danger of toppling trickily balanced arc lights. No one 'discovered' Connery during this jerky run: critical reviews scarcely mentioned him and the only press coverage worth bragging about was a rather banal interview about the '*South Pacific* star' in a home-town paper. Connery didn't mind, though Julie Hamilton probably did. For Connery, the actor Robert Hardy says, 'the joy was always the work'. During the Oxford run of *The Bacchae* Connery was pleased to boast about 'driving back to London late every night to rehearse *The Square Ring* for TV in the daytime, and then driving all through Saturday night to play football for the Showbusiness team on Sunday. I didn't feel I was being done out of free time. I was enjoying myself. I believe a lot of people would enjoy themselves going hard at it if they had the kind of work they liked and created the kind of surroundings they could respond to.'

By the end of 1956 Connery was in no doubt that he had found exactly the kind of work he liked. But he was less sure of Julie who, in the words of a colleague, had learnt 'the knack of making a nuisance' of herself in Connery's company. The lean time at the beginning of the year had taught Connery a lesson about showbiz that crowned the advice Henderson had given and sketched a very clear pattern for future survival: very little about showbusiness was 'a giggle'; one must study and one must toil, and one must scrimp and beg and push. Such effort required *all* one's energy. Connery had an advantage over others in tilting at success. He had the spiritual strength derived from fighting the swamp of Fountainbridge, and the physical stamina acquired on building sites. If he could merge his strengths and *push*, he might grow to live out Henderson's dream. But a wife, or a live-in lover, provided distraction and presented problems. Connery had great respect for Julie but, Henderson believes, she began to make demands he found difficult to cope with.

In the spring of '57 Connery was doing well enough in theatre and bit-part TV to discharge himself from the dole queue. An agent had even been secured, in person of the zesty young Richard Hatton, then making a good name for himself with the television companies. Connery was building up a few pounds' savings again and signs were good for a new suit or two, maybe even a new motorbike, by summer.

At the BBC, Canadian producer Alvin Rakoff was in pre-production on an American play, Rod Serling's *Requiem for a Heavyweight*, scheduled for live transmission from Studio D of the new Wood Lane Television Centre at 8.30 pm on March 31st. A variety of top name artistes had been considered for the lead part (boxer Freddie Mills's name was mentioned) before Rakoff settled on Jack Palance, the craggy American star who had featured in the American version on TV and had had a monster hit with the movie, *The Big Knife*, a year before. Ten days before transmission, three before rehearsals, Palance's agents cabled the BBC to cry off: a Hollywood engagement would delay the star, there was nothing they could do. Rakoff grabbed the casting directory and rushed into conference with his assistant Kay Fraser and Drama Chief Michael Barry. With rehearsals set for Monday, March 25th, Rakoff drew up a list of three major actors he thought would fit the bill. He saw each on the Friday, and had not decided on the Saturday morning when, on his way to the BBC, his girlfriend Jacqueline Hill (who starred in the play, and later became his wife) mentioned Connery's name.

Rakoff had used Connery already, employing him for some three small parts in *The Condemned* the previous year. Connery had originally been assigned one bit-part, that of a soldier, but he was 'so full of ideas, so keen', Rakoff recalls, that his function was extended. On location at Dover Castle Rakoff gave him the part of a soldier who throws a grenade . . . and the bandit who receives it! Later, for studio taping in London, Connery took another role. Rakoff had not been particularly impressed by Connery and asked Jacqueline why she thought he might suit. Jacqueline was to be the 'love interest' in *Requiem* and she replied chirpily, jokingly, that 'every woman would like to watch Connery'. Rakoff went to his office and pondered. He tossed the idea out and received a generally positive response. People remembered the Scotsman who had been 'interesting' in *Dixon* and had just won himself a little part (with Richard Hatton's help) in a little movie called *No Road Back*.

Rakoff decided to interview Connery.

CHAPTER SIX

Heavyweight Success

IN THE SUMMER of '56 Connery had earned his first few
days on a film set, auditioned and employed by second-
feature writer-director Montgomery Tully to play near-
silent stooge to Alfie Bass' unfortunate villain in *No Road
Back.** Korda's old assistant Steven Pallos's Gibraltar Pictures understood exactly the market they were feeding:
rattish gangland thrillers facelifted by the appearance of
a 'name' American star – in this case Skip Homeier – were
always popular Bs, no matter how improbable the story
or incompetent the cast. In this case Tully's task was made
immeasurably easier by a reasonably original storyline
(even a credible sub-plot love story) and the crack performances of Margaret Rawlings and Canadian Paul
Carpenter.

No Road Back went on circuit release belatedly and was
guaranteed oblivion by its rigorous adherence to current
convention in conception, style and promotion. Connery
understood that fully, as did everyone else involved. For
Alfie Bass, the movie was just another exercise in thriller
playing; but for Connery it was a memorable first – the
break into the rarefied acting life, the cinema, where
everything was Big Screen, Big Stars, Big Glamour. 'I
doubt if Sean was paid much,' says Bass, 'because a system was popular then whereby studio chiefs giving breaks
to newcomers smartly drummed down fees. I'd suffered
that myself a few years before when I was contracted to

---

*Connery is known to have done some film 'extra' work, appearing in
crowd scenes during location shooting. A crowd part in *Lilacs in the
Spring* (1954) was his first before-the-cameras performance.

Sidney Box. It was very nice and above board, but by the time all sorts of considerations were out of the way one was coming out with pennies. The interesting thing about Sean, though, was his intelligence. We had a lot in common; my background was, in a roundabout way, in cabinet-making too, so we could talk shop easily. At Pinewood, where the film was shot in about six weeks, we shared a dressing-room. Sean liked to natter and it came clear nothing less than *making it* was on. He had great ambitions. And talent. He was competent, he never forgot a line.' Emphasising the impact the eager newcomer had on the movie-weary veteran, Bass elaborates: 'How able was Connery then? Let me say this. I'm known as the shrewdest git in the business. And I would have happily become his agent.' Connery was relaxed and comfortable on the movie set and, instantly, he saw it as some sort of terminus. The stage, TV – they were fine, bristling with challenge. But the movie world was the pinnacle. Stage stars belonged to the toffee-nosed of Edinburgh's West End: movie stars were for Fountainbridge, for everyone. Connery also liked to observe the fuss around Homeier and Carpenter, the big cars at the studio, the smell of wealth wafting from others' dressing-rooms. At the same time, he wasn't so success-obsessed as to be impervious to the side-show offerings. Bass remembers 'one thing everyone knew about Sean very soon: he wasn't queer.' A couple of days after he started on the film he was befriending young starlets and production assistants. Inevitably, he was asking Bass to vacate the dressing-room at the convenient time. 'He wanted to entertain some bird,' says Bass. 'And a half-hour was all he needed.'

Toronto-born Alvin Rakoff, later to emerge as one of TV's preeminent directors of the Sixties, had one major credit behind him in the National TV award-winning *Waiting for Gillian* (1955) when he set out to tackle *Requiem for a Heavyweight* in 1957. A thrusting, sure-footed young director, he had a reputation for taking chances and whipping up irrevocable fast decisions, a course which did not exactly endear him to some BBC lords but which, whether

72

they liked it or not, produced the results. He had not seen Connery's debut in *No Road Back* but knew his TV work. In pondering Connery at first, the actor's build and potentially-dangerous appearance appealed to Rakoff. Later, when they met again for the first time since *The Condemned*, Rakoff was struck by the actor's new confidence. Rakoff was left in no doubt of Connery's ambitions, nor of the basic intelligence which dressed itself in showy, half-educated patter. He liked Connery and cast him, after readings, as the main character in *Requiem*, Mountain McClintock. The significance of Rakoff's risk in taking Connery, especially in light of its repercussions for the actor, is easy to miss. In 1957 the BBC was carefully pioneering refined TV drama, with the newly-formed ITA shambling far behind. 'Format' drama, with its Punch-and-Judy casualness was quite established, but the focus of art in the new technology fixed principally on the two 90-minute slots the BBC gave every week to major works. For a long time the technology of film-making became an obsession: on one hand whenever technically 'abstract' productions were attempted, they inclined towards eye-boggling gimmickry; on the other, elements filched from voguish neo-realist European cinema became achingly boring in their regularity. When techniques failed, as they did again and again, the tendency among perplexedly bemused programme-makers was to run for safety. New writers with new ideas were tossed aside, innovative directors promptly harnessed. In 1957 *The Times* noted that both the BBC and ITA 'seeming to despair of obtaining new plays of any value, are relying on alternative sources. For their serious productions the independent networks tend to mount adaptations of established stage works. The BBC do this rather less often; they regularly present dramatised novels and, having discovered the Victorian idiom to be apt for television, return to it again and again.'

Some writers resisted the fail-safe Victorian 'atmosphere' plays and soldiered along the edge of rejection, among them in Britain Elaine Morgan and Iain MacCormick and in America (where things were not much better)

Paddy Chayefsky and Rod Serling. These writers acknowledged Chayefsky's theory that 'television drama cannot expand in breadth, so it must expand in depth' and that TV writers should concentrate on intimate dramas – 'intimate meaning minutely detailed studies of small moments of life'. Morgan, Serling and the others kept their cherished ideal alive in their plays and passed the problems – technical and commercial – squarely over to the producer/directors. Some balked at the dangers of trying out their audience, others stirred. In undertaking Serling's *Requiem for a Heavyweight*, Rakoff knew he had a difficult production on his hands – an even-paced tragedy about a fallen boxing star that made no concessions to glossy entertainment but could easily become maudlin if handled badly. There was nothing to be gained and everything to lose in 'livening up the production' with slick camerawork and fast scene changes, so Rakoff grew to believe success depended on the workings of a close-knit, true-to-life acting team; the callous old manager (George Margo) must have cunning in his face and manners, the thick-ear boxer, Connery, must move, look and sound like a down-and-out with hopes. Rakoff created *Requiem* in his casting. His on-the-night direction was minimal, but brilliantly understated even at that.

At rehearsals on the Saturday afternoon and Sunday (from 11.00 am onwards) everyone felt a quality production was on the cards. Warren Mitchell and Fred Johnson as trainer and ring doctor were powerfully good and Connery's relaxation was quite remarkable. He was not intimidated by the centrality of his role, or the huge amount of lines, nor did he seem in any way conscious of his mistakes. He blundered and was corrected: it was as simply professional as that. Rakoff was more sure than ever he had talent; others considered him a bit slow, too raw. Michael Barry, the much-liked Drama Chief, watched on rehearsal and was frankly disappointed; he didn't think Connery 'had it'. 'Far as I was concerned,' says Rakoff, 'what he didn't have could be fixed by clever camerawork, switching from one camera to the other at the right time and so on.'

There were no hitches or tantrums – then the big night came. Rakoff was in his control box, readying himself for transmission time, with the actors simmering on the floor. Just seconds before 8.30 a gaggle of grey-suited BBC men stormed in, led by Michael Barry. 'They looked like Mafia,' Rakoff recounts, 'and I didn't know what the hell was going on. I asked Michael, but he hushed me and before we knew it we were rolling, the show was on.' Everything cruised smoothly: 'I missed only one shot, and that was where Fred Johnson was stitching some of Sean's facial cuts. I wanted a close up, but Fred's hands were shaking so bad I couldn't do it. The pressures of live TV took their toll on everyone.' Halfway through the ninety-minute play Rakoff found a quiet time to whisper the question again to Michael Barry: what were the grim-faced BBC execs doing scattered round the studio? Barry explained tensely: studio electricians were threatening strike action and there were fears the plugs would be, literally, pulled. The junior executives had agreed to stand by to 'push the plugs back in. Half the nation was watching us. The show *had to* go on.'

At home in Fountainbridge Joe, Effie, Neil and a neighbour friend from down the hall, Mrs Pearson, watched on Joe's new 17" TV set. It was the first time any of the family had seen Tommy on screen. Neil, an impressionable eighteen-year-old, drank in every growling syllable of the drama and, he says, Effie was moved close to tears. When the play ended Joe seemed lost for words. The best he could manage was, 'By heavens, that was smashing.'

Viewers across the country and critics, it soon emerged, unanimously agreed with Joe's assessment. BBC Drama received appreciative letters and the top journals afforded broad space to Connery's performance. As Mountain McClintock Connery portrayed the unbeaten hero of 111 fights who, because of eye damage, is ordered out of boxing for good. A manager desperately hounded by creditors tries to trade on his name by urging him into show wrestling, finally humiliating the fallen fighter and losing his loyalty by asking him to appear as a clown wearing a coonskin cap. J. C. Trewin in *The Listener* slavishly, mockingly, recorded the dialogue's propensity towards repetition. 'At first I thought I might take the count ignominiously in the first minute,' he wrote. But those who, like him, hung in 'were grateful for . . . the oddly wistful performance of Sean Connery as the man who was once almost heavyweight champion of the world . . . too modest, too bewildered, and too naturally kind to be a connoisseur of the cauliflower ear.' Trewin was less kind to Serling: 'This is neither a fragrant little play nor a tribute to the noble art. . . But its producer, Alvin Rakoff, let it have every chance, and the dramatist ought to go down on his knees to Sean Connery.'

In the *Evening Standard* the Boulting brothers lavished praise on Rakoff, Connery, the concept. *The Times*, outrageously, thought Connery 'physically miscast as the fighter', but praised 'a shambling and inarticulate charm that almost made the love affair (with Jacqueline Hill) credible.' Six months later *The Times* was still warmly recalling *Requiem*. In an article about the problems plaguing modern TV drama Iain McCormick pointed a finger of blame at English acting. Stage actors, he claimed, lacked the capacity to underplay correctly for TV. 'This,' *The Times* rambled on, 'is overstated; the recent BBC production of Mr Rod Serling's *Requiem for a Heavyweight*, to take only one example, displayed ensemble acting of precisely the type Mr McCormick recommends.'

Before leaving Television Centre on that wet Sunday night Connery knew he had pulled off a fine coup: he did not need Julie or any of his friends to tell him. Rakoff was pleased – 'but drained, as everyone was after such a complicated, multi-set live play' – and the small technical crew impressed enough to extend genuine congratulations. The usual post-transmission knees-up took place in the nearby Black Prince pub but that night, because everyone was dizzy with excitement, a small party in one of the dressing-rooms sufficed. 'Then,' Rakoff says, 'everybody went off into the night and caught their bus. It was the norm to take a long lie-in the following morning, to recover. I remember I didn't come alive till midday, then I bussed back to the Beeb. I read the evening papers with the glowing tributes on the bus. Later on, Sean phoned me with a thanks.'

The Monday review in *The Times*, just one of the countless ultra-positive responses, highlighted one noteworthy aspect: *Requiem* had differed from the usual Serling/Chayefsky in that the central character was 'intrinsically dramatic'. Rakoff agreed, and his real achievement with the production lay in casting Connery who, in the ignorance of his inexperience, interpreted 'intrinsically dramatic' as heroic, mimicking every muscular dab he had seen at the Blue Halls, and overlaid the whole with a smattering of the intellectual whimsy Henderson had pushed on him. In *Requiem* Connery unknowingly struck the golden vein that would eventually lead to his colossal success as James Bond. McClintock was a kind of juvenile, socially bankrupt Bond, and his memory lingered on and on in people's minds.

At the one-room flat in Brondesbury Villas, Kilburn – probably arranged by Julie – where Connery was now living, celebrations after *Requiem* were no grander than a hot stew – Connery's favourite meal: with lots of tomato flavouring – and a glass of beer. The pay cheque for the play was £25, but that was to represent the tip of the iceberg in terms of material pay-off. The very day after transmission, according to Connery, the film companies shuddered into wakefulness. 'Not unusual,' says Rakoff. 'British films, though they didn't realize it then, were giving their dying gasps. Movie people watched TV and culled whatever of quality they could from it. I knew what the direction of Sean's career after *Requiem* would be, I told Richard [Hatton] so.' Rank were the first on the phone to Hatton, suggesting a long-term contract. Connery impulsively passed the message along that he would 'think it over': terms were vague and complex and by now, balancing what he had learnt from co-workers like Alfie Bass, he was wary of involved contracts. There were a few independent inquiries, up-and-coming producers with their own companies – and, best of all, the international major, 20th Century-Fox, then moving well enough, made overtures. But Connery hedged. Already, as a result of *No Road Back*, he had had engagements for two other movies at Pinewood and Beaconsfield, both bit-parts. So there was no urgent need to dash into any contractual trap. Connery suddenly wanted breathing space, time to meditate and orientate himself. At Brondesbury Villas the people he shared the house with recorded his cool and mature reaction to the exciting shock waves of *Requiem*. No one was perturbed when he took time off to go home, with Julie, to Edinburgh.

At this key time in his career, when choosing the right avenue to take caused much suppressed concern, Julie's demands overreached. In Fountainbridge he introduced her happily, but the confrontation that others observed to be brewing developed quickly in what must have been, for Julie too, an unusually strained environment. Neil recalled that the incident that ended the love affair concerned the Scottish 'masculine prerogative' – a jar in the local pub. The family was gathered round the fire in the butt-and-ben, with Julie chatting to Effie, when Connery silently gestured to Neil his desire for a drink. Both brothers slipped quietly away, crossed to the Fountain Bar and ordered their pints. 'We had no longer settled ourselves with a drink apiece,' Neil said, 'than Sean's girlfriend put in an appearance.' Julie was insulted at being left behind and let Connery know it. There was a row and 'that did it . . . that was another of Sean's romances that died the death.'

To most, it seems, Connery and Julie outgrew each other. Over the year-and-a-half of their friendship, as they drew closer so they recognized the facets of each other's lives that did not match their needs. If there was any anger or sense of failure at the break-up, it was tepid regret. They parted, and Julie went back to the thriving London life and Connery to his chances.

Connery's second movie role, in Cy Endfield's *Hell Drivers*, at Pinewood, gave him no chance to shine, though the film was above average in every way. The prolific and action-minded writer John Kruse, who later went on to inject such vitality into the TV *Saint* series – and feed Leslie Charteris some ideas – devised the simple story of a road haulage company whose crooked manager forces aggressive competition on its lorry-driving staff to the point where personality conflicts flare and murderous emotions grow. Connery played Johnny, one of a half-dozen loud-mouthed blackguard drivers who race along death-trap roads. Connery had no more than ten lines, mostly thrown over Sidney James's (as another driver) shoulder, but he looked convincing in scenes where he could easily have half-tried – particularly his longest scene, where the truckers enjoy a boisterous night off at a dance-café and an all-out fist-fight, with Connery to the fore, breaks out.

Rank distributed *Hell Drivers* through the Gaumont chain of cinemas and, while it played to moderately good business, it failed to win the kind of recognition director Endfield had hoped for. Within the production business, the film was admired for its racy pace and good photography by Geoffrey Unsworth, a cinematographer bound for glory with classics like *2001: A Space Odyssey* (1969). Chastened but not deterred by his first major in Britain (he had directed second-features in America), Endfield went on to a few slicker and more generally successful films, notably *Zulu* (1963), considering *Hell Drivers* to have been an excellent market gauge that pointed him away from gritty thrillers.

Side-by-side with Endfield's film, Connery did a few hours on *Time Lock* for the Gerald Thomas-Peter Rogers director/producer team, then just months away from *Carry On Sergeant* and the beginning of the outstandingly popular comedy series which would, in its quiet way, be the only consistent rival to Bond during the sixties. Made at Beaconsfield Studios, *Time Lock* concerned the nail-biting attempts to rescue a six-year-old boy accidentally trapped in a Canadian bank vault with a time-device lock set to spring days hence, after the weekend holiday. Connery was last on the cast credits, appearing as '2nd Welder', his smallest film part to date, and his screen impact was negligible. But *Time Lock* was a good vehicle, and association with it helped.

Before *Hell Drivers* or *Time Lock* had made their appearance in the late summer of '57 Connery had hammered out a contract deal, under Hatton's guidance, with 20th Century-Fox. The bind was long-term but Connery had reason to be optimistic: Fox, above most, held a fearless high profile in international production and had ambitious projects on the go in Britain and the States throughout '57; Connery had no reason to believe they would do anything other than use him – and promote him hard, to get return for their meaty investment. And the Fox investment was considerable. By '58, Ian Bannen reckons, Connery was 'taking in £120 a week from that contract, but he was doing nothing . . . in today's terms you're talking about a contract actor sitting back and taking in, say, a thousand a week.' At Brondesbury Villas and among his small circle of not-too-intimate friends Connery's initial reaction to the Fox signing was described as 'silent delight'. His landlady recalled, 'Any other actor would have been delirious at the sudden upsurge in his fortunes, but not Sean. He took the whole thing very calmly. He did not even celebrate.'

The silent delight hinged on sudden wealth: Connery did not advertise it loudly but his professional friends were aware of the deep satisfaction triggered by real financial security at last. Counter to that, however, was a troubling awareness which seemed to blossom very swiftly that Fox, in spite of their outlay, in spite of *Requiem* and all the bit-part work, were not about to fling their neophyte 'star' into any star dressing-rooms. There were a few interviews, an audition or two with important directors, even talk of detailing Connery opposite Ingrid Bergman in *The Inn of the Sixth Happiness*, a part given eventually to Curt Jurgens. Connery was disgruntled. He wanted to work, he wanted to prove himself, even *try* himself. It was then, he complained, he suffered his 'Too' period. 'For a while I was too big, or too square . . . whatever. I just couldn't fit the parts they wanted to fill.' One part he did fit: director Terence Young was casting *Action of the Tiger* for fledgling producer Kenneth Harper's company, to be released through MGM. Through contacts Connery offered himself for a role and was given the part of Mike, a dishevelled ship's mate whose most taxing pitch is a pass at sexy Martine Carol. Connery travelled to Southern Spain for brief shooting in the early part of summer.

The story was, at least, geographically ambitious. Van Johnson played Carson, a philanthrophic mercenary, persuaded by Carol to help her sneak her political prisoner brother out of Communist Albania. Johnson fumbles through a tangled skein of misadventures before finally escaping to Greece with Tracy (Carol), the brother and a string of refugee children in tow. Young made a game effort at direction but the screenplay was never right and Johnson coasted as though wearily anticipating the kind of critical stick the humdrum aspects of the yarn would give rise to. The best parts of *Action of the Tiger* revolved around the displaced children and feckless bandits; indeed some of the very minor playing was exemplary. But, as so many reviewers were to note, the cinema had not quite got to grips with the Cold War and efforts like these to tell political parables usually foundered in caricature. In an important sense, though, *Action* is interesting as an extravagant, if not necessarily original, cinematic blueprint of anti-Communist 'entertainment' propaganda. In the spirit of détente the later James Bond movies, from *You Only Live Twice* onwards, veered away from contentious East-West relations but the early films, especially *From Russia With Love* and, more circumspectly, *Goldfinger*, based themselves on the Cold War tensions and fears. In this regard, *Action of the Tiger* is a distant cousin of Bond – a dry run, if you like, at spiked political thrillers.

To director Terence Young's thinking, he had personally botched the movie. Never a man to show his weaknesses on set, he kept a brave face while filming and was perhaps the most excitedly animated creature within a mile of the location. Privately he expressed his doubts and later, in many interviews, he unabashedly confessed it had been 'a pretty awful film'.

Connery, meanwhile, displayed his complete (and understandable) lack of discernment in movie matters by suggesting to friends and others his belief that he was onto something good. Alvin Rakoff, on reflection, is not at all surprised by this: Connery, in his eye, was 'rough-hewn, with scant understanding of how the industry operates'. As the film neared completion Connery approached Young, speculating on the likely success of the movie. The role had been his biggest so far for cinema and he clearly had confused visions of another *Requiem*-like hit. 'Sean equated the foreign locations, big stars (Johnson was the highest-paid performer he had yet worked with), and the recognized director with success,' says a colleague. 'He definitely considered this movie to be important.' Young was sympathetic towards the actor's naive expectations. 'He came to me and said in that very Scots accent of his, "Sir, am I going to be a success in this?" ' Aware already that he had irredeemably 'mucked it up', Young was blunt: 'No,' he told Connery, 'but keep on swimming. Just keep at it and I'll make it up to you.'

Young was to remember his promise four years later when two visionary producers arrived on his doorstep with what they considered a viable project. It was the film script of *Dr No*, which they wanted him to direct.

CHAPTER SEVEN

Another Place Called Hollywood

THE 'GLAMOUR' OF success that interested Connery in a secondary side-line kind of way became a very palpable reality in the middle of '57 when Lana Turner walked into his life. The Sweater Queen of MGM had just been fired after eighteen years with the studio and her career was nosediving. Paramount, never one to miss a bargain, picked her up cheaply and found the ideal vehicle for her, a fire-and-ice love drama that embraced both her sophisticated acting style and her reputation as a man-eater. Turner's love life was, to say the least, checkered. Her five marriages were incident-filled, her romances – with Fernando Lamas, Sinatra, Howard Hughes, gangster Mickey Cohen – legendary. Tyrone Power, it was known, was her truest love but Lana's thirst for varied male company was unquenchable. In the spring of '57, after the break-up of her marriage to 'Tarzan' Lex Barker, Johnny Stompanato, formerly Cohen's bodyguard, entered her life. Stompanato, according to writer-director Kenneth Anger, had been in big demand from certain prominent film ladies on account of his own 'prominent endowment which had earned him the sobriquet "Oscar".' Stompanato was a harsh and arrogant lover but Turner, it was widely reported, craved excitement and wasn't averse to being knocked a round a bit: she had been thrown downstairs by one husband, struck in public by another, drenched in champagne at Ciro's by another. Stompanato's toughness satisfied her needs and when they separated for her trip to Britain to make the Paramount movie, *Another Time, Another Place,* her love letters home reportedly made explicit her yearnings for his rough treatment.

83

Though Fox were profiting nicely with films like *The King and I* and the seemingly endless Monroe money-spinners, no one had yet come up with a suitable niche for their beefy new contract player, Connery. 'One of his main problems,' a Fox associate recalls, 'was that damned accent. Sometimes it seemed tolerable, but when he speeded up, like all Scotsmen, you couldn't interpret the babble.' Hatton and Connery kept the pressure up and finally Connery was auditioned for the Paramount picture. Turner had co-star approval and she watched Connery's test, and liked him. In build and looks, many noted, Connery and Stompanato were not a million miles apart. Fox made the formal settlement for the loan to Paramount and Connery had his first major Big Screen part, in an incredible stroke of luck, friends thought, featuring opposite and making love to a Hollywood goddess.

Turner's initial response to Connery personally was favourable, though it was reported he had caused her some embarrassment by picking her up for an early social date on his motor-scooter, clad 'in T-shirt and slacks while she was in formal fur and jewels. It was something of an embarrassment . . . but they got into her car, or at least one she'd managed to commandeer, and things went along all right.' Rumours circulated very fast that romance was in the air. Unquestionably Connery did date Turner and told friends he liked her and her professional advice was helpful. At that time there was no special woman in his life, but distraction was provided by the small mews house in North London he had bought and was beginning to renovate, and by the nightmare atmosphere on the set at MGM's Borehamwood Studio. 'The script was not entirely satisfactory,' Connery says, 'and they were rewriting as they were shooting. So they started with the end first, and I was dead at the end . . . so by the time they led up to me I was a picture on the piano. The picture wasn't very good. It was beautifully lit by Jack Hildyard, but dreadfully directed by Lewis Allen.'

In fairness, Allen was working with a tricky story – a movie that divided neatly in two, the unbalanced halves seeming to belong to different genres. Connery had fourth billing, playing Mark, the dashing BBC war correspondent who seduces American newspaperwoman Sara Scott (Turner) in London in 1944. Their brief affair is passionate, then Mark is killed flying to Rome to cover the German surrender in Italy. Devastated by the news, Sara is hospitalized and on her release makes a pilgrimage to Mark's hometown in Cornwall. Pursued by her devoted boss (Barry Sullivan), she evades him and makes friends with a Cornish woman (Glynis Johns) whom she discovers to be Mark's wife. The shock of discovery that Mark was married and has a son, and Sara's attempt to share the wife's memories and grief make up the latter part of the movie – a turgid, at times exhausting 50-odd minutes. In contrast, the first half – where Connery hides behind sandbags reporting unexploded buzz-bombs and wriggles in and out of bed-like couches with Turner – is nimble and, with Sidney James's American-accented roguery pointing up the nonsense, fun to watch. Taking into account the chronology of shooting, it seems Allen perked up as he went along. Then again, the chemistry between Turner and Connery (who vanishes entirely after the first half-hour) might be the secret. At any rate, taken as a whole, the film is neither *Peyton Place* (1958) nor *Imitation of Life* (1959) – both Turner hits-to-come – though it vacillates between the types.

As shooting advanced and Connery's friendship with Turner deepened, out of the blue Stompanato arrived in Britain. Turner fixed a house for him in west London but friction swiftly burned between them. More than once Stompanato arrived unannounced at MGM studios, frequently insisting on overseeing the love scenes between Connery and his co-star, to the obvious chagrin of Allen and Turner. 'It doesn't take imagination to understand Stompanato's rage,' a technician comments. 'He'd been in Hollywood and around film people long enough to know when make-believe is make-believe. But he knew Sean and Lana were getting too close for comfort.' Old friends of Connery's broadly hint that the friendship bloomed to impassioned affair: Tommy had Hollywood incarnate in his arms and he did with it what he did most effortlessly – he made love. His intention wasn't the chilly calculation of making a friend and looking for a nepotistic leg-up, rather the idea of proving something to himself; rough-hewn and all as he may still appear, he was capable of slotting sweetly into the star world. He could cope with the work hassles, and the intellectual demands – and he could cope with the capital egos too. Kenneth Anger in his *Hollywood Babylon* suggests that Stompanato outranked Connery in giving Turner the kind of treatment she wanted. He pushed her hard, warning her, 'When I say HOP, you'll hop! When I say JUMP, you'll jump! I'll mutilate you, I'll hurt you so you'll have to hide forever.' Anger describes Stompanato's arrival on the set, brandishing a gun, ordering Connery to 'stay away from Lana'. 'Connery decked him,' says Anger and the studio, with a little help from Scotland Yard, had Stompanato put out of England.

Though Connery was still fond of Turner – 'a lovely lady,' he remembered her twenty years later – he was relieved when the film ended and she flew to Mexico for a reunion with the gangster boyfriend. The publicity he had gained while co-starring was welcome but he was personally unhappy with the movie. His professional associates had told him this was the *key* film, the one that would get wide distribution in the US and could make his name overnight, but he knew before he saw the release print that everyone had, in the words of a technician, 'blown it'. 'Sean is not a patient man when it comes to incompetence or stupidity,' says director Richard Lester – and, in the case of *Another Time, Another Place* he was annoyed that rich potential had been crippled. The script, Turner, possibly Connery himself in his•newness to star playing, were contributive factors, but Lewis Allen took the brunt of Connery's blame.

At Wavel Mews in North London where Connery had his new home – a spacious three-room affair above a huge garage that he later converted into a sitting-room – he defused his disappointments by embarking once again on a strenuous get-fit programme. It served a dual purpose: it helped work off the needling frustration and it reminded him of home, of adolescent pleasures from a life that seemed rosier from afar. Ian Bannen was close as anyone to Connery during this period and, while he too was into weight-training, he saw himself as 'a total amateur' compared with Connery. 'He had all the equipment, the weights and expanders and bars, and he was deadly earnest about it. I spent quite a bit of time at the house, very ordered and pleasant it was – that was Sean's way, he liked things tidy – but sometimes it was like a gym!' Despite his sizable weekly earnings from Fox and his admiration for the movie glamour-world, Connery still favoured a style of living that was not far from frugality. 'He went around on this motorbike,' says Bannen, 'which remains in my memory only because he was always falling off. Didn't seem he could go down a bloody road without hitting some tree or something.' He ate simply too, confining his lavish sprees – which in themselves were never extreme – to occasional weekend binges. Michael Caine, whom Connery had met for the first time on *Requiem*, where Caine was a walk-on extra, was himself struggling during '57–'58, with only 10th billing on the limp *How To Murder a Rich Uncle* (1957) to boast about. 'It was hard and worrying obviously,' Caine says, 'but Sean never showed any weakness. He had a star temperament, he knew what he was about.'

During the decidedly grim time of *Another Time, Another Place* Connery did not despair because, in his own simple explanation, 'I was eating regularly.' Others from cosier backgrounds might have vented alarm, but Connery, outwardly anyway, kept his cool. He had had two big non-starter flops so, to rekindle his sense of purpose, he turned back to beavering at television. His most exceptional part came in August '57 in the ATV Playhouse production of the Pulitzer Prize-winning *Anna Christie*, the explosive O'Neill play that had fared so well at the Oxford Playhouse (and other venues) the year before. The role of the prostitute struggling for redemption, haunted by the sea, was given by producer Philip Saville to a Big Screen actress, relatively new to TV but very able, the ash-blonde Diane Cilento. Connery portrayed her lover. A taxing and wordy play, *Anna Christie* required extensive rehearsal to establish the proper rapport between the major characters. Since Connery had the upper hand of familiarity with the work, he suggested to Cilento they rehearse after hours, in their free time. Cilento was married to Italian writer Andre Volpe and had a baby daughter Giovanna, but the couple's living arrangements were loose – friends suggest they were on the point of separation even then. So Connery was invited to Cilento's flat, where work commenced.

Two more different people, socially and academically, it would be difficult to find – and yet, temperamentally they had a lot in common. Cilento was from the top of the social ladder, a 24-year-old multi-linguist whose deep love was for writing. Her Italian-born father, Raphael Cilento, settled in Queensland, Australia, since long before Diane was born, had been honoured with a knighthood for his services to medicine; Lady Caroline, her mother, possessed a bright artistic flair and was herself by profession a physician. Diane's early life in Queensland was one of luxury, but at fifteen a gypsy spirit akin to Connery's led her to New York where she started drama studies. Later, studying at RADA in London she rejected her parents support allowances and earned her own way working in a wine shop and, for a spell, at a circus. Her first film part was in 1952, four years later she was high on the billing working with director Lewis Gilbert, and by the time she met Connery she was being described in the popular press, rather mindlessly, as 'a high IQ sex kitten'. Robert Henderson remembers her as 'a tough, independent little cookie'. Her crusty core, combined with fierce single-mindedness, appealed to Connery and he later admitted that, from the beginning, 'she swept me off my feet.'

Initially Cilento's reaction to Connery was unexciting. Quite apart from the shadows of her marital ties she found him a jagged-edged personality, too free with a lashing critical tongue and, beyond the passionate range of the character he was depicting, a shade heartless. 'My first opinion of him,' she said, 'was that he had a terrific chip on his shoulder. He'd come to my place and stretch out on the floor. I felt he was trying to see if he could make me angry, so I purposely didn't react. Finally I realized he had no ulterior motives, that he was just being himself.' An actor friend who knew both paints a different picture: 'Maybe he didn't admit it to himself, and he could be stubborn, so that wouldn't surprise me – but Sean was in awe of assured actors and actresses. Lana, Diane – he saw them as some sort of challenge to his ego as women. They were the best any man could get, so he wanted them for that reason. But, as well, there was this need to assert *his* talents against theirs. In those circumstances Diane considered him to be overweening.'

But Cilento thawed, and a close friendship sprung out of *Anna Christie*. Artistically the play was a success, not exactly *Requiem* league but certainly, to Connery's mind, the best thing he had done in half a year. He was pepped up, not only by the quality of the results but also by the nature of this new relationship. Cilento, he told colleagues, was like no one he had yet met in the business. In effect, he was saying she treated him – as she did – with the kind of respect he believed was an artist's due; raw and all as most considered him, she, the experienced movie actress, had relied heavily on his support during the play. He was flattered, but enthralled too by her manifest competence, her self-possession, her iridescent intelligence. They dined together, and enjoyed a few social evenings and she encouraged him to talk about his fears and ambitions within the business. 'Diane was his first real confidant in the industry,' the actor friend says. 'Up till then, with the exception of Hatton, he kept troubles to himself.'

Cilento pushed Connery towards formal dramatic training with a cautious generosity that aroused no suspicions. He enrolled, alongside her, in Yat Malmgeren's 'movement' school – an extraordinarily pointless exercise, Robert Henderson believed, because, 'even from *South Pacific* days Sean's grace in movement was amazingly good.' Malmgeren, a Swede, was not an actor but former dancer in the Kurt Jooss Ballet Company. 'He taught the study of action – attitudes and drives,' Connery said. 'It was based on the concepts of time and motion evolved by the Hungarian dancer Rudolf von Laban. . . I used to go there three times a week, doing theory. We learnt a cohesive terminology that applied to the whole group, so that there was no problem of communication as there so often is with expressions that mean one thing to one person and another to somebody else. It was a remarkable period for me. It proved that with the proper exercises you can reshape your physical structure. Nothing like the weight-lifting exercises I'd done, but attacking yourself from within, from the head through to the base of the spine – to awaken yourself physically, completely, so that you become a much better tuned instrument.'

Under Cilento's influence he read more widely, extending himself to the fullest with Stanislavsky and the Shakespeare he hadn't covered during the last touring months of *South Pacific*. For a time, with friends, the tone of his conversations changed: he became 'heavyweight' and seemed to disdain the philistinism that attended commercial movie-making. There was nothing pretentious about this apparent 'new Sean'. On the contrary, having suffered disillusionment in his first run of movies, he was sensibly reassessing the requirements of theatre and arty TV, the media he was, conceivably, best suited for.

Early in '58 he concentrated his energies on renovating his home and resumed small theatre work, but the bitterness of cramped opportunity returned. Fox's cash was nice, but there seemed something indecent about earning ten times what Joe was pulling back home, for doing no more than sitting by a phone. Then, out of the gloom, there was sudden sunshine. A casting crew from Walt Disney studios in Hollywood touring the British Isles in preparation for a major feature saw his Paramount movie, auditioned him and, with Fox's blessing, offered a contract for *Darby O'Gill and the Little People*, to commence shooting at the Burbank Disney Studios in May.

Connery was ecstatic. Stanislavsky wasn't forgotten, but for the moment he was pushed aside. Robert Henderson recalls: 'I was appearing at the Coliseum in *Damn*

Yankees and I wanted to see *Madame Butterfly*, a new production of the opera, which was opening at Covent Garden. I couldn't get along at night, so I was given permission to attend dress rehearsal in the afternoon. I'd just arrived when a phone call came through to the box office and it was Sean saying, "Robert, I've got to see you right away. I've been offered the chance to go to Hollywood for a Disney and I want to know I'm doing the right thing." I told him a Disney movie was good for anyone, and I suggested he come right over to the theatre if he wanted a chat so desperately. About a half-hour later he arrived and I came out to the lobby just as the marvellous first act climax was on. . . We had our talk and he decided himself happily on taking the Disney offer.' Even in his heady glee, Henderson reflects, Connery showed that 'specialness', the divine curiosity that distinguished him from the bunch. Overhearing the strains of *Madame Butterfly* as they discussed Hollywood, Connery suddenly asked, 'What's that?' 'Well, that's the next step to becoming a powerful actor,' Henderson replied. 'That's grand opera, Sean. You're earning a little money now. So why don't you buy a ticket and go see some, learn about it?' Connery did, to Henderson's eternal joy. 'Soon,' Henderson says, 'he was able to tell *me* about Maria Callas and the whole business. That encapsulated Sean's attitude. He didn't just want to make it big in Hollywood or wherever – he wanted to learn too, he wanted to be big *and* good.'

While Connery was packing his bags for Hollywood and preparing to hand over his house to Ian Bannen for the duration, *Another Time, Another Place* opened, inevitably, to terrible notices. British papers revelled in the fiercest criticism, tagging it melodramatic, confected, unreal rubbish played 'without style or enthusiasm' (*Monthly Film Bulletin*). By the time it opened in America Turner was in trouble. On April 4th 1958 Cheryl, fourteen-year-old daughter of Lana and inbetween husband Steve Crane, fatally stabbed Stompanato, having eavesdropped a furious row in which the gangster seriously threatened to 'cut up' Turner. Cheryl was charged and brought to trial, with Turner as a defence witness. As it turned out, a jury which retired for only twenty minutes pardoned Cheryl by finding her guilty only of justifiable homicide. But for the months the case held public interest Turner was pilloried, her scarlet past raked over and over. The pietistic sets in the States saw to it that none of this new-found notoriety helped *Another Time, Another Place*. Box-office takings were bad and reviews across the country unsympathetic. Connery's first big chance to win American attention which he reckoned would fail anyway, was largely buried under an avalanche of dirty linen. The esteemed Bosley Crowther in the *New York Times* film review tore the picture to shreds, stating it was 'a long way from making any contact with interests that might serve to entertain. . . This one was made in England . . . evidently as a part of the current Go-Home-Yank plan.' A few critics did notice Connery. One New York observer said, 'The BBC commentator is played by a newcomer to films called Sean Connery who will not, I guess, grow old in the industry.'

For all the wounding flak, Connery arrived in Hollywood in a mood of breezy optimism – not quite childishly wide-eyed but, in the words of a co-actor, 'zinging with drive.' 'Disney was a benevolent despot,' says Michael O'Herlihy, technical adviser and dialogue coach on *Darby O'Gill and the Little People*, 'but he was a fine boss and many people, like myself, were fortunate in getting a break from him. Once he took to you, you were his for life. He took a fatherly interest in everything his employees did. After *Darby* I did a spell with Warner Brothers. I did a long run on *77 Sunset Strip*, and broke into directing. In '66 Walt gave me my first chance at a feature – *The Fighting Prince of Donegal* – and I was quite amazed that he'd seen *everything* I'd done in the intervening years. He was a very caring, charming man, and I think he quite liked Sean . . . but in an average kind of way.'

The working atmosphere at Disney Burbank studios cheered Connery immensely. The 'ensemble' spirit of the acting team – Janet Munro, Kieron Moore, Albert Sharpe, Estelle Winwood – relaxed him, recalling rep and *Requiem*

92

and all the successful things he had done; the weather was superb; the California girls a revelation. Everything was shot within the studios, the Irish backgrounds matted in. Disney visited the set every day, chatted with Connery about his Scottish life and theatre experience, even gave him a tip or two. For a first exposure to the Hollywood machine, Connery had landed on his feet. 'I suppose he, like so many, had a vision of a licentious, crazy holiday camp governed by demigods,' says co-star Kieron Moore, 'but in fact Hollywood was a duty-conscious business town. People went to bed early and arose early: there was work to be done and the standards were high. It was a town for professionals, Disney was the most professional, and Sean admired that.' The problems of a rather dull, unconventional director were leavened by Disney's charm, the professionalism and the jollity of the group sharing lodgings at the Burbank motel actor Jimmy O'Dea had christened 'Fatima Mansions', after a slum estate in Dublin. Robert Stevenson was an Englishman with an all-American outlook, directing a bog-Irish fairy story (the 'little people' were, of course, leprechauns), largely from story-board, picture sketches of scenes as opposed to written script. 'He wasn't, let's say, bursting with imagination,' Kieron Moore skirts deftly. O'Herlihy is more to the point: 'Stevenson didn't talk to actors, that was his trouble.'

Connery, however, bore up well. From his experience with Lewis Allen he had learnt the trick of conserving energies while bumbling directors wrestled with themselves. Privately he felt the story was good and his third billing part afforded him the chance to drift through a variety of light but interesting emotions. In the film he played Michael McBride, prospective lover of Katie (Munro), daughter of the deposed caretaker of a massive estate, Darby O'Gill (Sharpe). Fearful of his daughter's standing in the community because he has lost the estate job, Darby connives with the King of the Little People (Jimmy O'Dea) whom he has captured to ensure that McBride, who will take over as caretaker, falls in love with and marries Katie. Pony Sugrue (Moore) contests

McBride's job and love for Katie, but is eventually outdone in a spectacular fight scene. As children's entertainment it was Disney at his near-best and what script did exist (written by Lawrence Edward Watkin) was, Connery thought, beautifully judged. He even had an opportunity to sing – the first time since *South Pacific* – and though Stevenson contemplated dubbing him, his rendition of *Pretty Irish Girl* was left on the soundtrack.*

Ironically, the aspect of the film's shoot which vexed most of the leading actors didn't perturb Connery at all. Stevenson's most aggravating quirk was a penchant for 'the buckshot theory' whereby eighteen to twenty takes were called before a selection of the best one or two for printing was made. In the heat of the Californian sun Irish tempers grew distressingly short. 'It was tiring for the actors,' O'Herlihy says. 'There were make-up problems and continuity and some [of the actors] were floored by the time a scene was declared in the can.'

In the evenings the tradition of rueful Irish revelry was maintained in 'wakes' at Albert Sharpe's favourite nearby pub, known by all as The Skid Lid. 'Sean was brave all day,' says O'Herlihy, 'then he sank a few at night – like myself. I won't say I ever saw him flattened, but he had fun.'

Well aware of the rumpus surrounding former flame Lana Turner, Connery, without advice, made no effort to contact her. With a similar calculated prudence she avoided him, but a fair amount of muffled gossip circulated during June and July. 'Sean never spoke of Lana,' O'Herlihy says, 'and as far I was concerned he was just another contented bachelor in the best town on earth for bachelors to live in.' With a few white lies and his British motorcycle licence, Connery managed to rent a flashy American car. He learnt to drive around Burbank and took his casual dates for nerve-shredding spins. Once, on

*Connery's only singing record, *Pretty Irish Girl* (Top Rank JAR163) was released in Britain in April 1959. On the disc he duets with Janet Munro. Ruby Murray and Brendan O'Dowda cut a cover version (Columbia records) which was more popular.

a wall on Sunset Boulevard, he was shown the scars of what was patently gunfire. He inquired, and was told someone had tried to assassinate Mickey Cohen, firing from a passing car. Knowing Cohen to be a former lover of Turner's and cognisant of the spread of rumours about his London affair with her and the row at Borehamwood with Stompanato, ex-guard of Cohen's, Connery was shocked. 'He didn't have the sense to be alarmed,' an actor friend says, until somebody who knew Turner and understood the shady subterranean life of Hollywood phoned him up and spelt out the dangers. In his calm indifference to locale, the caller suggested, Connery was offering himself as a sacrificial sitting duck. Mickey Cohen, still faithful to Stompanato's memory, wanted to see blood spilled. Connery saw the light: 'He was out for revenge. Apparently he didn't believe that Cheryl had killed Stompanato. He thought the killing had been engineered in some other way. My pal warned me: "You don't know how these boys work out here. They play for real. Anyone who had any association with Lana Turner and Stompanato in London would be wise to get out of the way." '

Towards the end of the fifteen weeks of Disney, Connery moved out to lodgings in San Fernando Valley, several miles safe from Hollywood. 'Disney himself must have known about the rumours,' a colleague says, 'but I doubt if he knew before his scouts employed Sean. I'm not saying Sean had any charges of misconduct to answer, but Walt Disney had an image to preserve. Let's put it this way: Disney would no more have employed Lana than Mickey Cohen – right?' Whatever troublesome gossip persisted, Connery evidently managed to quash it discreetly and to Disney's approval. By the time work on the picture ended Disney, like Stevenson and the rest of the technical crew, were pleased with this new Scotsman's input and were on the best of terms with him.

Complicated effects and process work remained. 'A helluva job,' O'Herlihy says, 'superimposing the "little people" and faking the magic; at one stage we overloaded every circuit and blew every dynamo in Burbank.' But the big people had given their best and discharged themselves with honour. Connery found first-time Hollywood 'a great experience'; and the compliment, it appears, was returned in kind. Forgiven for *Another Time, Another Place*, America had given him another chance and he had, Kieron Moore was in no doubt, pulled it off creditably'.

CHAPTER EIGHT

Faltering Fox and the Classic Anchor

As BEFITTING THE nature of the project and the conscience of a man who claimed to be a descendant of a General Disney who fought on the 'right' side at the Battle of the Boyne, Walt Disney premiered *Darby O'Gill* in Dublin in June 1959. The film was Connery's first hit and though he later parried attempts to analyse his work on it he told the journalist Freda Bruce Lockhart, 'I wish I'd had a share in the profits.' Probably because of the surfeit of family-orientated and fantasy films on the market at the time Disney, whose praises had been deafeningly sung through the early fifties was, a publicist describes, on the critics' hit list at the time. Despite the huge business the movie did all over the world very few journals reviewed it favourably. For *The Times*, the whole thing was 'fatally lacking in lightness and charm' – an evaluation that suggested to a heartier reviewer *The Times'* man was facing the wrong way in the theatre. Connery's notices, along with those of the leprechaun king Jimmy O'Dea, were good, though the inevitably dissenting voice of the *New York Times*, in person of A. H. Weiler, branded him 'merely tall, dark and handsome'.

Disney's magic spell worked, as Robert Henderson had anticipated, very quickly for Connery. Within weeks of completion of the movie Paramount were seeking to borrow him again, this time for another heroic-fantasy epic, a *Tarzan* feature. 'He was a rich man then,' Bannen says. 'The tables had turned since I'd met him in the foyer at Kew. Here was I, still on the boards, and Sean hopping from feature to feature.' Bannen vacated the mews house and Connery began converting the garage into a thirty-five-foot sitting-room. Diane was still around – 'in the background', friends say – as were Yat Malmgeren's dramatic movement studies. The Paramount picture, *Tarzan's Greatest Adventure*, was conveyor-belt stuff, made at frantic pace by the formidable John Guillermin. Connery was pleased with the calibre of his co-stars – Anthony Quayle and Gordon Scott – and, though he had no illusions about the class of material, he was appeased by the respect that association with Disney had engendered. After the invaluable experience of Hollywood he was, a colleague says, 'brilliant in the junk' of *Tarzan*.

'His sense of proportion was precocious,' says an actor friend. 'Even at this early stage – and let's face it, he was still *new* – he could divine good from bad and assess the *amount* of effort individual projects were worthy of. His delight at being accepted in the business goes without saying but he always showed an uncustomary fussiness. It might or might not have been *Tarzan*, but I remember him brooding over an early script, learning lines I think, then tossing it into an armchair. "What's it like?" I asked, suspecting he was less than blissful. "Lots of lines," he grinned sardonically, "just lots of lines." ' The same friend recalls the books littered round Connery's rooms: 'It was funny, really. You had this great mountain of a fellow lifting body weights and checking out his muscles in the mirror . . . and on the shelf, in a chair, you'd see something heavy, some Russian writer, or Balzac . . . and it wasn't just effect, he read them, I swear.' Yet, the friend adds: 'Often you felt he was embarrassed about his aspirations. You'd say, "What's this, Sean? O'Casey?" and he'd give you a twitchy look and say, "Let's have a pint." '

Curiously, however deep the artistic conflict ran, Connery in the immediate aftermath of Disney was at peace with himself. Through '58 he had had little or no time for TV (he did no BBC work: he was hotly fond of the BBC and liked their standards), but as soon as a decent meaty part came up, coinciding with a free period, he leapt at it. *Riders to the Sea*, a mildly successful play in mid-'59 was his first 'respectable' achievement since *Anna Christie*. 'He enjoyed that TV work,' Robert Hardy says. 'I'm sure it had nothing to do with his relative lack of success in cinema till then. I think he just liked the austerity, the technical restrictions that invited a disciplined man to do his best.'

In '59 too he returned to the Oxford Playhouse stage where his champion, the gifted producer Frank Hauser, carved parts for him in the classics. 'He wasn't always good,' says director Lewis Gilbert about those early sallies, 'but he was always interesting.' Joan Littlewood, whose trend-setting Theatre Workshop was consolidating, quietly prided herself in the discovery and coaching of half-formed talents like Michael Caine and Richard Harris, whose celebrated break was in Littlewood's production of *The Quare Fellow*, 1956. She saw Connery on stage and, like Gilbert, found him interesting. She was in advanced planning for her Workshop *Macbeth* tour of Russia and Eastern Europe and, seeing Connery's malleable potential, considered him ideal for a principal role. Through friends she approached Connery – and to the same friends' surprise, he turned her down. 'He spoke to me about it, giving no hint of his reasons,' Robert Henderson says. 'It was a wonderful offer, but maybe he'd committed himself secretly to the cinema solely by then.' It is equally possible Connery's growing love for Diane Cilento obstructed *Macbeth*. In '59 she fell ill and tuberculosis was diagnosed, a harrowing shock that began for Cilento what she later called 'a two-year re-think about my life'. For a while she was gravely ill and Connery was never far from the telephone. Producer Samuel Bronston (*King of Kings*, etc) and director Anthony Mann, in the throes of planning the eleventh century Spanish epic, *El Cid*, a vehicle intended to project Sophia Loren to a wider international audience, favoured Connery for one of the four lead roles – probably that of Count Ordoñez, later given to Raf Vallone. But again Connery rejected. 'In that case,' a colleague says, 'he wanted to do Pirandello's *Naked* at Oxford. Yes, he understood the high designs of *El Cid* – but Diane was well then and she wanted to do it, so he had to be by her side.'

While Cilento was fighting TB with Connery always

near her bedside *Tarzan's Greatest Adventure* opened with a decidedly gaspy whimper. The sanctity of such matinée 'junk' was so entrenched in the tenets of light cinema criticism that just about no one dared to call it bad. The *Observer* and *The Times* circumspectly *described* the movie and the *Monthly Film Bulletin* even hedged with 'the production values are above average and the various villains suitably larger than life; Jane is non-existent, the natives and the chimpanzee comedy element are restricted to one short scene, and a literate and grammatical Tarzan gives vent to his famous war cry only at the finish . . . if the same team comes up with a better story the next Tarzan might be more worthy of the tradition.'

The story, in fact, was the problem. It was a too-many-cooks effort, overbaked by Berne Giler, Guillermin and Les Crutchfield with a modicum of a Burroughs' sub-plot thrown in. Tarzan (Gordon Scott) played man-hunter, trekking up river to find and bring to book the villainous Slade (Anthony Quayle) and co-killers like O'Bannion (Connery). Slade is hellbent on scooping a hoard of diamonds from a hidden mine known only to him, and has killed ruthlessly to advance his aim. Encumbered with Angie (Sara Shane), an action-woman plane crash survivor-of-convenience, Tarzan plods through the too obvious trail, kills O'Bannion in a thoroughly unexceptional fracas, is rescued from ineptitude by the much-suffering Angie and finally corners Slade. The humdrum showdown has treachery in Slade's camp – Slade naturally kills the traitor – and a clifftop struggle between Tarzan and Slade, with Slade plummeting to his death. Predictability kills almost all tension in the story and, though Gordon Scott articulates his Tarzan nicely, his pallor (in Technicolor) and that crease-browed, well-shaven look irritatingly conjure images of pin-stripe suits and furled umbrellas ensconced in bamboo wardrobes back at the tree-house. In about thirty minutes of screen time Connery relates no more to his audience than the cub philosophy that makes O'Bannion a killer, though occasionally his grace in the action sequences holds the eye.

Measured against its class, *Tarzan's Greatest Adventure* could score no better than a six out of ten and it inspired some discussion in the summer of '59 about Connery's future with 20th Century-Fox. *Picturegoer* journal speculated whether they would drop him, and a few close friends reciprocated by passing round the word that Connery's patience had run out. The game was uneven, Connery suddenly felt. He had 'pulled off' Hollywood and was consistently proving his talents in a vast range of disparate parts in theatre and TV, yet Fox were only sporadically tossing him scraps of hints of projects that *might* be coming or auditions elsewhere he should try. In 1960 on loan again, now to Anglo-Amalgamated, he was returned to the gangland thriller, this time accepting *The Frightened City* only because of an unquestionably able cast and a good script by Leigh Vance, later more popular as a TV writer with *The Saint*, and others. The film's publicist, Brian Doyle, says, 'Sean gave the impression of being pleased with the movie, and he was terribly professional – that's what I recall more than anything. All told, working relationships were good. Our goal was a better-than-average thriller entertainment, Sean went along with that fully, and I think we reached our objective.'

The Frightened City, directed by John Lemont, was the peak of Connery's pre-Bond cinema efforts though, very strangely, it failed to gain anything like the recognition most involved with it felt was its due. Connery was thirty when it was made, amply experienced and splendidly aggrieved by Fox's mishandling: the new profound bitterness about Fox's lassitude brought a tight-lipped ferocity to his part as the protection-racketeer enforcer that made the entire business strikingly credible once he sidled onto screen. He was Paddy Damion, a soft-hearted, hardheaded crook employed by Harry Foulcher (Alfred Marks) to collect protection money from London clubs and cafes in a slimline protection scheme devised by the ostensibly respectable accountant Waldo Zhernikov (Herbert Lom). Damion is a complex, tragic figure worthy of a latter-day Shakespeare: he is scrupulous in his loyalties but confused by the blurred borders of right and wrong; he works out in a rundown gym organized by 'gentle' villain Alf Peters (David Davies) – a member of Foulcher's racketeer team, whom he devotedly respects – but accepts the immorality of forced collections only because he needs an income to look after his crippled pal (Kenneth Griffiths) and to court Sadie (Olive McFarland). When Foulcher murders Peters, Damion quits his commitment to close dependants and revokes his former principles. He kills Foulcher – but acting in defence – and is on point of executing Waldo when the police (led by John Gregson) step in. In the penultimate scene Damion is led away in custody, his gestures and monosyllabic grunts underpinning the perfectly-struck image of a senseless, faithful beast lost to understanding in the concrete jungle.

Everything Connery had filched, stumbled upon and been taught in six years of acting was piled in ideally concentrated measures into *The Frightened City*. The much-commented-upon 'rawness' that was the inevitable legacy of Fountainbridge, the movement techniques of his studies, particularly noticeable in his hand gestures, his laconically witty speech deliveries learnt from longtime film performers like Diane, all blended to create a powerfully memorable character who, as Henderson always hoped for, looked one thing – indomitably tough – but was another – humane. Those who acted with Connery on the movie reckoned he deserved good notices. Brian Doyle believes he 'just about dominated the picture' – but the rewards just didn't come. On the circuits *The Frightened City* did very average business and though the popular dailies flagged it 'the toughest crime exposé ever made', just such a commendation assured box-office disaster. Dosed to drunkenness with the annals of Scotland Yard at work round London's docks, moviegoers were refreshing themselves with the sour medicine of middle-class life-as-it-is in kitchen-sink dramas like *Saturday Night and Sunday Morning* (1960) and *A Taste of Honey* (1961).

After *The Frightened City* Connery's relations with Fox were reportedly very strained. David Shipman in his encyclopaedic *The Great Movie Stars* confesses that the facts about the termination of the long-term contract are 'muddy', but it does seem the bond of mutual interest had come unstuck by the time Connery took his first leading role, that of the gormless gag-feeder to a rather gormless Alfred Lynch in Cyril Frankel's *On The Fiddle*, based on a novel by R. F. Delderfield, a laughless comedy that could have ended a lesser actor's career. Ben Fisz, producer of *Hell Drivers*, and Anglo-Amalgamated had confidence enough in Connery and the property, to pair them with an investment of a few hundred thousand pounds. The movie flopped, but it did serve to win Connery his first prominent notices – if not all good – and bring him to the attention of people like Dennis Selinger, the agent who, under the aegis of the influential International Creative Management, would direct Connery towards great successes of the post-Bond years like *The Man Who Would Be King* (1975). For Selinger, Connery was 'quite fun' and, allowing for the bumpiness of the vehicle, 'undeniably in possession of something one could only term star quality.' Close associates attest to the fact that Connery has always liked the notion of working in comedy but the role of the dumb foil, most felt, was misjudged. The director Guy Hamilton, who was soon to direct *Goldfinger*, summed up the flaws in concept and acting in *On The Fiddle* when he said, apropos of Connery's talent: 'His power as an actor is built on strength: it can be shaded down to suit the circumstances of a scene – but Sean is greatest as a strong character.' The plot of *On The Fiddle* is wafer-thin. Horace Pope (Alfred Lynch), tricked into joining the RAF during the war, joins forces with gypsy recruit Pascoe (Connery) and, for laughs and cash, starts up a lucrative conning racket among his colleagues. The no-gooders eventually show their wily bravery when they make accidental contact with the enemy in France, and end up as much-decorated heroes. Paradoxically the divergence of opinion about the movie and Connery's effectiveness yielded fruit. By the summer of 1961 magazines and dailies all over the British Isles had commenced a rowdy 'will he, won't he succeed in movies?' debate, which Connery tactfully participated in. 'It is a real mystery to me why no film company has built Sean into a great international star,' wrote

103

Freda Bruce Lockhart in *Woman*. '[In a TV play] Sean reminded me of Clark Gable. He has the same rare mixture of handsome virility, sweetness and warmth. His attractive speech . . . has the vigour which many find lacking in the pinched vowels of London-trained actors. Above all, Sean has *size*. I don't just mean . . . height. I mean, too, the breadth and all-embracing effect of his personality.' Connery cooperatively griped: 'They'll offer me anything on TV, as opposed to stage or films.'

In her feature on Connery in the doldrums, Lockhart concluded with word on the newest TV venture. BBC producer Rudolph Cartier had chosen Connery to play Vronsky opposite Claire Bloom in *Anna Karenina*, a prestige production scheduled for November 1961. Before that there would be a West End play, Anouilh's *Judith*, at Her Majesty's Theatre. 'I hope Cartier's production brings him luck,' Lockhart cheered, 'for it is my conviction that he is one of the biggest hopes among promising present-day actors.'

Diane Cilento was in full agreement, but Fox were smugly preparing to close his file and wave him goodbye: in their eyes budding talents galore peopled the pubs and billiard halls of Shaftesbury Avenue, all awaiting dotted lines to scrawl upon; most would be more indulgent and less tetchily ambitious. Sean Connery proved himself – sure; but in the words of a Fox man, where in God's name could one fit him? Who wanted a Scottish giant in kitchen-sink drama? As for Hollywood? – well, Disney had not asked him back and Mickey Cohen was still alive. Sean Connery might never make Hollywood again.

'When I directed Sean in Shakespeare's *Henry IV* in the spring of 1960, eighteen months before James Bond, he was already a star,' says Michael Hayes. 'You knew that by his behaviour – instantly. He wasn't loud or showy but compared to the other fine people we were using – Esmond Knight, Julian Glover, Patrick Garland – he was gold-plated. With the exception of Esmond, of course, who had vast experience, we were all new young bucks trying to make our way. Sean was different. He had a car . . . in fact, several over the time I knew him. I remember

104

once he'd bought a little Fiat, around the time of *Henry IV*. I asked him, just in passing, what had become of the other model, which had been very respectable. "The ashtrays were full," he retorted. Sounds like a cliche star story – but it's true.'

Everyone close to Connery rejoiced in his success as Hotspur opposite Robert Hardy's Prince Hal in *Henry IV*, one of the fifteen hour-long live Shakespeare plays that ran under the banner title *An Age of Kings*, produced by Peter Dewes and described by *The Times* as 'an astonishing achievement'. Among those round to kiss him congratulations was Julie Hamilton. A worker on the series recollects meeting Julie at a Wavel Mews party after the play. While stressing that there was no lady-in-residence, he elaborates that, with Julie, 'there was some up-and-downing, that's for sure. I know their close friendship was ended, but there were reverberations right into '60, perhaps even later.' Recovering well from her TB, Cilento was work-active again but discreet about the extent of her relationship with Connery. 'Of course I knew *about* Diane,' says Michael Hayes, 'but I didn't know her. Sean brought only one face to the studios: that of the consummate pro. One was left in no doubt about his priorities then.' Did he display angst about his jerky movie career? 'Not overly,' Hayes says. 'And in context of *Age of Kings* it would have appeared churlish. I mean, he was more renowned than the rest of the cast. He was a star with a star's outlook – what more could he have wanted?' Hayes was pleasantly surprised by Connery's ease with live Shakespeare. 'Hotspur's speech is not versified in the way others' are, so Sean had the advantage there, but he carried it off with such dash. His *relaxation* – that's what I remember; that's the gift he brought to us from films. Technical proficiency that allowed him to bawl.' Robert Hardy had a wider knowledge of Shakespeare, stretching back to the Histories at Stratford in '51, where he had understudied Richard Burton's Prince Hal. Hardy felt he was 'in presence of a man who had the capacity to be truly great; he had charisma. Hotspur is a difficult character temperamentally, many people express their doubts about him. And indeed, after *Age of Kings*, many people complained about Sean, saying they found his accent hard to swallow. But I think it lent something to Hotspur which *was* Hotspur. We were lucky to have Sean.'

And then came *Anna Karenina*, the giant production journalistic bright lights like Lockhart had mumbled predictive hopes about. 'Sean was anxious and excited about it more than anything he'd recently done,' a BBC worker says. 'A lot of it probably concerned Claire Bloom, who had come to pictures via the Old Vic, done all the classics where Sean had done just a handful, and had big screen triumphs in *Look Back in Anger* and others. Sean was racing then. He was keen to get more classic roles under his belt. We'd had him in a Terence Rattigan (as Alexander the Great in *Adventure Story*) and he was regularly at Oxford – but *Anna Karenina* was a milestone.'

'Discontinuous recording' (in the BBC's phrase) of the play by Marcelle-Maurette, adapted by Donald Bull, started on Friday, June 23rd, 1961 at Television Centre Studio 3, and went on till Sunday night. Cartier, who had previously directed Connery in *Adventure Story*, struck a cracking passionate atmosphere that forced the best from the leads; Bloom, Jack Watling, June Thorburn, Connery. 'Sean had a childlike regard for Cartier,' a technician explains, 'and was most over-anxious to please. But Bloom counterpointed beautifully. There were many retakes, but the whole thing was so *intense* it had to be good.'

While awaiting transmission of the Tolstoy classic, scheduled for November 3rd, Connery did a short run in the West End biblical play *Judith*. 'He was the one who, in the Bible, slays Judith,' Robert Henderson says. 'He hadn't got much to say but he attracted attention because he was almost naked on stage, wearing only a loincloth. Never before on the legitimate stage had he the chance to show off that remarkably beautiful physique.'

Judith was panned by many critics and its run was cut short, but the chance afforded Connery to exhibit his near-nude body paid dividends. One admirer in the audience at Her Majesty's was director Terence Young, already in discussion with two restless foreign producers about a strategy to emulate the success of Ian Fleming's James Bond books in movies. The first name mooted as a possible screen Bond was David Niven, Fleming's favourite actor, but in months of negotiation the idea had cooled. Fleming, who had power of veto by virtue of his supreme literary standing, now fancied the notion of a newcomer – someone with charm, grit and intelligence who might, in some way perhaps, mirror himself, Bond's true alter ego. Young watched Connery from a half-full theatre and mused. He remembered his promise to the Scotsman on *Action of the Tiger*; he also recalled that he had told friends even then that Connery would 'go places'.

After a spate of angry wrangling that marked the end of their contractual marriage, Fox at last mustered a jumbled project, *The Longest Day*, that allowed Connery a minute 'star part' – virtually hidden in a forest of forty-three stars of current cinema. No fewer than four directors vied to leave their imprint on this well-reconstructed (but dry as old toast) account of Operation Overlord, the Allied invasion of Europe on June 6th 1944, and Ken Annakin directed the Juno Beach British sequence in which Connery plays Private Flanagan, 'the seasoned veteran whose Irish temperament saw him through the landings'. Connery was passable, but the strain of mounting this gargantuan production – two years in the making, nine months and seventeen days in principal photography, thirty-one locales, almost one hundred main actors – shows in almost every foot of every reel. Bosley Crowther, the famed American reviewer, liked it but appended the telling remark that 'no character stands out particularly as more significant or heroic than anyone else.'

To friends Connery dismissed his contribution: the film belonged to John Wayne, Mitchum, the megastars; Fox and their wayward son, Darryl F. Zanuck, about to return after many years absence as executive president, never saw it any other way. It was no compliment to his talent, or gesture of appeasement from the company.

All hopes pinned to *Anna Karenina* were fulfilled. Audience response was, according to the BBC, 'very satisfactory' and most of the dailies greeted it boisterously. The

Listener thought it deserved, if not prizewinning status as the year's best, then at least 'a distant salute'. *The Times* was unequivocal in its estimation of the winning factors. The writers involved, they judged, achieved 'variable success'; but, 'most successful was Mr Sean Connery, a headlong, passionate Vronsky.'

Harry Saltzman and Albert R. Broccoli, the producers who had acquired the rights to film James Bond, watched *Anna Karenina* on the advice of Terence Young. But, while they were intrigued by the old-trouper tricks this new boy employed to knock Claire Bloom right off the screen, the exercise was essentially unnecessary. Connery was already top of their poll.

By the middle of November it was decided: Sean Connery, in contravention of what financial backers United Artists thought best, would be James Bond.

If, in Michael Hayes's eyes, Connery was already a star the glowing pride of achievement one might assume to be his was not as complete as most judged. Away from film journalists, away from production offices, he revealed his weary side. At the out-of-work actors' gathering places he loved to frequent – the Buxton Club in the Haymarket, the Arts Theatre, the Salisbury in St Martin's Lane – he was, as Michael Caine says, 'still the struggling young fella, unknown outside the profession, looking for the right break.' Ian Bannen was aware of the frustrations of faltering movies too: 'Sean was slaving at theatre and the classics, using them as a kind of anchor in the storm.'

With the Bond break the storms of uncertainty were about to abate, to be replaced by a tempest of frenetic adulation and unstoppable fame.

CHAPTER NINE

Enter the Walking Aphrodisiac

THE FIRST ATTEMPTS to put James Bond into movies failed. Under the intended sponsorship of millionaire business-man Ivar Bryce and his one-cylinder Xanadu production company (their sole venture had been Kevin McClory's financial failure *The Boy and the Bridge*), Ian Fleming, McClory and top British screenwriter Jack Whittingham developed a plot – which later became *Thunderball*, book and film – but abandoned it when Bryce and Fleming got cold feet. It had been Fleming's hope that established producer-directors like Anthony Asquith or Alfred Hitch-cock would take up the rights of the *Thunderball* treatment, but when Hitchcock flatly rejected it Fleming decided to withdraw. Jack Whittingham's fee for the final script was £5,000 and the project was shelved indefinitely. Fleming wrote to Bryce: 'Showbiz is a ghastly biz and the last thing I want is for you to lose your pin-stripe trousers in its grisly maw . . . nor, of course, do I want the first James Bond film to be botched.' A literary perfectionist with a penchant for collecting rare classics but reading trash, Fleming had more in common with Sean Connery, the man who was to breathe life into his dream-hero, than many recognize. Compared with Connery's upbringing, Fleming's childhood was crème de la crème – country seats, town houses, Eton, Sandhurst – but both men shared an ambition which, to some, was almost ugly in its fury; both enjoyed risk-taking, both acquired sophis-ticated tastes. 'Don't be misled by Sean's lorry-driver press,' says Honor Blackman; 'the man exuded high-living refinement when I got to know him.'

Within a few months of Fleming's postponement of

screen Bond, the Canadian producer Harry Saltzman, acting on the advice of his and Fleming's lawyer, Brian Lewis, optioned the existing Bond novels. Saltzman's option covered seven books in print. One Bond title, *Casino Royale*, was unavailable, having been sold to Gregory Ratoff for $6,000 in 1955. Another title *Moonraker*, had been purchased by Rank, but Fleming's agents, Music Corporation of America, retrieved the rights in 1960. Saltzman's track record was superb – he had been the driving force behind Woodfall, the production company partnership with John Osborne and director Tony Richardson – and had been partly responsible for the success of new-wave cine-realism, hawking such projects as *Saturday Night and Sunday Morning* and *The Entertainer*. He was also, Honor Blackman recalls, 'a hard man, a dedicated deal-maker.' With Bond, however, his deal-making prowess did not show. Having paid Fleming $50,000 for a six-month option, twenty-eight days before expiry he was at sea, no nearer a financing deal than he had been at the start. It was then his writer friend Wolf Mankowitz introduced him to Broccoli, the 50-year-old New Yorker who was himself a longtime Bond admirer, and whose contacts in financing circles were impressive. Broccoli's experience was every bit as colourfully wide as Saltzman's, though he was irritated by the relative lack of success of some recent endeavours. A good scholar and avid reader, he had a degree in agriculture and a spell as assistant to Howard Hawks behind him when, after the war, he transferred operations from Hollywood to London and started a series of adventure films in partnership with Irving Allen, earning the distinction of producing the first ever Anglo-American features. Saltzman's proposal for a partnership arrangement to launch Bond was based on his belief that, after kitchen-sink, people wanted 'something different, strong plots with excitement, fast cars, bizarre situations, drink and women' – the antidote to a post-fifties malaise which resounded with the memories of the leanness and suffering of the Second World War's aftermath. Broccoli needed no persuasion. In 1959 he had been tentatively negotiating for Bond: he wanted in. A fifty-

fifty deal was eventually struck, though Saltzman would have preferred terms more favourable to himself. All that then remained was choosing the book to film, drafting the screenplay and casting the essentials – Bond and his bedmate.

Richard Maibaum, who had written Broccoli's *The Red Beret*, dashed to work, initially on *Thunderball*, while Broccoli commenced talks with film backers in May 1961. Columbia Pictures considered the Bond offer, then turned it down. Maibaum switched to *Dr No*, having received word that the High Court action taken by McClory against Fleming's rights in *Thunderball* complicated the ready availability, and Broccoli approached United Artists. On June 20th 1961 in a brief boardroom meeting at UA headquarters in New York, backing was at last agreed upon. David Picker, later to run United Artists but then London chief, was the Bond fan in the UA camp who swayed company president Arthur Krim. Broccoli and Saltzman asked for a million dollars to put *Dr No* on screen, but were given $800,000. In a frenzy of excitement the jubilant producers winged back to London and started scouting for their director and crew. Disappointments marked the beginning of their work: first-choice directors Guy Green and Bryan Forbes refused the project; Guy Hamilton, later to take the challenge with *Goldfinger*, rejected 'because of intrusive private affairs'. Finally Terence Young was approached, a little uncertainly, because his recent films had been, in the vernacular, 'uneven' – specifically, financial flops. United Artists agreed to accept Young provided the movie's budget was guaranteed with a completion bond; i.e. if the film took longer to shoot than anticipated, the producers would foot the bill for the additional costs incurred. Saltzman and Broccoli did not hesitate on the bond, reassured by Young's able and economical work on *The Red Beret* (1953) for Broccoli.

Casting for *Dr No* was in progress before Young was officially assigned to the movie. Indeed, Sean Connery was already in the running – along with people like Patrick McGoohan, Roger Moore and Richard Johnson. Fleming, who was quite happy with the professionalism and

111

generosity of Broccoli and Saltzman, still promoted the idea of an established name lead.* He mentioned Michael Redgrave and Trevor Howard but, after the fiasco of *Thunderball*, was very content to 'stay away from all this side of the business and all those lunches and dinners at the Mirabelle and the Ambassedeurs which seem to be the offices for all this huckstering.' By the time the search for Bond was at full throttle, according to Connery, Fleming was keen on the idea of an unknown, someone who would would not overshadow James Bond.

Saltzman and Broccoli had first met Connery at a party, and liked his looks. Broccoli enjoyed his thick accent in particular and had further food for thought when, in Hollywood, he had viewed *Darby O'Gill and the Little People* and observed his wife's enthusiastic response: like Jacqueline Hill on *Requiem*, Dana Broccoli found Connery's macho aura inescapably attractive. By coincidence, in London, film editor Peter Hunt who was to edit almost all the Bond movies, was recommending *On The Fiddle* to Saltzman, and Terence Young in his role of friend to the producers was starting to bellow for Connery too.

Saltzman phoned Richard Hatton, and Connery was called in for interview. He approached Saltzman's South Audley Street office casually, expecting nothing. He had been through the casting maze too many times to believe that cheery grins and spirited animation won any prizes. Instead he stepped out of his small car as though heading for the dank office and familiar foursquare grilling of the BBC. He wore a brown shirt, brown suede shoes and no tie – garb befitting the Buxton on a Friday night, hardly a million-dollar movie audition. In their first floor office Broccoli and Saltzman greeted him coolly and Saltzman, ever the inquisitor, fired the questions. Connery's answers came pat, in the perfect animal burr Broccoli found

*Financially Fleming did reasonably well by the film deal: he was guaranteed a minimum of $100,000 per picture, with 5 per cent of the producers' profit. By the time he died, in August 1964, he had probably made about $¼ million from the movies. In his will he left some $½ million.

rivetting. Yes, he had read Fleming – *Live and Let Die*, some years back. Yes, he thought the concept of a Bond series viable. No, he didn't regard himself exclusively as a classics actor, or a stage performer or whatever – he had yet to find his niche. The warm and candid tone of the chat altered only when Broccoli queried Connery's style and dress sense. At one juncture he told the producers, 'You either take me as I am or not at all.' Saltzman may have had reservations – according to one associate he 'liked his subordinates to know their place' – but Broccoli found Connery's authority a very definite plus. 'He pounded the desk and told us what he wanted . . . we agreed, he walked out of the office and we watched him bounce across the street like he was Superman. We knew we had got our James Bond.'

Other had yet to be persuaded.

Connery started testing at Pinewood, opposite an un-ending queue of aspiring female leads. When some of this test footage was sent to New York, UA glanced over Connery and cabled back:

SEE IF YOU CAN DO BETTER.

Broccoli and Saltzman ignored the cable because they had already committed themselves to Connery, signing him in November for a multi-picture deal that would engage him till 1967, allowing one non-Bond picture a year. His up-front fee for *Dr No* was £6,000 – 'a fortune', to Robert Hardy and other friends.

Connery had not undertaken *Dr No* and the long-term deal lightly. When the offer was made he took time to consider it, consulting Hatton and Cilento. It emerged that, after Disney, he had been offered another long-term contract, to join either the *Maverick* or *Wyatt Earp* TV series being churned out, supermarket-like, in Hollywood. That deal wasn't exactly bounteous in rewards, but it would have granted him the permanent access to the Hollywood hit factory which he hungered for. He had turned it down then by private decision, firstly because he thought he would be short-selling himself to run-of-the-mill TV and secondly because he wanted to be near Diane. Now, with

113

Bond, Diane took a hand, giving forceful advice. Fleming's books were immensely popular, with yearly sales nearing the million mark. It was significant too that they attracted praise from all sections of the community, and had been likened to Buchan, Sapper – the best of twentieth-century popular fiction. Raymond Chandler had written glowingly about Bond; the poet William Plomer had been instrumental in seeing him through to publication, advising both Fleming and publishers Jonathan Cape; Somerset Maugham was an admirer. . . Agonizing over submitting to another long contract, Connery confessed his greatest fear, that of signing his services away for the crucial period of most actors' lives – his thirties. Looking back on Fox he explained the frustrations of his misuse as feeling like 'a man walking through a swamp in a bad dream'. He knew if he was to make it internationally it must be soon; he saw himself initially as a romantic lead, not a character actor. He wanted to be successful while he was fit and young enough to exploit it.

Cilento urged him to take Bond. 'If it were not for me,' she told an American magazine writer in 1964, 'Sean might never have become James Bond.'

Reflecting on his casting interview with Saltzman and Broccoli, Connery admitted he had 'put on a bit of an act' in swaggering and pounding the desk and grunting reluctance to screen test (a verbal agreement to do Bond had already been made when Connery screen tested: 'his' test was run under the pretext of testing the female co-lead). Intuition carried him through the game: though he hadn't worked out pros and cons, he had sensed he wanted Bond just as, seven years before, he sensed *South Pacific* was right for him.

With shooting scheduled for January 1962 Terence Young and his assistant Joanna Harwood entered a pre-production arena that gave every indication that disaster was looming. There were five different scripts, all scrappy, and Broccoli, who had been largely absorbed with casting, was at war with Saltzman, in charge of the writing. Young recalls that, in the end, Broccoli's nerve went. Flinging the mountain of wildly derivative scripts aside he shouted to Saltzman, 'Look, we've paid all this fucking money for this James Bond book and we're not using a word of it. Now, Terence is a writer, he's the quickest writer I know. He's got ten days to put it back. He can take all the scripts we have . . . and whatever he writes we're going to be stuck with and Harry, if it's bad, it's your fault.' Young and Harwood took a room at the Dorchester Hotel and began rewriting, going day and night. Meanwhile, Saltzman had equal reason to lose patience with Broccoli. 'Cubby was the tit 'n' bum man,' Guy Hamilton says. 'He had fixed ideas about the *type* of girl he wanted in Bond's bed. And one thing he wanted was good tits.' Julie Christie, among a score of others, failed the tit test. Broccoli had seen her on TV and summoned her. No one doubted her talent, least of all the discerning Cubby, but, close up, her bust just didn't reckon. Finally, in a stack of new star photographs, Broccoli came across Swiss-born Ursula Andress. In the cheesecake publicity shot she was wearing a wet T-shirt that moulded her hard-nippled breasts. Glancing over her curriculum vitae, Broccoli was encouraged: she was the right age, twenty-five, and height, 5' 9", had made films in Rome – which stood for nothing in talent terms – but had been briefly on contract to Paramount. Without meeting her, Broccoli wired a Hollywood friend seeking testimonials and received exactly the affirmative response he wanted. Interviewed later, Saltzman unwittingly mocked the casting process that had cost so much concern and cash: 'We chose Ursula because she was beautiful and because she was cheap. We didn't have the money to spend on anyone else.' Andress received £300 per week for the scheduled six weeks. The film overran: she claimed she was not paid dues for extra work.

Among Connery's friends at the West End actors' clubs word was out that Fleming's 'Establishment hero' super spy was his. 'I was amazed,' Michael Caine states candidly. 'I was sure they'd give it to Rex [Harrison], because he was your living image of upper-crust good-living.' Robert Hardy thought it, 'oddball casting, but a tremendous

115

compliment to Sean . . . everyone banked on something contrived and Englishy, but Sean presented one with an entirely fresh perspective on British cult heroes.' The *Saturday Evening Post* quoted a movie director who knew Connery saying, 'He was on the garbage heap of acting,' until Bond. Connery himself experienced what might best be termed polar affections once news circulated. 'Actually it was a bit of a joke round town,' he conceded; there were those in the Buxton club who thought Bond a backward step, B movie stuff, and those who imagined Sean Connery clad in anything other than Levis and beatniky suede shoes a travesty. But Diane Cilento, who was closer than anyone to unrolling events, understood that *Dr No* was to be no Monogram or Republic conventional B, but rather a force-fed mini-epic. All of Connery's artistry and cunning would be called into play and the end result would be the most stringent acid test of his durability.

Young hurried Connery into a crash course in social graciousness that made cynics snigger. 'Terence was James Bond,' says Zena Marshall, who starred as the murderous sex-tigress Miss Taro in the film. 'When he cast me, all he said, the way he behaved, told me he was projecting himself as Bond. He had incredible style and complementary gentleness and strength.' For sure, Young's background was closer to Fleming's outline for the superspy than Connery's. The son of Shanghai's Commissioner of Police, he was educated at Harrow and Cambridge and served in the war with the Guards' Armoured Division. His tastes were for the good things of life. 'Terence loved to be surrounded by pretty furnishings, champagne, attractive people,' says Molly Peters, whom he cast in *Thunderball* three years later. He had also worked, for a short time, as a helper to Hitchcock, as, significantly, had screenwriter Richard Maibaum. (Though Young and Harwood rewrote much of *Dr No*, with Berkley Mather, Richard Maibaum received the main screen credit. He went on to write nearly all the Bond films.) Elements of Hitchcock infested all the early Bond movies, by way of tribute rather than accident.

'I sent Sean to my shirtmaker,' says Young. 'I sent him

116

to my tailor. I used to make him go out in these clothes, because Sean's idea of a good evening out would be to go off in a lumber jacket. . .'

Feeling much out of his depth by the curious workings of this curious film world, this same domain that had defeated him two years before, Fleming's reaction to progress was confused. At first he wasn't happy with Connery, though he kept up a brave face when he cabled Bryce about Saltzman's conviction in the 'absolute corker, a 30-year-old Shakespearian actor, ex-navy boxing champion, etc, etc.' With Young, whom he knew through mutual acquaintanceship with Noel Coward, he was more cruelly honest. At a UA London function he squared up to the realities of an untested director guiding a half-known ex-labourer star into James Bond's elegant world. 'So they've decided on you to fuck up my work,' he charged Young. Young was not shaken. 'Let me put it this way, Ian. I don't think anything you've written is immortal as yet, whereas the last picture I made won a Grand Prix at Venice. Now let's start even.'

Dr No 'started even' with location shooting in Jamaica on Tuesday, January 16th 1962 and Andress joined the team some ten days later to film her Crab Key sequences on the north shore. Her husband, John Derek (later self-styled 'creator' of third-wife star Bo), accompanied her and she fitted in well, though Young found her 'strangely built . . . she had the shoulders, stomach and legs of a boy, but with this great face and breasts.' Shooting her to advantage was not as easy as it might have been, though by Connery's side her bulky proportions looked about right. Connery liked the Dereks, and laughed a lot with Ursula. She had a waspish, rebellious side to her that brightened the mood of relentless time-is-running-short tension and though her squeaky accent caused trouble from Day One, her disciplined approach impressed him. Later he called her his favourite Bond co-star – and indeed she proved an invaluable asset to the yearly rethreading of the Bond mythology: for a million Bond fans Andress, white-bikinied with hip knife on a Caribbean beach, became the symbol of luxurious, sexy, inviting adventure.

Pleased with Connery's work in Jamaica, Young brought the team back to Stage D at Pinewood in the middle of February, where Ken Adam, a longtime associate of Broccoli's, had been labouring on some imaginative set designs with a budget of only £14,000. Here the interiors would be shot, and the famous introductory scene, where a suntanned Connery announces himself as James Bond to Eunice Gayson's Sylvia across a gaming table, went in the can on the second day. A few days later the seduction of busty, dangerous Miss Taro was filmed. Zena Marshall recalls: 'I spent the entire day in bed with Sean, so you could say it was fun! But it was hard work too. Ian Fleming came on the set and had several words with me. He seemed to think my role important, this enemy agent making love to Bond, each tacitly knowing the other is out to kill them. There were a few retakes, because Terence wanted us to relax into the mood of love-making, and we did some sections twice for the different markets. In Ireland, for example, they couldn't see my tits, so a more covered-up shot was run. . . Sean was very rough and raw, but his charm was exceptional.'

Day by day Young preached etiquette. Once he checked Connery for eating with his mouth open (during dinner with Dr No), on another occasion Connery's accent thickened in the excitement of a scene. One or two 'errors of class' slipped through: Bondphiles blast the sartorial blunder of Connery at Strangways' house, buttoning down the last of his suit coat buttons, spoiling the cut of a finely-figured outfit.

The film story of Dr No, Fleming was relieved to see, differed only in small detail from his novel. Young considered the yarn ordinary, Connery thought it good. John Russell Taylor, the film historian, isolated the formula shrewdly: Bond spends one half the movie getting into the villain's clutches – and laying the girls on the way – and one half fighting his way free. In Dr No the journey into trouble begins when Strangways (Tim Moxon), our man in Jamaica, is murdered while investigating the 'toppling' of American rockets from nearby Cape Canaveral. MI5 agent Bond is yanked away from his current flame

(Eunice Gayson) and ordered into the inquiry. Following Strangways' trail, he meets the treacherous duo Professor Dent (Anthony Dawson) and Government House secretary Miss Taro and, after their conspiracy to kill him fails, he executes Dent and has Taro arrested. Dent's plot leads Bond to Crab Key, the island fortress of Dr No (Joseph Wiseman) where, after incarceration and a bold breakout, Bond thwarts Dr No's latest attempt to topple an American rocket and kills the villain. His accomplice, from the middle of the second reel, as it were, is the lovely Honey Rider (Andress), a shell-collecting island-drifter.

The completion of the film in March marked an occasion for muted celebration. Small problems rankled: Andress, it was decided, would have to be dubbed throughout. Monty Norman's music score was incomplete; fresh thematic music was needed. Connery was good, *but* . . . UA officials flew in from New York to watch a preview in a private cinema in Mayfair in Connery's absence. Saltzman liked the picture well enough, 'but then I liked *Look Back in Anger* . . . and that died the death of a dog.' The distribution money-men silently watched ninety minutes of Sean Connery then, in unison, grimaced. He was all right, average detective hunk, self-conscious in the close-ups. Reportedly one top-ranking executive said, 'I can't show a picture with a limey truck driver playing the lead.' Somebody else vocally took consolation from the fact that Broccoli and Saltzman had only overspent by $110,000. 'We can't lose *too* much . . .'

Thus decided, UA would splash nothing on promoting *Dr No* in America. The film would, no doubt, get some rentals and earn a few bucks, but the likelihood of financing for a follow-up was a little less than slight.

Connery, on the other hand, liked to pretend resolute optimism. He told friends the film was 'bloody good' and, no matter what UA felt, he was prepared to 'sit tight and wait'. Sue Lloyd, the actress, had become friendly with him, having met him at the Buxton, and shared a few loving evenings with him at her flat – 'never his – I never saw the inside of his place, and only had the vaguest notion he lived somewhere in the NW region'. She found

119

him 'quietly optimistic'. A few weeks after completion she met Andress at Shepperton Studios where both were vying for an upcoming part in a minor movie. 'Ursula had no idea what the repercussions of *Dr No* would be. We were chatting and she said, "I've just been in Jamaica enjoying the sun, doing this thriller with Sean Connery" – and it might have been any thriller, with any actor. It meant nothing to her beyond another job. She held no hopes for it.' But James Bond remained, at least, a literary institution and Connery was intent on doing his share of pre-promotion. He gave a few interviews, stressing his pedigree (the whistle-stop *Macbeth* he had done for Canadian TV the previous autumn, just before he signed for Bond, figured large), and promulgated a James Bond philosophy. He told the *Daily Express*: 'I see Bond as a complete sensualist – his senses are highly tuned and he's awake to everything. He likes his wine, his food and his women. He's quite amoral. I particularly like him because he thrives on conflict – a quality lacking in present-day society.' With wary respect for UA he added, 'I've been asked if I'm worried about getting tagged as Bond. . . Bond is a "bracket" for me. It's a £1 million production [sic] and the people who set up and cast the film have a healthy respect for a pound and dollar tag.'

While professionally Connery sat tight during the summer of '62, in his private life tumultuous changes were underway. The desultory love affairs that filled the vacuum of an actor's 'resting' days – brief flings with model Joyce Webster, Sue Lloyd and others – were suddenly, stout-heartedly replaced by a new and vigorous relationship with Cilento. 'As far as I was concerned,' an actor friend says, 'Andre Volpe no longer existed. Diane's marriage had been over quite a time, but now divorce proceedings were going and she and Sean were settling down together. They spent several nights a week with each other and we waited for the knot to be tied . . . we waited for a move from Sean anyway, Diane was another kettle of fish. You see, Sean, under it all, was a one-woman man. Diane, well, she had a career to be catching up with.' At home in Fountainbridge, in the same stair, Effie and Joe were told of Sean's new love in a phone call. Later, briefly, Sean brought Diane home and the family reunion was serene. Effie read between the lines and guessed the seriousness of the affair. She smiled when, in the autumn, she read a national newspaper interview where Sean extolled the bachelor life: 'No one to tell you what to do . . . I can leave my socks on the floor, play poker all night, come and go as I please . . . I couldn't ask any woman to put up with that.'

By the time the interview was published Diane Cilento was several months pregnant, expecting Connery's child, and he was about to apply himself to the difficult task of persuading her to marry him.

United Artists were stunned. Having sidestepped the option of a fanfare premiere in Chicago or New York, they opened *Dr No* in the Midwest where, if destined, it could die the quiet death. By the time of the American opening it was a massive European success. Premiered at the London Pavilion on October 6th 1962, with Paul Getty in attendance, by the clever news-conscious design of Saltzman and Fleming, gross receipts amounted to almost £1 million within a few months. Unstinting superlative reviews sung paeans of hope for a British cinema with American values (at last!) and reversed anything ever breathed in blasphemy about Connery's talent. Shocked by the trendsetting zest of the escapade, the MGM-at-its-peak style decor, the Fritz Lang echoes, *Films and Filming* could only pant, 'There hasn't been a film like *Dr No* since . . . when? There's never been a *British* film like *Dr No* since . . . *what*?' 'Carefully, expertly made,' bleated *The Times*. 'Magnificent mayhem,' agreed the *News of the World*. Connery's personal reviews were no less enthusiastic. Peter Green in *John O'London's* believed there was 'no doubt that Sean Connery with his Irish good looks, splendidly hairy chest, and tough but elegant charm, embodies this modern male compensation factor [James Bond] better than most actors could.'

At the premiere, where Zena Marshall took Connery's

121

arm, and Saltzman for once sat back to allow his movie to speak for itself, audience response was mysterious enough to be electrifying. Zena Marshall, viewing the whole assemblage for the first time could not but be impressed. 'The theatre was deadly silent at the beginning, but as it went on they were shouting for Bond. Sean's performance was so smooth he riveted the eye. I remember Anita Ekberg was there, sitting just along our row from Sean. Throughout the movie she couldn't keep her eyes off him – not on screen, *in person*. Later at the reception at the Ambassadeurs it was the same. Whatever effect he'd had on women up till then was doubled: James Bond made him a walking aphrodisiac.'

The clutter of features and reviews that cascaded round the New York opening at the Astor, the Murray Hill and other theatres in the 'premiere showcase' group in May firmly and irrevocably stamped approval on Connery, the Star. Bosley Crowther recommended the film as 'lively and amusing' though 'not to be taken seriously as realistic fiction or even art, any more than the works of Mr Fleming are to be taken as long-hair literature.' A *Variety* reviewer predicted, 'As a screen hero James Bond is clearly here to stay. He will win no Oscars, but a lot of enthusiastic followers.' Tongue crushed in cheek, *Time* magazine gave an unprecedented leader to the British import: 'Agent Bond, in short, is just a great big hairy marshmallow, but he sure does titillate the popular taste . . . at last the scarlet pimpernel can be seen on screen. He looks pretty good. As portrayed by Scotland's Sean Connery, he moves with a tensile grace that excitingly suggests the violence bottled in Bond.'

There were quibbles of course, most, like the Queequeg article in *The Spectator*, beefing about script departures from Fleming's original. But, overall, throughout the world, *Dr No* succeeded. By the time the New York journals were card-indexing Connery, Sean, the 'new' actor, *From Russia With Love* was already filming at Pinewood, backed by $2 million from a humbled UA; on the home front Connery was decorating his new property, a three-storey mansion overlooking Acton park, and worming

into married life with Cilento and a ready-made family –
step-daughter Gigi and five-month-old son Jason.

Fame had taken its time. But in some regards some
matters were moving too fast.

CHAPTER TEN

Hitch, Effortlessly

'I DON'T THINK I'm meant to be married,' Diane Cilento told an interviewer in March 1961, propounding tersely the reasons for the failure of her union with Volpe. Two years later, six months after marrying Connery, she was reminded of that conclusion. Asked to comment she replied tartly, 'I got married.'

The beginnings of the new marriage were not auspicious, though the affection and regard Connery and Cilento held for each other is beyond question. By her own admission, Connery had to talk her into tying the knot. Beneath the dedication to his craft and his pugnacity of purpose, Connery in his thirties was surprised to find 'the old John Knoxian influence' working away – a realization that struck him whenever, after long absences, he came back to Fountainbridge. On discovering Cilento was pregnant in the summer of '62, shortly after just such a refresher trip to Edinburgh, he promptly set a course for marriage. Time and circumstances were right for him: with his Bond contract he was assured good money for a few years; his existing savings were considerable; he was past thirty, and tired of philandering; most importantly, Diane was a supreme career navigator, blessed with a conscience that divided good from bad irrefutably. He proposed, but she refused. 'I didn't want to get married,' she said later. 'Having made a bodge of it already I didn't rate marriage. I thought it was too stifling.' Discussions about alternative life styles stretched into September, but Connery was adamant in his reluctance to settle for separate lives, with the new child farmed on loan every other week. 'Sean was never enamoured of the idea of children,' a friend says, 'but he was anxious about the baby once he knew the die had been cast. And he loved Diane, remember. He told people she reminded him of his mother – bright, strong, firm.'

In the dazzling afterglow of the *Dr No* premiere, over dinner, Connery finally persuaded Cilento to agree to his proposal. He had already made a major gesture of resolve: he had purchased for £9,000 a twelve-room house in Centre Avenue, Acton, formerly the home of twenty-five nuns of the Order of Adoratrices; he had drafted in an interior designer and decorators, and he was building a nursery. Cilento was flattered, but she laid out preconditions. She told the *Sunday People* later, '[Sean] was so sure we could make a go of it . . . I wanted us both to retain a fair amount of freedom. I don't like ownership in marriage. I don't like too many promises either. There is no way of being sure you can keep them.'

Days after Cilento had accepted Connery the wedding ceremony took place in Gibraltar. Gibraltar was simplest for many reasons: in Britain the couple would have had to wait three weeks after the posting of banns, and the bush telegraph that operates through registry offices would have meant unwanted press coverage; as it was, certain jaundiced circles were still a-buzz with the scandal of a scarlet lady, just one month divorced, seven months pregnant and hopping in and out of love with Connery. 'She jilted him a few times,' one acquaintance says. 'He was never too sure of her.'

At first in Gibraltar Connery thought he'd got the ultimate jilt. Cilento was in Spain, staying with friends, and arrangements had been made by telephone for her to meet up with Connery at the appointed registry office. Connery, on his British passport, had no trouble entering the colony but Cilento, travelling on her Australian documents, was delayed at the frontier. The ceremony was postponed for a few hours, new witnesses had to be roped in – two taxidrivers, for convenience – and, at last, vows were exchanged. Connery's humour was foul, but Cilento thought the whole affair 'like a funny TV show. He was all feet, all thumbs, frustrated.' Nerves were not allowed to settle for long. It was suggested a trip up the Rock might be appropriate – a chance to watch evening falling on the Mediterranean, bask in the sun sliding down over Africa, romantically tip a glass to the future. But they stayed atop too long, and strayed into a military preserve on their way down. Locked in, with night descending, they were lucky to find a sentry with a sympathetic ear after an hour. According to Cilento, they repaired to their honeymoon hotel exhausted, facing a night of anti-climax after the dramas of the day.

Six weeks later in London on January 11th Jason was born, by which time the family – with Gigi looking ever more on Connery as Dad – had moved into Acacia House in rough 'n' ready Acton. Connery personally supervised the several thousand pounds' worth of reconstruction, frequently haggling with the builders and challenging costings. 'I'd been on building sites,' he said, 'I knew how corners could be cut, what was feasible and what wasn't.' Space and colour were the main considerations. For the thirty-seven-foot living-room Connery insisted on 'bright red carpet, white paint, lots of very bright cushions . . . colour is necessary.' A year later he was watching Jason 'reaching for the lights and the brightest colours and laughing . . . he will grow up to memories and experiences that will be . . . inescapable.' The simple sentiment revealed the naive but idealistic urge to displace Fountainbridge for once and for all. 'Sean was never ashamed of Edinburgh,' says Ian Bannen, 'but he acquired a liking for good material things. I suppose he tried to impose it [on Fountainbridge] in some ways. For instance, I remember he took me home there and he'd bought this very modern gigantic fridge for his parents. Huge thing. It was crammed into this tiny room where everyone had to squeeze round it. It was quite ridiculous.' With the upfront money for *From Russia With Love* he was now trying to lure Effie and Joe away from the stair. He offered them a flat in London but Effie pointed out that she needed to be near Helen and Neil, her parents, then living in Corstorphine, and very dependent on family help. The fact that McEwans' Brewery was beginning to annex nearby properties did not deter Joe. 'This is so handy,' he told the *Sunday Express*, fending off his son's offer, 'London is such an enormous place, and there's always so much bustling and hustling.'

But now, with Cilento's guiding influence stronger than ever, bustling London was the place to be – a thoroughly managable empire falling, street by street, cinema by cinema, to his advance. *Dr No* ran virtually non-stop, somewhere or other, during 1963. Back in Fountainbridge, old friend John Brady saw it and thought, 'That's it – Tommy's made it for life.' United Artists were a little less sure, but they were certainly investing more executive interest, as well as cash, in *From Russia With Love*. They (and Saltzman and Broccoli) even stood behind born-again director Terence Young when, over several months, he mulled over perfect casting, determinedly seeking the perfect villains for Fleming's enigmatic Red Grant and Rosa Klebb, easy enough in Robert Shaw, who had to put on weight and muscle, and Lotte Lenya. He also wanted a heroine to outstrip – in every sense – Ursula Andress. Young commuted sleeplessly between European capitals, according to press reports, looking over some 200 girls for the role of Tatiana, the turncoat Russian. Among those in the running were Austria's Elga Anderssen (dropped by UA decree when she spurned an executive's advances), Roman Lucia Modogno, English roses Margaret Lee and Sally Douglas, Pole Magda Konopka, Yugoslav Sylvia Koscina and a Miss Universe 1960 runner-up, Italian Daniela Bianchi. In March Bianchi was told she had the job and on April 1st filming began, again at Pinewood's Stage D, utilising most of the proven technical talents from *Dr No*.

Over sixteen weeks Young took his team from Pinewood to Turkey, Scotland and Madrid, shooting more extravagantly than he had on the first Bond, and running more takes. Halfway through, returning from arduous weeks in Turkey where there had been union troubles and minor cast illnesses, Connery was exhausted but he perked up when director Basil Dearden approached him, offering a lead role in the upcoming *Woman of Straw*, co-starring with Ralph Richardson an actor he had admired since he was a child. Connery agreed without seeing the script, and revived for Bond.

As a consolidating choice, the one to secure the Bond series, *From Russia With Love* was evidence of Broccoli and Saltzman's matured market sense. Perhaps Fleming's most ambitious and strangely-structured book, he himself had reservations about its worth. Before the book was in proof in 1956 he wrote to his publishers about his fear of staleness and the contrivances 'to fill the vacuum created by my waning enthusiasm for this cardboard booby'. As it turned out the public, and President John Kennedy to boot, loved the novel and turned it into a perennial best-seller. Dick Maibaum, the screenwriter, wisely chose to retain as much as possible of Fleming in his script, a punch-heavy story of a plot by an international crime organization, SPECTRE, to kill Bond, steal a decoding machine and confound both British and Soviet spy services. Tatiana (Bianchi) is the bait, duped by Russian Rosa Klebb into believing she is serving the Motherland by luring Bond to Istanbul to hand over the prized decoder. Tatiana is ready to defect for the love of Bond and double-cross Klebb but psychopathic Grant is despatched to stop them as they travel westwards across Europe on the Orient Express. In a brutal clash aboard the train, Bond kills Grant and later does down Klebb in like fashion.

Superb photography by Ted Moore, richly daring editing by Peter Hunt, Bianchi oozing sensuality with every timid arch of a brow and the martyrdom of President Kennedy six weeks after the London opening of the film hoisted *From Russia* into the realms of stellar immortals. Effie and Joe came to London to join Diane and Connery for the premiere and party and were floored by the extent of anticipated success. Effie maintained that deadpan aloofness that had kept her through the bleak days of the Depression, but Joe was fully at a loss. The crowds, the glaring manifestations of a wealth he could only have dreamed about in drunkenness, the autograph hunters screaming for Tommy – it was all too much to digest. At the reception after screening he told a film journalist he

128

believed his son would 'get quite popular' in the immediate future. Already at work on *Woman of Straw*, Connery seemed almost unaware that film history was in the making: *Dr No* could easily have been a fluke, but with the successful premiere of *From Russia With Love* a heavily-backed series was guaranteed. Forced to give an account of the singularity of his technique in making Bond work on screen, Connery himself gave way to a hyperbole he soon grew to detest. He spoke of the lack of humour in Fleming's novels (a gross unfairness in the eyes of Fleming and those familiar with the undertones of black humour in the books), and of his, and Terence Young's, attempts to lighten the material with one-line gags and some self-mockery. Hyperbolising was the order of the day. Fleming, who had privately expressed doubts about 'the labourer playing Bond', was now reported as saying Connery was much as he had imagined Bond; were he writing the books all over again, he stated, Connery would be his clothes-horse.

Champagne had, literally, flowed day and night during the making of *From Russia* – Young liked the good-living atmosphere on his sets. In the wake of the October premiere, floodgates opened. As a feat of technical virtuosity – the American production values – the movie defied any negative criticism. More significantly, its subject matter outlandishly teased the super-highbrow critics prone to analysing cinema as a mirror of life. Quite rightly, Philip Oakes in the *Sunday Telegraph* catalogued the voyeurism, sadism and lesbianism stacked in the film and suggested: 'It is a movie made entirely for kicks. Guns go off; girls get undressed; people have sex; people die. Happening succeeds happening, but nothing and no one is of real significance.' As *From Russia* started to do the Odeon rounds in Britain, the Beatles were reenforcing their position as the new icons of the youth culture. In Wilson's Britain, all you had to do to be heard was to shout *differently*. Although the Beatles were initially seen as rebels and Bond as representing establishment values, the irony that they were both 'made for kicks' was overlooked. But Bond was an unshakable point of reference where 'the illusions of sexual prowess, indestructibility, glamour and force are ritually enacted' (*Queen* magazine). *The Daily Telegraph* saw *From Russia* as a quasi 'reflection of an ugly, totalitarian world . . . [viewed] not only with recognition, but with what ominously looks like approval'. After the assassination of President Kennedy on November 22nd, the Cold War intensified. *Playboy* magazine, sub-literary voicebox of all America – young, liberal *and,* in its own way, conservative – adopted Bond as its standard-bearer instantly, and in so doing assured colossal popularity through all strata of society during the confused sixties. *Playboy* earned the distinction of serialising Fleming's last few novels prior to book publication. It also specialised in features on Bond movie girls, running nude or topless shots of Ursula Andress (*Dr No*), Martine Beswick (*From Russia, Thunderball*), Margaret Nolan (*Goldfinger*), Molly Peters (*Thunderball*), Mie Hama (*You Only Live Twice*) and Lana Wood (*Diamonds Are Forever*). Revealing exclusive articles and interviews with Fleming, Connery, Dick Maibaum and Roald Dahl, who wrote the script of *You Only Live Twice*, also frustrated lesser journals keen to cash in on the Bond boom.

Connery's personal notices for *From Russia* jousted for pride of place with those of the lovable Pedro Armendariz as Kerim Bey, villain Robert Shaw and Daniela Bianchi, who was endearingly waiflike throughout (in her first starring role, very consistent, though she was dubbed by Barbara Jeffoed). In America, where the film opened in April '64, the acid pen of hard-to-please critic Manny Farber decided the winner, though backhanding equal honours to the runner-up. In an article in *Cavalier* magazine he waxed eloquent on 'Robert Shaw's scene stealing . . . which is done alongside Sean Connery, who is a master in his own right in the art of sifting into a scene, covertly inflicting a soft dramatic quality inside the external toughness.' Bosley Crowther meanwhile at the *New York Times* was screaming 'Don't miss it! . . . Just go and see it and have yourself a good time.'

'About halfway through *Woman of Straw,*' a film colleague relates, 'Sean's attitude to acting and stardom changed – overnight. Diane was behind him, so was Harry Saltzman maybe – though he lived to regret it – but suddenly Sean was *it*.' Strengthened by financial security and the gradual realisation of his greatest ambitions, Connery did appear to alter tack during the winter of '63–'64. One magazine article of the period quoted a press agent ranting: 'Sean Connery? You want my honest opinion? Sean Connery is a great, big, conceited, untalented, wooden-headed ninny'. Whispering tales were already circulating about his greed and big-headedness ('You couldn't drag him to a party unless there was something in it for him'). At Pinewood Studios, filming with the short-tempered Gina Lollobrigida, Connery was apparently asserting his equal-star-billing status. The on-set mood was horrendous and technicians reported daily conferences, where director Dearden cast oil on troubled waters. Connery was constantly suggesting script rewrites, though his friend Stanley Mann, whom he later grew close to, had co-drafted the original. Friends suggest Cilento had much to do with proposed alterations. 'Her stock was high,' says one. 'She'd just finished Tony Richardson's *Tom Jones* and gotten herself an Academy Award nomination. She was full of energy, and full of ideas for making Sean an "artist".' On location in Majorca cast relationships deteriorated alarmingly. Connery was allegedly 'sick and tired' of Lollobrigida's lapses. One scene called for him to roughen her up with a shake and a face slap. Furious after an earlier argument, Connery hit Lollobrigida too hard, sending her reeling. He later apologised, claiming accidental force, but expanded in an interview, 'Acting is a job, like carpentry or building roads. There are 100 people involved in putting you up there on screen. The trouble with a lot of stars is that they develop heads as big as their close-ups.' His own head, he made clear, was unchanged by good fortune. 'If I wore hats,' he snapped, 'I think you'd find I still take the same size.'

Very intimate associates bear up Connery's proclamation. His home life was unpretentious, he kept one secretary whose function was to answer mail; he drove a Volkswagen (later a second-hand Jaguar), while Cilento had a small Austin Healey; his major luxury was good-eating. 'Sean loves his grub before everything,' says John Boorman. The only appreciable change concerned his attitude to the work on offer. 'It must have been after the first or second Bond that he decided to quit the stage,' says Ian Bannen. 'He said he never wanted to do it again . . . all that shouting hurt his throat. Simply, he wanted to do first-class films. Only.'

Michael Caine says, 'He'd brought to Bond the gift every star actor has: he'd made Bond his own – doesn't matter what Ian Fleming originally visualised. Sean was Bond. But he knew his talents were bigger than that. Of course there was lots more he wanted to do while the going was good.'

In December '63, just after *Woman of Straw* concluded, and distressingly early in the day for Harry Saltzman, Connery was telling *Photoplay* the extent of his unease at the prospect of typecasting. 'I remember once going to see a casting director for a role in a picture,' Connery said. 'When she asked me, "And what *type* of actor are you, Mr Connery?" I just got up and walked out . . . an actor hates to be typecast . . . I don't want to be Bond all the time. It riles me when people call me Bond off the set. . . That's why I'm making pictures like *Woman of Straw*, in the hope audiences will accept me in other parts.' But there was caution in such soul-baring too. Around the same time he was deriding the 'socially conscious plays and scripts [that treat] working men as noble savages.' He told the *Daily Mail*, 'There's so much bull about written by armchair socialists.' In that regard, by current cinema standards, he was lucky to be playing Bond, a decently concocted, high-carat sub-superman.

Woman of Straw, as it turned out, did nothing to enhance Connery's reputation beyond Bond, though its critical assessment and damnation, many feel, was unfairly based on the expensively plump production values of the Broccoli-Saltzman pictures. Predictably, Ralph Richardson earned all the praise managing, by *The Times* reckoning, 'to extract slight fun from the glum proceedings.' The film was phrased, it is true, as pseudo-Hitchcock, and gave the impression of being penned originally for stage (the later stage version by Catherine Arley and Ian Cullen worked better, capitalising on an easier evocation of claustrophobia). In the story nurse Maria (Lollobrigida) is persuaded by Anthony Richmond (Connery) to marry his unsympathetic invalid uncle (Richardson) and so, in due course, inherit and share out the uncle's fortune, estimated at many millions. Maria grows to care for the old man, but when he dies prematurely she is convicted of murder. The denouement is straightforward: Anthony has tricked her, murdered the old man and, as next of kin, plans to net all the money for himself. The final scene has a rather predictable showdown with the police, unexpected evidence from the black butler who has come to like Maria, and the tables turned on Anthony. The *Monthly Film Bulletin* approved of Connery, but wished greater inventiveness with the material – the names of Welles, Losey and Hitchcock were invoked – but the *New York Times* blamed everything on Lollobrigida. 'Try as the script and camera may to convince us that Miss Lollobrigida is the most irresistible of females, she stubbornly remains her placid, matronly self – hardly the type to draw a passing snort from an old lion like Sir Ralph. No wonder Mr Connery double-crosses her in the end.' William Peper in the *New York World-Telegram and Sun* complained that Connery cut 'a handsome but rather colourless figure. . .' and, inevitably, that he was 'much more fun as James Bond.'

Connery's immediate response to the poor reception for his first major role since Bond was submerged in the pre-production of the third Bond, *Goldfinger*, and, more excitingly, the frenzy of work on yet another inbetween feature, though this a somewhat special one, called *Marnie*. 'I wasn't all that thrilled with *Woman of Straw*,' he said afterwards, 'although the problems were my own. I'd been working nonstop since goodness knows how long and [was] trying to suggest rewrites while making another film (*From Russia With Love*). . . It was an experience, but I won't make that mistake again.'

Connery and the press were unfair to *Woman of Straw*,

which stands staunch in retrospect, removed from Bond comparisons. As in *The Frightened City*, the seething aggression that Connery displays in restrained laughter and bravado explodes like a hammer on the ascetic rigidity of Richardson and Lollobrigida, sending sparks everywhere. No matter what the *New York Times* says, La Lollo is sinful in slinky black satin, and the staging is good.

Several years after its release, *Woman of Straw* was still ringing on the tills for producer Michael Relph and distributors and backers UA, bearing up well in its own right. It could not, of course, keep pace with Bond. Within twelve months *From Russia With Love*, which had cost exactly $2 million, had grossed $12½ million, smashing everything else at the British box-office for '63–'64, and *Dr No* was already $5 million in the black. Sean Connery was in demand across the world and, understanding fairly well now the peak he was arriving at, he reached for the best he could get.

Almost two years precisely after hoofing out of his little Fiat and signing on for *Dr No* at £6,000, Connery and agent Richard Hatton were writing a thank you to Alfred Hitchcock and Universal for $400,000, the negotiated lead fee for a pet project of Hitch's, *Marnie*. *Marnie* began life as a novel by *Poldark* author Winston Graham, was purchased by Hitchcock in 1961 as the ideal property to reintroduce Grace Kelly, Princess of Monaco, into films and had Universal's backing from the start. Joseph Stefano, who had so brilliantly adapted Robert Bloch's *Psycho*, wrote the treatment and Grace Kelly accepted Hitch's velvety persuasion. But at the last minute word of the project broke in Monaco, the princess's subjects were enraged and the movie ground to a halt. Hitch shelved *Marnie* and rushed into *The Birds*, testing the lead-playing potential of a new discovery, 26-year-old New Yorker 'Tippi' Hedren (Hitch always insisted on the single quotes round Tippi). *The Birds* did well enough to encourage Hitch to try Hedren in a stronger character role and, very abruptly, in 1963 he reactivated *Marnie*, engaging a woman writer, Jay Presson Allan, to develop the female title role for his new star. Connery had probably come to Hitch's attention in *Dr No*,

134

which he is known to have watched with interest, having rejected Bond two years before; at any rate, once decided on his young male lead he was prepared to pay whatever asking price. $400,000 was a lot for a relatively new star, but Hitch could swallow that. Less digestible was Connery's second stipulation: Hatton conveyed the word timorously – Connery wanted to read the script before committing himself. Hitchcock thought twice, concerned at the possibility of being hampered by the condition he despised above all, the star ego. But, as Michael Caine points out, 'no matter how it was for Sean, he never was one who had time for the accoutrements of ego: in that sense he was always an actor's actor.' Hitch clearly caught wind of this and scoffed the prevailing gossip from certain quarters that still insisted Bond-Connery was becoming a monster. He told associates Connery had the perfect combination of youthful sexiness *and* relative inexperience which he sought always. He could mould Connery, he was certain.

In London the popular press paraded the story of Connery's 'gruff individualism' with kiddish glee. Hitchcock's London agent had allegedly told Connery, 'Even Cary Grant doesn't ask to read a Hitchcock script.' To which Connery was supposed to have replied, 'Well, I'm not Cary Grant.' The Bondian devil-may-care tone was inescapable, and the media were intent on pursuing it, much to the satisfaction of Saltzman and Broccoli. Even *Time* magazine in the States took up the *Marnie* propaganda line, declaring, 'Connery's individualism is just right for Bond, who makes steely love, is a wine snob, and likes to rub people out without leaving blood on the carpet.' Candidly, Connery dismissed the fuss over his asking for the script. For a start he was exhausted, having worked without a break for more than a year, first promoting *Dr No* throughout Europe on personal tour, then flashing through *From Russia* and *Woman of Straw*; and, much as he honestly revered Hitchcock, he wanted to be sure *Marnie* was not some sub-Bond possibly forced on Hitchcock by Universal, who were reportedly less than delighted with *The Birds*. Protesting about the to-do over what one

135

newspaper described as his 'failure to conform to the established patterns of the film business', Connery explained, 'Look, for the first time in my life I can ask to read a script, and if you had been in some of the tripe I have, you'd know why.' In the end, he got the script, glanced through it and saw immediately Hitchcock knew what he was about. *Marnie* was, simply, the finest thing he had been offered since *Dr No*. And – best lure of all – Hitchcock was giving him Hollywood again.

Before Christmas '63 Connery flew to Los Angeles alone and was picked up by two Universal VIPs at the airport. He refused the chauffeured limousine placed at his disposal and asked for a small runaround 'like my Volks back home'. Taken to the fashionable Chateau Marmont, according to press reports, he seemed horrified. 'Nice place,' he grunted, 'but what's wrong with the motel I stayed at in Burbank six years ago? Easy to get in and out of and very inexpensive.' And so he was whisked to Jimmy O'Dea's beloved 'Fatima Mansions', the flat-roofed shack originally laid on by Disney. 'It was the same little game about restaurants,' one American magazine mourned. Asked how he felt about Chasen's or LaScala, Connery bluntly stated his preference for American hamburgers. His idea of entertainments too caused surprise. No, he didn't want to take in local strip shows or star parties or touring musicals. He wanted to swim a bit, knock a golf ball round (he had just been introduced to golf by Terence Young), maybe collect a suntan more in fitting with the swanky American businessman he was to play.

Whatever lingering fears Hitchcock and Universal had about 'star temperaments' must have dissipated within hours. Connery was not likely to shirk the discipline of the job. He had come back to Hollywood to work.

From their first meeting Connery and Hitchcock got on famously. Hitchcock was a trifle unsure of Connery's blatant lack of social grace in some areas, but he enjoyed the Scotsman's appetite for work – monumentally more important in his eyes – and his speed with lines. Connery, for his part, liked the respect afforded him, not just by the master himself, but by the serious film press. There was talk of Bond, but intelligent questioning too. Later he guessed the reasons for his smooth professional acceptance was that: 'most of the younger British actors today, like Finney and O'Toole and me, are more organic, down-to-earth actors than previous generations. In America there is much more feel for realism than in Europe, where there is still a conception of an actor as being somehow divorced from real life, and in Britain, where acting is still often associated more with being statuesque and striking poses and declaiming with lyrical voices.'

But Bond was taking America by storm while Connery was making his declaration of independence and, because a minimum of three Saltzman-Broccoli pictures lay ahead of him, he was forced to make some concessions for the light press. Between takes at Universal Studios and on brief location in Maryland he was photographed with busty aspiring actress-models and an informal chat with Hitchcock about the relative merits of British and foreign women received massive, nonsense cover. Hands contemplatively clasped around his paunch, Hitchcock restated his devotion to chilly English women: 'They are three dimensional . . . the other type of beauty, the Italian, big voluptuous figures may look 3-D but, believe me, they are just cut-out dolls.' Connery retorted, 'You've just described my type.'

Marnie, the film, progressed well. A rift between Hedren and Hitchcock half-way through slowed proceedings for a day or so, but Hitchcock had been through the mill so many times he could, in the words of a technician, 'direct with his eyes shut and his cigar stone cold.' The plot had been doctored to accommodate a young lead – in the book the Connery character was an elderly man. Connery plays Mark Rutland, a rich company executive, who discovers that a junior in his employ, Marnie (Hedren) is a kleptomaniac. When he discovers her criminality he covers for her and forcefully cajoles her into marriage, believing loving attention will change her. But he finds her frigid and incapable of love. Challenged, he explores her behaviour and background, eventually discovering her to be the daughter of a prostitute who murdered a lover before the child's eyes. The neuroses explained, Mark leads Marnie off to a better life. Hitchcock outlined for Francois Truffaut the attraction of the storyline. He wanted to make the movie, he said, because of: 'the fetish idea. A man wants to go to bed with a thief because she is a thief, just like other men have a yen for a Chinese or coloured woman.' Mark was, to Hitchcock, mildly neurotic too – though none of this was relayed on set or in script to Connery. 'I had a great time with Hitchcock,' Connery said. 'He tells you on the set what moves he wants. The only major direction he gave to me . . . was when I was listening to what somebody else was saying in a scene, and he pointed out that I was listening with my mouth open – as I often do – and he thought it would look better shut.' But of the neurotic slant to Mark: 'He never got into anything like that. He used to tell me funny stories before a take quite often, but he never dwelt upon the psychology of the character. . . His humour is pretty schoolboyish.' At one stage Hitchcock told Connery, 'If I'm paying you as much as I am and you don't know what you're doing, then I deserve what I get in the way of performance.'

For the latter part of the picture Cilento flew out to Hollywood with the children and the family rented a modest $1,000-a-month Bel Air cabin complete with swimming pool where Cilento bathed naked daily. From there Connery made provisional arrangements with John Ford's agents to take the star part in the planned film biography of playwright Sean O'Casey, to start rolling in Dublin towards the end of '64 when, hopefully, *Goldfinger* would be comfortably in the can. Cilento liked the ring of class to the project and backed up her man, as she did when he refused to don a Bondish Savile Row suit and set the cornerstone of MCA's new skyscraper, opting for a golf round with her instead. 'The atmosphere was heavy with integrity and sophistication,' says a friend, sardonically perhaps. 'Here was Diane carrying round her Academy nomination and Sean working for Hitchcock and chatting to John Ford. There was a bit of hypocrisy, though –

because Sean was already pretending that Bond was just the sideline, the money-taker, when in fact Bond was *his success*.'

Marnie, in its final cut, displeased Hitchcock to some degree. He felt the neurotic conundrums had not been delineated sharply enough and, though Connery had sailed through complex emotional variations quite effort-lessly, aspects of the character which *seemed* to work on set did not carry to celluloid. In his published conversa-tions with Hitchcock Truffaut suggested that the role of Mark had been miscast: Laurence Olivier might have reached the subtler heights. Hitchcock was inclined to agree: 'I wasn't convinced that Sean Connery was a Phila-delphia gentleman. You know, if you want to reduce *Marnie* to its lowest common denominator, it is the story of the prince and the beggar girl. In a story of this kind you need a real gentleman, a more elegant man than we had.'

The comment was no intended insult to Connery per-sonally. As a capable pro, Hitchcock had admired Con-nery more than many of his leading men, rating him somewhere below Cary Grant or Jimmy Stewart, but above Rod Taylor and Paul Newman. The technicians on *Marnie* shared the maestro's joy. When the picture wrapped up, they presented Connery with a memento of the good times – a gold watch valued at $1,000. Connery found the sentiment 'rather touching', though he was less than touched by the post-script: on reentering Britain in March, en route to start *Goldfinger*, the Customs de-manded £25 duty on the 'luxury goods' import.

Marnie opened in the summer of '64 to mixed reviews and reasonable business, helped, like *Woman of Straw* by the oblique Bond link. For Eugene Archer in the *New York Times* it was, regrettably, 'a clear miss . . . the master's most disappointing film in years.' Connery worked, he judged, 'commendably and well . . . but inexperience shows.' *The Times* was more kind. Its critic believed the film, 'manages remarkably well . . . it is easy to see why the plot outline should have taken Mr Hitchcock's fancy: it is essentially *Spellbound* turned inside out . . . moreover,

139

the film has plenty of material for the nuttier French Hitch-cock enthusiasts: a dash of *amour fou* in the hero's obses-sive devotion to a beloved he knows to be from the outset almost impossible; lots and lots about the crucial word which can set free (shades of *Under Capricorn*) and the exchange of culpability.' Mr Sean Connery, for *The Times*, 'escapes quite effectively from the James Bond stereotype.' Almost all reviewers – and early audiences – joked about unusually bad process work, back-projection and obvious painted backdrops, the final set of the street, where Mar-nie's mother lives earning derision everywhere – like something Trauner might have cooked up for Carné in the good old days, *The Times* jeered.

In later years the very factors that damned *Marnie* were to be instrumental in elevating the movie to the cult elite: it was, film historians reckoned, a picture that resided outside time, a compendium of all Hitchcock films, 'an illuminating portrayal of the delicate balance between sickness and health in everyone.' (Dr Donald Spoto, in *The Art of Alfred Hitchcock*).

Connery, however, suffered the grey realities of the present. He had revelled in the optimism of the Califor-nian winter, and disliked returning to the damp drudgery of another Bond at Pinewood. Hollywood was twice as attractive the second time round, because now there was the deep cushion of cash and recognition, and Lana Turner was small fry in the deep and misty past. But, bound to Bond, Hollywood was as far away as ever.

A very foul-humoured and irritated Connery faced up to *Goldfinger* because, colleagues claim, expectations were not realised in Hollywood. *Marnie* proved stodgy and Cil-ento did not win an Academy Award: in her nominated category, Best Supporting Actress, the award went to Margaret Rutherford for *The VIPs*. Apart from Ford's prof-fered *Young Cassidy* – which was destined to fall through anyway – the kind of offers dreamt of had not materialised.

Back at Acton the fans were huddled round the high walls of Acacia House, as they had been intermittently for months, anxious to catch a glimpse of the Establishment super-stud hero who was cheekily outpacing the Beatles in the rapid-growth-phenomenon stakes. They saw instead a balding, angry man in a heavy overcoat, glowering, ready to do battle with Harry Saltzman and Cubby Broccoli.

CHAPTER ELEVEN

Agony and Ecstasy and. . .

'JAMES BOND CAME of age with *Goldfinger*,' says new Bond director Guy Hamilton, 'but in so doing stirred up a bit of a hornets' nest.' Greed, ruthless ambition, pomposity and a pervasive fear of failure almost strangled the Bond series at this bountiful time. The spring of '64 was not a peaceful spring for anyone associated with Bond or the Broccoli-Saltzman company, Eon. Terence Young, who had been preparing the new script with Dick Maibaum, fell out with the producers because he demanded a cut of *Goldfinger's* profits, and was replaced by ace action director Hamilton whose credits included *The Colditz Story*. A new screen-writer, the esteemed Paul Dehn, was summoned, and Hamilton began daily work at Dehn's Chelsea flat, re-building Maibaum's 'loose' script. Saltzman, always the gadget man, was at gentle war with Broccoli, ever the tit-and-action man, though both felt, in line with Hamil-ton's thinking, that the best and worst of the first two movies must be sifted with the positive elements exploited hard.

Amidst this tumult, this icy strategy to get richer faster, Connery sauntered in with his gripe. 'Sean had risen to stardom very fast by most standards,' Hamilton says. 'Only six, seven years before I'd been watching him as an extra in the Oscar-winning *Mr Roberts*, and we were nod-ding acquaintances at Gerry's Drinking Club, opposite the stage door of Her Majesty's. I didn't think he had too much going for him, but by *Dr No* he was proving his salt. He matured rapidly then, and the difference in per-formance between *No* and *Russia* is vast. And so, with the Bond success he was picking up offers here, there and everywhere. But the big problem, the cause of his disillusion before *Goldfinger*, was that the offers he could consider were restricted by the contractual commitments of doing Bond. Those Bond pictures took a hell of a time to do, and Cubby and Harry weren't, naturally, prepared to allow Sean go after other jobs as they arose. *Woman of Straw* and *Marnie* gave Sean no particular satisfaction because they weren't the kind of films he wanted to be doing. He was concerned about his craft. He came back from Hollywood wondering what he was . . . he wanted to test himself and see if he was more than just Mickey Mouse as James Bond.'

Connery also wanted greater compensation for cramped opportunity. He had grown to dislike Saltzman intensely – 'mistrust him', in the words of a Bond director – and was suspicious of placating suggestions made by Eon. Finally, reluctantly, he accepted £50,000 plus a percentage for *Goldfinger*, stemming his annoyance by putting out word, via Hatton and other close business friends, that he was seeking original, typesmashing parts. The 'integrity' other associates snigger at seemed quite real: though uneasy with *Goldfinger* in principle and eager to stretch, Connery turned down the first draft script of *Young Cassidy* submitted by Ford, at which time Rod Taylor was marched in to plug the gap. 'After this one [*Goldfinger*],' Connery told an actress friend over dinner, 'it's got to be something away from the sauve gentleman; it's got to be a classy part.'

Physically, making Bond was tougher than ever, though Hamilton was a more ordered director than Young, the kind who preplans every move, allows little improvisation and believes 'sorting out the locations is the hardest part'. Shooting began in March at Pinewood in an atmosphere co-lead Honor Blackman describes as 'furiously professional'. A man of incisive vision and great daring, Hamilton more than anybody was responsible for the huge success of *Goldfinger*, the movie that rechannelled Bond from the edge of earnest amorality to untouchable U certificates. 'The difficulty was often the divergence of opinion between Saltzman and Broccoli,' Hamilton says.

143

'It became a case of why-is-your-idea-better-than-mine? One had to sit around for hours awaiting decisions. But once that obstacle was overcome, it was fine. I had my say in casting. I believed Bond must play opposite someone strong, someone to draw out his strengths. That's why I wanted Gert Frobe, the German actor who was very accomplished, and Honor. With Honor, who is a powerful actress, there was a certain amount of "Oh my God, she's *The Avengers* girl and how do we overcome that?" . . . and they said she looked like a rattled bag compared with some of the young frillies they'd used. But I said, don't worry, she's a fine actress, that's what is important – and we can shoot her with filters to make her look whatever way you like.' Blackman herself was in no doubt that she had been assigned because of her wide experience – *plus* the personal following she had trapped with her kinky, leather-costumed Cathy Gale in TV's *The Avengers*. 'I'm sure the appeal of macho Bond versus kinky me was at the back of the producers' minds,' Blackman says, 'and it obviously worked on screen, this strong female persona – it substituted for the lesbian aspect of the heroine Pussy, which it had been decided would be understated in the movie.'

Pussy Galore is Bond's first crusty lover, a lesbian gang-leader who assists megalomaniac Auric Goldfinger (Frobe) in his ambitious attempt to penetrate the gold depository at Fort Knox, Kentucky, and contaminate the contents by exploding a nuclear device, thereby incalculably increasing the value of his own gold reserves. Bond, against the odds (indeed, against character credibility), seduces Pussy in a hay-barn and, aided by her perfidious swing against Goldfinger when all else has failed, wins the day. Simple fare – but with the strong and imaginative hand of Hamilton, some spiky Dehn dialogue and the creation of prototype sub villains (Oddjob, played by Harold Sakata) and outrageous diversions introduced mostly by Saltzman (the gadget-laden Aston-Martin DB5), the movie took on an extra dimension hitherto unreached even in the fantasy labours of Bond. 'I was helped, naturally, by what had gone before,' says Hamilton. 'I wasn't, for instance, prepared to shoot miles of film and leave half of it on the floor, as had been the case. In *Goldfinger* Bond was sweetened, I suppose, by the perfection of formula. There were only about twenty shots that never appeared on screen. Myself, Sean – we all knew what we were aiming for.'

To Honor Blackman, Connery cut an impressive figure in two ways. Firstly he was 'downright perfectionist, as am I; I liked that. He would never expect one to buy a bad take. If he fluffed, he was first to call a halt. But he wasn't a directorial voice. Guy had full command – so much so that he didn't balk at putting me in my place! There were elements of the lesbian character I would have liked to try out, but he said no; an in-joke or two was fine – like me calling my co-pilot girl Harry or Joe – but that was enough for Guy.' Blackman observed Connery's edginess with the publicity machine too but believed the cause was primarily his shyness. 'He was a reserved man,' she says, 'confident, but private. As the film went on, obviously we got to know each other better. I found him attractive, sexy. . .' She laughs darkly. 'I think he's got a pair of the best eyes that have ever been seen on screen, apart from anything else he might have that's good – and there's plenty of *that*.'

Shyness alone was not the root of Connery's troubles with publicity. Hamilton is quick to emphasise that, regardless of threatened rifts with the producers, Connery was keen to outdo *From Russia With Love*. His perfectionism was not helped at all by constant interruptions at Pinewood, where publicists brought casual journalists onto the set. In one incident, during a key scene a French writer was guided across to a meditative between-takes Connery. The lady writer began to shoot questions. 'First she asked what the film was called,' says Connery. 'I told her. Then what part *I* was playing. I told her. . .' The back-breaking straw came when the journalist jotted Gert Frobe's name on her pad as chief villain. "I've never heard of *her*," she mumbled. Connery exploded. 'I just blew up and walked off the set,' he recalls. 'So I suppose I'm considered rude by that person. Well, I consider *her* disrespectful and incompetent, and both are definite sins. If

145

someone treats me rudely or dishonestly, you see, I repay them an eye for an eye.'

As she had done with *From Russia* and the later films, Cilento coached her husband through *Goldfinger*, helping him learn his lines in his study at Acton by sitting in as Pussy or Jill (Shirley Eaton in the film). She confessed she enjoyed the Bond girl parts, but thought them fundamentally too facile and scant: she herself would never wish to star in a Bond. As it was, her own recently rocky career was stabilising – with Jason growing spirited and independent she had room to breathe again – and good parts were available. *Rattle of a Simple Man*, a minor movie that attracted good notices, was her first worthwhile occupation since *Tom Jones* and, now, Carol Reed was offering a prestigious role in *The Agony and the Ecstasy*. Cilento was delighted with the new script and keen to have her husband star opposite her, but the movie was already fully cast, and he was stuck on Bond anyway. An alternative, for the future, was sought. At the ideal time friend Terence Young appeared as saving angel. He was preparing his own movie version of the Defoe classic *Moll Flanders*, and was agreeable to the notion of pairing husband and wife in the leads. No sooner was Connery's appetite for challenge whetted than the idea was dashed. Reed's film was booked to start in Italy in June, but no definite finish date could be given; Young must start rolling in the autumn. For a few days it was heart-rending stalemate, then Young moved on with other actors and the Connerys lost their chance. Cilento flew to Rome with her mother and children, *Goldfinger* duly wrapped up in July and an atmosphere of ambiguous gloom settled on the Eon camp. 'We knew Sean was vexed with Bond,' a publicist says. 'We knew the series was threatening what he regarded as his actor status. I think probably he wanted out there and then but, like Harry and Cubby, he was kind of mesmerised by the potential. He was thinking, all right, it's a bore, a madhouse, but how much bigger can it get? Will *Goldfinger* earn – what? – $5 million? How much could *I* earn if I stuck with it? He was divided between what he

146

was at heart, an old-fashioned, learn-up-your-lines actor, and a businessman with his hand in a honeypot.'

United Artists pushed out the red carpet for *Goldfinger*, promoting it massively and planning close major premieres in London and New York (September and December respectively). Connery, meanwhile, began his first holiday in nearly two years, flying to Rome to join Cilento with a script in his briefcase that he had first turned down when *Moll Flanders* was in the air, but which now interested him more than a little. The script was an adaptation of Ray Rigby's stage play, *The Hill*, about a North African detention camp for would-be deserters in the Second War, and had been given to him by Pinewood-based producer Kenneth Hyman. The instant appeal of *The Hill* was its projected starkness, and the true-to-life grit of the central characters, of which Connery might be the lead. Sidney Lumet, the celebrated American director of disturbing films like *The Pawnbroker*, was to take the reins – another alluring plus. In Rome Connery made his positive decision to do *The Hill*, and overnight the post-Hollywood, post-Bond depression lifted. Further talks with producer Doc Merman to co-star husband and wife in a movie version of the best-selling novel *Call Me When The Cross Turns Over* in Sydney, Australia, early in '65 cheered the Roman summer all the more.

The paparazzi and scandal-thirsty Italian journalists inevitably fastened onto Cilento, Connery, Cinecittà and the shortest distance between those points while 'James Bond' was in residence in their capital city, but excitement was hard to find. Cilento was a dutiful and admired actress, liked by co-stars Charlton Heston and Rex Harrison and almost too obedient to the camera call. Connery stayed in the pretty pink villa in the hills, reading, idling, going shoeless day and night, growing a moustache for *The Hill*, tending Jason, chit-chatting with the cook and Lady Cilento. A French journalist who spent a free lunchtime with the happy family reported them 'ideally suited, as content as any young family could hope to be.'

Connery found preparation for *The Hill* more satisfying than any movie he had yet made. He ascribed his profound pleasure to 'the time to prepare, to get all the ins and outs of what I was going to do worked out with the director and producer in advance, to find out if we were all on the same track.' There were minor rewrites, but Rigby's script was so good and Lumet's envisioned treatment so assured that Connery felt insistence on some small alterations he would have liked churlish.

Just before he departed for Spain for location news came through that Ian Fleming had died in Canterbury after a heart attack. Connery had liked Fleming – 'a dreadful snob, but a marvellous companion . . . we shared many fascinating conversations and his knowledge was vast'. Word of the death came while Connery was playing golf with Rex Harrison at Rome's Olgiata championship course. In apt tribute, the two stars played an extra 18 holes, Connery teeing off with a Penfold Hearts ball, the variety Fleming dictated for James Bond in his match against Auric Goldfinger in the novel. 'It seemed appropriate,' Connery said. 'I think Ian would have liked that.'

Fleming missed the triumph of the *Goldfinger* opening by just five weeks. For the first time mob-style crowds crammed Leicester Square for the grand Odeon premiere, attended by Honor Blackman 'wearing a solid gold finger cast, quite stupid actually, and flanked by big security men'. Autograph hunters stalked everywhere; fans ripped down poster hoardings and chanted for Connery; TV news picked up the opening night story. Bond was of age, all right – bigger in stature that Eon could ever have hoped for, even on the strength of previous successes. The financial rewards were astounding, in terms of immediate box-office. The *Evening News* reported that 'Nothing like *Goldfinger* has happened in films since they discovered the word "stupendous" '. For the last week in September the Leicester Square Odeon took £17,327 and the Hammersmith Odeon, which averaged £2,000 on its biggest Hollywood attractions, totted £10,000. In New York, weeks later, the phenomenon was repeated and embellished. *Goldfinger* cost $2,900,000, taking artistes' fees into account and all; *Variety* reported it had become the fastest money-maker in the history of motion pictures, grossing $10,374,807 in fourteen weeks in the United States and Canada. United Artists took the unprecedented step of announcing its expectations: by the time the movie ended its engagements in the US, about $20 million in receipts was expected, and this a conservative estimate. On the critical front response was neatly divided between the perspicacious and the snobbishly begrudging. *Punch* was open-handed in praise: 'The whole thing is glossy, entertaining, often funny nonsense.' In *The Spectator* Isabel Quigly was worried about the movie being 'the most overtly fascist of this insanitary series', but had to admit the audience approved, clapped, laughed, cheered its head off – and 'not just a hooligan patch of it'. *Saturday Review* admired Hamilton ('who has paced the action . . . faster'), Fleming and Connery ('who has the role down pat by now'). Penelope Houston devoted a huge chunk of *Sight and Sound* to in-depth analysis, concluding that *Goldfinger* was 'rather a symbolic film' which, as Penelope Gilliatt had suggested of the Bond boom, encapsulated 'the brassy, swinging, ungallant taste of the sixties.' The *Daily Worker*'s comment that the entire business was 'one vast, gigantic confidence trick to blind the audience to what is going on underneath' was given short shrift. Leonard Mosley, always discerning, gasped, 'Even for eggheads, I swear this film is worth a visit. Honor bright. My word is my Bond.' *The Times* dryly observed: 'superb hokum . . . Ian Fleming would have enjoyed it' and Alexander Walker thought it, and Honor Blackman especially, the best thing since spliced film. In America *Newsweek*'s lofty commentators annotated Freudian undertones and wagged a heavy finger with the deduction that Connery-Bond was 'the only guy in the world who has satisfactorily resolved his Oedipus complex. It is an odd entertainment when the hero's strength is as the strength of ten because his gender is pure.'

Connery – the purity of whose gender had never been in doubt – was unmoved by all the tub-thumping. He was glad to repair to Almeria in Southern Spain, away from prying flashbulbs and rubbish questioners, to join Lumet and his cast for what was to be his most physically gruelling film to date. Leaving his family so soon might have presented problems, but Cilento was still contentedly dug into *The Agony and the Ecstasy* and Lady Cilento was there to be surrogate parent.

Ken Hyman, the producer, had expressly made clear the likely strenuous demands of *The Hill*. With his construction crew, headed by art director Bert Smith and manager Dick Frith, he had been in and out of Almeria for three months preparing the ground. The exigencies of film-making made it more feasible to base the production in Spain rather than North Africa, where writer Rigby had been a PoW during the Second War – *The Hill* was based on personal experience. But Almeria was no easy alternative. The entire action of the picture takes place within a wired stockade under blazing sun, but the ideal site was hard to find. Smith and Frith finally found a sandy wasteland at Gabo de Gata where, over ten weeks, an area of 500 yards by 200 was cleared (one sand dune, 200-feet square and 15-feet high was bulldozed away), and the punishment hill of the title was built, using 10,000 feet of imported tubular steel, and more than 60 tons of timber and stone. From midsummer the sun was fierce and relentless – temperatures never fell below 115 degrees – and conditions improved not at all when the cast arrived.

'We were in the bloody desert,' says Ian Bannen, who was starring on screen for the first time with his old pal, 'and the water and food were ghastly. It'd be hard to find words to describe the location. Tough, that's all I can say. Real tough.' 2,000 gallons of pure water were shipped in to keep crew and cast alive, but that didn't stave off unavoidable dysentery. In the beginning, after the rest in Rome and buoyed with the enthusiasm for breaking from type, Connery bore up while others fell to sickness. The actors' working day was long – ten hours or more, six days a week – and fitness was the prime requisite. 'If Sean was uptight about Bond, Sidney (Lumet) kept him smiling,' Bannen says. 'I think *Time* magazine summed it up when it said Sidney makes love to his cast and crew, he's a great sweetener. Sean was fine at the start – despite the fact the location was as smelly as Aberdeen on a hot day. Fishy, that's what it was like, fish-smelling. Awful.'

Eventually Connery did fall ill, flattened by a combination of the heat, the rigours of running round and 'Spanish tummy', but he was on his feet in a day or two and not much shooting time was lost. 'It was the one picture I was on where there was no yellow, pink and blue (script amendment pages),' says Bannen, 'and that pleased Sean a lot.'

Connery, in fact, rated Lumet, the picture and the passion of purpose very highly. Despite the deprivations of Almeria, he loved every minute of the seven week shoot – five in Spain, and two for interiors at Metro Studios in Borehamwood. Later he saw it as 'an example of a film which wasn't a success by the public's standard but eventually became, in terms of acceptance, a supposed classic. . . The idea was to make an ensemble movie, and we made it. The writer, the director, the cast and myself all agreed we'd succeeded in making the movie we wanted to make.'

The Hill, Bannen observed accurately, was a man's film in many ways. The cast was all male, the story uncompromisingly frank and brutal. In a British military stockade errant prisoners are repeatedly forced to climb an almost sheer man-made hill, weighed down with full kits, tongue-lashed by vicious sadists like Staff Sergeant Williams (Ian Hendry). Joe Roberts (Connery), court-martialed for striking an officer, is one such prisoner, pushed beyond endurance, but fighting 'the system' to the end. Bannen, who played righteous Sergeant Harris, thought the film a winner as soon as he had seen the rushes at Borehamwood. 'But you can never tell from the bits and pieces. As it happened, it didn't take in the money and we were all, I'll confess, disappointed. Sean more than most, I'd say. There were things that maybe were misjudged. The black and white photography was aesthetically fine but the American drive-ins don't like it. On the other hand, the movie was a big hit in Europe. I saw it, as a paying customer, in France and Italy. I was doing a Tony Richardson film, cruising the Mediterannean on a schooner, going from port to port. I remember seeing *The Hill* in Greece. It was incredible. I've never witnessed cheering and applause like it in a cinema before. The Europeans really appreciated it. For America, I think the director should have dubbed it and got out some of that background "left-right, left-right" . . . but it stands, I think, as a sound, good film.'

The release of the picture early in 1965, overlapping early production on yet another Bond, *Thunderball*, gave Connery his best serious personal reviews since TV. The *Sunday Express* recognised 'a masterpiece . . . (with) Sean Connery reminding us what a really splendid actor he is.' The *Sunday Citizen* observed 'tremendous performances by Ian Hendry and Sean Connery.' The *Sun* considered Connery 'startlingly good', and the *Daily Express* capped the lot with 'a devastating film . . . Sean Connery gives one of the most disturbingly effective performances of the year.' The *Daily Telegraph* granted its finest commendation: 'A more powerful film has not come out of a British studio for many a year . . . a superb all-male cast.'

To Connery's intense annoyance, once back in London, publicity surrounding *The Hill* focused more on the fact that he had cast aside the toupee he had worn since *Marnie* and allowed the bushy eyebrows that had been cropped for *From Russia With Love* and later films to flourish again. The fan magazines splashed 'Bond in *The Hill*' over double-page spreads that bullheadedly resisted distinction of character, and the tabloids published sneak shots of 'James Bond at play', disguising the disharmony between Connery and Eon by hinting that the drawn features and scraggy moustache were but the jaded face of the dissolute 007. Having sweated blood on *The Hill* and withstood a fan mail deluge since *Goldfinger* it was all too hard to take. When Connery won a few thousand on roulette at an Italian casino, the papers screamed, 'Bond Breaks Casino Bank'; at the launching of Israel's branch of Variety Club International where Connery was voted to present the major cash donation, the *Daily Mail* headlined, 'Bond Hands over £103,000 for Israel'.

Trouble, intimate friends believed, was coming. 'Sean

makes a point of controlling his temper,' Cilento said. 'Only twice since we've been married have I seen his wrath.' At the time these comments were being bandied about, culled from syndicated articles worldwide about married life with Mr Bond, the secret seams of the two-year-old marriage were already coming unstuck. Suddenly, in the run up to *Thunderball* in the spring of '65, vague murmurs were stuttering out about family unrest. 'I don't know how it started,' says a friend off *The Hill*, 'but I will say Sean was a fairly faithful type. Diane, though, was a tough egg. When it began to look like their differences were going to open up into a real split, I guessed Diane was the one who wanted to end it.' Another colleague says, 'Diane was jealous of the Bond success and she didn't hide it. Sean was jealous of the high-brow society Diane attracted. She was a *real* actor, he was hammy. Of course there was more than that. From the beginning she'd said she wanted freedom in marriage. I don't know if any husband could have given her enough. But certainly Bond gave her none. She was Mrs Bond – and she would have none of it.

Thunderball compounded the marital difficulties of Connery and Cilento in more ways than one. Worst of all, here were two people obsessed by the need for privacy attempting to resolve their problems in the eye of a show-biz publicity storm that was growing month by month. Legal hitches temporarily hindered *Thunderball* but by February the new script was ready, all production grievances settled and Connery, once again, financially seduced. His fee for *The Hill*, a relatively small budget feature, had been an astronomical £150,000, and for *Thunderball* was reputedly up by £50,000, with a percentage thrown in. Filming started in France in late February, by which time Connery had already met his female co-lead, another pneumatic sex-siren called Claudine Auger, at a London press party. Auger was neither the producers' nor director Terence Young's first choice. Saltzman had wanted Raquel Welch, having seen her overspilling a bikini top in the October '64 edition of *Life* magazine, and tentative arrangements had been made. But a phone request from Richard

Zanuck, a friend of Broccoli's and production head of Fox in Hollywood, to release her for the forthcoming *Fantastic Voyage* had been complied with. From Christmas '64 through February '65 a long line of glamorous half-known or unknown actresses were tested – by Eon's estimate, as many as six hundred. From them, after close misses by Yvonne Monlaur and dusky Gloria Paul, the former Miss France, Auger was given the lead part of Domino. Married to the French director Pierre Gaspard-Huit, twenty-five years her senior, Auger 'always felt I would become Domino. I had read the book about seven times and knew her inside out. I am very much a Domino sort of girl myself, a fun-loving extrovert. Whatever I am doing I enjoy doing it – loving, driving, riding. . .

Auger and Connery were photographed together at cocktail functions where she was quoted gushing fawningly about Connery's style and talent. Back at Pinewood in March rumours of romance started and on the second Friday of the month Connery quit Acton to move into a flat alone. The *Daily Express* conveyed a close friend's non-surprise: 'It is a great shame. They've tried to patch up their troubles, but it has not worked out.' The same article also reported that 20th Century-Fox had just disclosed the postponement of the movie Cilento and Connery were to star in together; Fox also added that Mr Connery would not now be acting alongside his wife. 'It isn't true to say Sean's mood after *The Hill*, or passing fancies on *Thunderball* or whatever else were responsible for the separation,' a friend insists. 'Anyone who understood their marital arrangement would know the process by which they broke up then. They were just two extremely independent types who had two very different-shaped careers. And Sean put his career before his home, and Diane did the same.'

A week after the trial separation had been announced Connery was back at their Acton home, sleeping overnight. The press pounced. Since his arrival from Spain he had been shadowed everywhere by cub reporters looking for a slice of Bondian wit or wisdom. Cilento brushed away the prattling flock. Were husband and wife to be permanently reconciled? Was there another woman in Connery's life? Did he intend to stay at Acton now? 'You must simply draw your own conclusions from what you know,' Cilento hedged. 'All I can say is that Sean spent last night at the house and will spend tonight here too. A reconciliation? If that is your interpretation, yes. I leave it to you.'

But it was not a reconciliation. Connery moved out again and, as the antidote to encroaching depression, flung himself inventively into *Thunderball*. 'He was lovely to work with,' says Molly Peters, whom Young had plucked from the crowd scenes of his earlier movie *Moll Flanders*, to star as Patricia, the smouldering health clinic masseuse who 'works over' James Bond. 'Very brotherly to me, because it was my first big part and I was desperately nervous – not only of the lines, but because there were these sexy bed and shower scenes I'd to do, one (the shower) where I was nude with him. He encouraged and never showed impatience – unless it was with outsiders who intruded, publicity people and the like.' Unlike Hamilton on *Goldfinger*, Young changed script day by day. Molly Peters's dialogue was altered and, in very un-Hamilton fashion, some eight takes of the nude shower scene were done. 'But Terence made it easy, he kept the atmosphere humorous and he so obviously got on with Sean that we were, in spite of all that was going on beyond Pinewood's lot, like a little happy family. For the shower scene the make-up people wanted to use sticking-plaster on my pubic area and nipples, which I thought more obscene, if anything. In the end, they just covered my front, and my bottom of course was bare for the scene where Connery presses me against the glass and you see the outline. I remember, after all the takes, Sean joked it up. We went into the steam for take number eight or so and when it was over Sean came out on all fours, gaga, with a bowler hat on. He could laugh. And he could make one feel important, that was nice. Once, after a spot of private life bother, I broke into tears just before a take. Sean came up and put his arm round me and said, "Who upset you? Tell me: who here upset you?" He was vexed

155

for me, and I'd no doubt he would have sorted out whoever it was if I'd said a name.'

Molly Peters, among others, observed Connery's attraction to 'glamorous women who came to the set, especially one fabulous Hungarian', but kept apart from his social encounters. A Bond girl says, 'Sean's attention was absorbed by Claudine. He went for continental types, and she suited him ideally.'

Late in March crew and cast flew to the Bahamas to resume filming and Cilento stayed behind with Jason and Gigi. The tiny archipelago was, in *Playboy*'s words, 'in a state of siege, occupied by an invading army of newspaper reporters, magazine writers and photographers from every major publication in America, England, Europe, Canada, Australia and Japan; TV crews from ABC, NBC and the BBC, silk-suited press agents and swim-suited starlets.' Auger kept Connery company discreetly, though they were pictured together daily, embracing, languishing in the warm Gulf waves, ambling along Love Beach. Perhaps the mandatory overt romance of Bond-and-bird was the most fortuitous natural cover; then again perhaps it was, as a film colleague says, 'a nuisance; Claudine was a good friend to Sean, they liked each other's company; but Sean wanted Diane to come out to Nassau, he wanted her back.'

Scheduled to fly to Nassau after protracted phone talks, Cilento cancelled out when, early in April, Acacia House was burgled and items of favoured jewellery were taken. Days later she caught a plane, accompanied by Jason and Gigi.

Connery met her at Nassau airport, suntanned, uptight, alone. Asked about reconciliation he played dumb. Pressed with queries as to whether he was pleased to see his wife he answered smartly, 'Yes, of course.' Then the reunited group skipped into a Cadillac and motored to a bungalow specially rented for them on Love Beach. *Thunderball* kept rolling through Easter and Connery made love, for the cameras, to slinky, sad-eyed Auger. The word 'reconciliation' fell from the reporters' barrage. The couple were together again, the radical marriage resumed.

156

Cilento told journalist David Lewin, 'I am through the other side now of being called Mrs Bond and although it still happens it cannot upset me any longer. Sean and I have our own lives to lead in our own way.' Ominously she warned, 'This industry can take hold of you and wrap you up like a piece of meat . . . neither of us will allow ourselves to become that involved. We are not going to let ourselves be merchandised.'

Connery, unfortunately, was already bought, packaged and sold. In succeeding with Bond he had, for the moment, lost himself.

CHAPTER TWELVE

You Only Live . . . Twice?

A KIND OF insanity overtook Sean Connery's life from '65 through '67, the period during which the basis of his fortune was amassed. In 1965, thanks to *Goldfinger* mostly, he was number one box-office attraction in America, an unparalleled achievement in recent times for a British cinema star. In 1966 he still topped the polls, and his fame had well and truly conquered Eastern and Western audiences. In Japan he was idolised, ranking high above the Beatles in cultist status. In Germany, Scandinavia and France his celebrity had injected new vitality into cinema-going.

'The French were the first to recognise the Bond films,' he told Tony Crawley, and other film writers. 'In some ways the French are insular because of their chauvinism towards film, but they have always been very respectful of effort in new directions.'

'I suppose many actors envied him for the breadth of his popularity,' friend Robert Hardy says, 'but the burdens must have been *too* extraordinary.'

Connery's fee per film touched a plateau of around $500,000 during the heady mid-sixties, but overwork marred some of his performances. *Thunderball* had him as Bond tracking down a stolen Vulcan bomber, equipped with atomic charges, to its sunken hideout in the Bahamas. Largo (Adolfo Celi) was the chief SPECTRE villain behind the enterprise and Domino (Auger) his unhappy mistress. As in *Goldfinger*, Bond beats the villain by the skin of his teeth, abetted by the disaffected girl. The ambience of holiday brochure skies and sand and haute cuisine came over well and the main trio of girls, Auger, Peters and Luciana Paluzzi, radiated a cruder sexuality which, in its gender-purity, should have delighted *Newsweek*. But structural faults, the tendency for the action to jerk as Bond hops from the tranquillity of a health clinic to gumshoeing in Nassau, to frenetic underwater escapades, are distracting. Connery too seems uneven, missing the beat of his regulated sprightly dash just when a pro (even playing 007) shouldn't – in particular in the gentler, romantic scenes. Notices for the movie were consistent with noisy public approval. Bosley Crowther's love-hate affair with Bond in the pages of the *New York Times* went on: 'Mr Connery is at his peak of coolness and nonchalance . . . even the violence is funny. That's the best I can say for a Bond film.' The cautious Dilys Powell, ever eager to dispense with the blindfold of hype, wondered whether mechanical ingenuity wasn't undermining human interests and the *Sunday Telegraph* stomped a heavy step further with the bold flyer: 'There's no story in *Thunderball*'. Later in this same review Robert Robinson opined, 'Bond is the magus to whom all things are possible, a sickly condition with a very poor prognosis, for once it is diagnosed by an audience it robs a character of individuality, and at last, of interest. Where there are no limits, there is no story, and novelty is offered as a substitute.'

Substitution seemed better than surrender in other areas of Connery's hectic life now. With Cilento invited to Hollywood to make *Hombre* opposite Paul Newman, Connery and agent Hatton plugged for an American deal that would allow reconciled husband and wife the chance of consonance in the same sphere for a bit. Since the Australian picture was off, the next best must be something near *Hombre*. Hatton tied down *A Fine Madness*, to be filmed on location in New York for Warners by Irvin Kershner. By coincidence Newman's wife, Joanne Woodward, had already been signed for the film. Though *Hombre*'s principal location shooting would be in Phoenix, Arizona, both liked the idea of commuting the short distance whenever possible to be together, though it was agreed the children would stay with Cilento. 'Sean was too jaded by Bond,' a colleague believes, 'to feel any jubilation at coming back to America for such a big picture.' Michael Hayes, the *Age of Kings* director, considers it 'quite astounding that, amid all that Bond uproar, he could trim himself to the finesse of *A Fine Madness*'.

Of the four or five movies that ripped after *Thunderball*, *A Fine Madness* is undeniably Connery's best, possibly because the character he portrays, Samson Shillitoe, the arrogant rebel poet, is an exaggeration of Tommy the Fountainbridge rebel – an overblown depiction of an overgrown rebel perhaps but no less interesting for the echoes it tunes in to. Samson is a wild beast, haunted by the epic poem he can't quite write and hounded by a wife he loves but, though he wants to, can't quite leave. Sacked from his job for blaring rudeness, he is chased all over New York for back alimony and falls into the clutches of a sophisticated Manhattan psychiatrist (Patrick O'Neal) and his wife (Jean Seberg) who try to help him. Corrupted to *his* hair-raising way of life, the sophisticates finally agree to release the untameable Samson and let him search for raucous peace with wife Rhoda (Woodward).

Hombre and *A Fine Madness* achieved more or less all their goals. Cilento and Connery restruck the link of mutual confidence and commitment. Both movies were critically well received and Connery utilised his time in New York and the comfort of his ten percent in *A Fine Madness* to steel himself for what was suddenly announced to be his last Bond, the Japanese-set *You Only Live Twice*, scheduled to start shooting in May '66. (*On Her Majesty's Secret Service* was originally to have been Connery's fifth Bond, and Guy Hamilton hoped to direct it, starring Brigitte Bardot as heroine Tracy (Hamilton's suggestion). The problems of coordinating production in time to use the spring snows of Switzerland, essential to the plot, stopped the project.)

A year earlier, reflecting on his gutsy role in *The Hill*, Connery had said, 'Some people thought I couldn't make a go of a movie without romantic interest.' That he so obviously had was proved not only by the favourable notices, but by the genuine new attention paid to him by lofty 'names' in New York. A producer who knew him at the time says, 'Sean made a go of fitting in to the Greenwich Village, arty swing of New York. He saw plays on Broadway, chatted with the moguls . . . even lived out something of his (*Fine Madness*) character. A certain clique took to him as artist, not James Bond, and he liked that. He was friendly with people like Sir Tyrone Guthrie, the stage director.'

Months later, Connery was at home with Cilento in London. Revelling in the New York reviews for *Madness*, like 'Give it A for effort and B for impudence and originality . . . Connery plays well' – the *New York Times*, he was bursting with fresh, Bond-busting, sane ideas. With a side-jab at Eon he was telling the press 'One should be paid what one is worth. Money gives you freedom and power . . . I want to use that power I now have as a producer. In Hollywood I asked Sir Tyrone Guthrie why he had never made a film. "Because no one asked me," he said. Well, I want to ask him. In the same way that Burton asked Zeffirelli to direct *The Shrew* when Zeffirelli had never made a film before.' Connery added, with the fresh perspective of time in New York, that what he was really tired of was 'a lot of fat slob producers living off the backs of lean actors.' He wanted to wriggle free of the slob producers who had him in their grisly grip and he wanted to go back to purist roots. He would, he said, direct a play on Broadway next year. 'Of course a lot of people say that's madness – when thirty-eight new productions out of forty-four have flopped on Broadway in the past season this is hardly the time for an untried English director to be welcomed. But I'm going because I like the play and I want to do it.' The determination was admirable but ill-founded and the play, London-based Ted Allan Herman's *The Secret of the World*, announced to star Shelley Winters, never materialised.

Before embarking on the last exhausting Bond Connery and Cilento took advantage of the lull to, metaphorically, put their house in order. They analysed and defused the conflicting aspects of their lives together. Cilento decided to retard her film career for a while and concentrate on novel writing. Her novel *The Manipulator* published in

1967, with the dedication 'For Sean', and the jacket designed by Connery, was a moderate success. The continuing violation of privacy at Acton, especially after the burglary, was deemed unacceptable. The house went on the market in April 1966, advertised openly under a rambling newspaper notice headed 'Sean Connery, the motion picture actor, offers . . . the self-styled queen of the suburbs'. The going price was £17,950 freehold. Connery explained his reasons for wanting out with typical frankness: 'People knew the house – after all, there aren't many actors in Acton – and would come and sit and stare at Diane and me in the main room. If it had gone on I'd have been found guilty of assault.' Renewed efforts were made to persuade Effie and Joe to quit Fountainbridge, but the best Sean could do was nudge Joe into early retirement.

Property in Spain – a few farm acres with a nondescript house – was secured and, to the couple's initial great pleasure, an attractive Victorian house on Putney Heath, slap in the middle of actor-land. Cilento homed on Putney while Connery, grimly, taxied to Pinewood for discussions about *You Only Live Twice*. 'After this,' he swore to reporters, 'I will only do the things that passionately interest me for the remaining thirty-five years of my life.'

Lewis Gilbert, fresh from the set of the blistering *Alfie* with Michael Caine – destined to give Bond a run for his money at the box-office throughout late '66 – approached his first commission on a Bond with reservations. 'In the beginning I turned it down,' he says, 'because four had already been done and the natural reaction was to say, well, what can I contribute, it's all been done. But then Cubby rang me again and said, you can't turn this down because you have the biggest audience in the world sitting out there waiting for you. And that *was* interesting. I mean, you can do the greatest picture ever and it will still not find an audience, but with Bond you are guaranteed. Then of course there was the investment. This picture would cost $7 or 8 million and, like a general in the field with his tanks and resources, that kind of back-up for a director is pretty alluring. So I decided I'd do this Bond, and try and contribute my own little something to making the saga different.'

With their fingers on the market pulse Broccoli and Saltzman saw the need to freshen Bond too, but their individual ambitions were dogged by personal unease. 'There was a dreadful divide,' a director says. 'Harry had wandered off into projects he whimsically wanted to do, like those Len Deighton spy films (Michael Caine as unglamorous agent Harry Palmer) and Cubby grew tired of Harry's irregular participation in Bond. Harry wasn't as fast on the uptake, ideas-wise, as Cubby – that was part of the trouble too.' Lewis Gilbert confesses he acted as 'a sort of go-between, keeping the peace' but stresses, 'Once the picture got going (the producers) were terrific. With their vast experience I had people to turn to when I was in doubt and, good God, at times on Bond you needed support.' During pre-production Broccoli and Saltzman allegedly came very close to dissolving their partnership. They finally parted in 1974, with Saltzman selling out to Broccoli and returning to theatrical management. A very close associate on *You Only Live Twice* says, 'They couldn't stand the sight of each other then . . . and things got worse when Sean's dislike for Harry blew up. It got so bad he wouldn't come on set in Japan if Harry was around. A, he didn't want to be in Japan doing Bond at all; and B, the last person he wanted looking over his creative shoulder was this hard-shelled old driver.'

Roald Dahl, the popular short-story writer who had never written a film, was engaged as an extraordinarily offbeat choice to screenwrite the Japanese film. Perhaps, Gilbert suggests, Noel Coward's observation about Dahl's 'fabulous imagination' with the 'underlying streak of cruelty and macabre unpleasantness and a curiously adolescent emphasis on sex' endeared him to the producers. Dahl humorously recounted for *Playboy* his early contacts with Broccoli. Never having heard of either of the producers and having only seen *Goldfinger* he believed the man trying to reach him on the telephone to discuss a possible commission was one Archie Lockley. Patricia Neal, his actress wife who had answered the phone, insisted, 'This one *is* Broccoli, head of the Mafia. You'd better watch out.' Dahl wrote his script in record time, ready for shooting in Pinewood in May. There were plot difficulties still, so Dahl and writer Harold Jack Bloom prepared to fly out to Japan in July for revisions.

'There were many, many difficulties,' Lewis Gilbert smiles. 'Apart from Sean's unease, we had a kick up over casting. Up till the very last minute there was no arch-villain. Harry swore he'd found a superb Czechoslovakian actor, but the man did a few days in Pinewood and we had to let him go. We roped in Donald Pleasence quickly. Then there was the hassle with the girls. These films are prepared on the highest diplomatic level – that's to say, Cubby was getting permissions to shoot at key sites in Japan by approaching embassies and all the rest. So, naturally the Japanese were insistent that certain requirements be met. First we tried to get our Japanese heroines in Europe, then Hawaii – but they were all brash or too Americanised or wrong. Then the Japanese people said, in effect, use our girls, or else. So we auditioned and picked two main girls Mie Hama and Akiko Wakabayashi, neither of whom could speak English. They went on crash courses, but the problem arose when Akiko picked up her English faster than Mie. Mie was lovely, but she just couldn't get her English down. So we decided to drop her, and I took Tetsuro Tamba (Japanese Secret Service chief in the film) aside and told him our situation and asked him to explain nicely to Mie. He was helpful, he took her out to dinner and told her and next morning he came to Cubby's office and we were having a meeting and we said, "Well, does she know?" "Yes," Tamba said, "I told her." "And how did she take it?" Tamba was very philosophical. He said, "She said OK, if she was out she'd commit suicide. She couldn't go home to Japan and face the loss of honour after all the pre-publicity. James Bond is king in Japan, and she's got the big role opposite him." Harry and Cubby looked at Tamba with mouths open. Then we all said, "Well, on second thoughts she's not *so* bad. She can keep at it and we'll fit her in.' Hama's part, originally to be the larger role of Aki, Bond's agent ally,

Left: Down these mean streets…
Freer Street, off Fountainbridge with
its busy 'stairs', much on the design
of the Connery tenement round the
corner.
(Aquarius/Scotsman)

Below: Fet-Lor Amateurs team
1949-50, Connery second from
right, second row from top. 'In that
game you're old at 25. I wanted to
go on a bit longer than that.'
(Courtesy Craigie Veitch)

Above: Success on television: Connery's first TV role, in Alvin Rankoff's *Requiem for a Heavyweight,* 1957. Connery, as ageing boxer Mountain McClintock, is tended by Fred Johnson as the Doctor and George Margo. *(BBC Copyright)*

Left: Success at home. At the King's Theatre, Edinburgh in *The Seashell,* October 1959. *(Aquarius/Scotsman)*

Right: Connery as Alexander the Great in Terence Rattigan's *Adventure Story,* BBC, June 1961. *(BBC Copyright)*

Above: John Gregson as the goodie, Herbert Lom as the evil Waldo, and Connery on a tightrope between the two. *The Frightened City,* 1961.
(Aquarius, London)

Left: Brushing up the Bond image. Connery outside his north London flat, shortly after signing the Bond pictures deal, December 1961.
(Aquarius/PIC London)

Left: At Heathrow Airport en route to Jamaica to commence filming of *Dr No,* with director Terence Young (in check coat), January 1962. *(Aquarius/PIC London)*

Below: Sultry Zena Marshall accompanied bachelor Connery to the *Dr No* premiere, October 5, 1962. But Anita Ekberg had eyes only for the star. *(Aquarius/PIC London)*

Left: The newly-weds. Connery celebrates with Diane Cilento, December 1962.
(Aquarius/PIC London)

Below: Not everyone was happy about *Woman of Straw* (1964), least of all Connery and co-star Gina Lollobrigida.
(Aquarius/Nova Productions)

Above: Clowning with 'Tippi' Hedren on the set of *Marnie* at Universal, Hollywood. *(Aquarius)*

Below: Hitchcock liked Connery but "wasn't convinced" he was the Philadelphia gentleman hero of *Marnie.*
(Aquarius)

Above: Star partnerships, and all running smoothly. Connery and Diane
Cilento, Saltzman *left* and Broccoli at the opening night of *From Russia With Love,*
October 10, 1963. *(Aquarius/PIC London)*

Left: For better or worse, Sean Connery *is* James Bond.
(Aquarius/PIC London)

Below: Blonde, Bond, bed. High-octane mix with the voluptuous Molly Peters,
rehearsing *Thunderball. (Courtesy Molly Peters)*

Opposite: Heir apparent? Yet to be offered that role of Bond Mk II, Roger Moore dines with Connery at Les Ambassadeurs Club, London, December 1969.
(Aquarius/PIC London)

Below: Connery-eye-view of the Bond boom. Photographers crowd the set of *Thunderball* during an interlude in the steamy bed scene with Luciana Paluzzi, at Pinewood Studios.
(Eon films Ltd/Aquarius, London)

Above: With Ossie Davis in a scene from *The Hill.* ''Some people said I couldn't make a go of it....'' But the film was a critical success.
(Aquarius, London)

Below: The Wind and the Lion won much praise too. Here Connery plays opposite Candice Bergen.
(Columbia-Warner)

Above: Director Michael Crichton discusses an early key scene with Connery and Lesley-Anne Down for *The First Great Train Robbery*. The cinematographer Geoffrey Unsworth who died shortly after completion of the film can be seen reflected in the mirror. *(Courtesy Seamus Smith)*

Below: Fred Zinnemann fulfils an ambition, directing a 'mountaineering story,' *Five Days One Summer*, with Connery.
(Courtesy Fred Zinnemann)

Left: Joe, Effie and Tommy – at home in Fountainbridge just before *Dr No* opened, September 1962. *(Aquarius/Scotsman)*

Below: Proud moment for a son of Edinburgh. Herriot-Watt University confers an honorary Doctor of Letters degree, 1981. *(Aquarius/Scotsman)*

Right: Family group. Sean and Micheline, sons Jason and Stefan. *(Aquarius/Scotsman)*

Below: Connery with second wife Micheline. 'It's a rare bird who will stay with you year in year out if you don't marry her.' *(Aquarius)*

Overleaf: Connery at 50, Switzerland, 1981. *(Courtesy Fred Zinnemann)*

was swapped with Wakabayashi's Kissy, the pearl-diving island girl Bond later falls for – a part that was less demanding in terms of dialogue.

Connery and Cilento tried desperately to make the three months of location shooting a holiday, they tried to distance themselves from the crazy circus of developments. While a chartered jet flew the cast and crew one way round the world, the patched-up couple chose the alternative route, going via Manila, a drastic mistake. In the tiny jam-packed city they were mobbed, pestered in their hotel, ultimately trapped. On arrival in Japan conditions deteriorated fast. The lobby of the Tokyo Hilton was crowded day and night by sweaty, camera-hung newsmen, chattering like geckoes in a swamp. The film trail led south, to Kagoshima – and the swelling, surging press followed along. Alan Whicker had accompanied the crew, travelling with his own, more subtly intrusive BBC camera team, and he had the good grace to sip his Kirin beer, play the far spectator and admit appalled amazement. Connery, he noted, had 'abandoned his fierce professional concentration and seemed indifferent to the film's progress'. Cilento in a jaded moment told Whicker: 'He's tried beyond normal limits, because everywhere you go there's always someone coming out from behind a tree . . . photographers follow him into the lavatory.'

After *Thunderball* Connery told columnist Sheila Graham only $2,800,000 plus a high percentage would buy him for another Bond, but when *You Only Live Twice* was over he said, 'I don't want to know. It's finished. Bond's been good to me, but I've done my bit. I'm out.'

'I can understand how he felt,' Lewis Gilbert says. 'If he seemed to be "cruising" in certain parts of our movie it was only because he knew the character was immovably second in line to the gadgets, and that bored him, I suppose. For myself, I tried to give Bond a human dimension. By introducing the emotion when the girl Aki is murdered, for example. But Sean had such a strain to put up with, with the fans. Once, when we tried to do a simple shot of him walking down the Ginza we decided the safest way was to hide our camera, let him slip out of a car and amble past – let him vanish in the street strollers. We tried,' Gilbert laughs loud. 'But Sean got out of the car . . . and was just pounced upon by a million fans.'

You Only Live Twice, a kind of advanced *Dr No* in storyline, did not sweep the box-office as its immediate predecessors had done. The reviews, by now, were token efforts, regurgitated superlatives primed to fill out entertainment pages in journals good and bad. Politically and socially Bond was now neutral – a labourer with bourgeois style in a high-living, to all purposes, apolitical universe. In *You Only Live Twice* Russia and America are testy brothers naturally vexed by the in-flight thefts of their respective manned space shots. The ubiquitous SPECTRE, led by Blofeld (Pleasence), is the real culprit, stealing the space capsules in hope of inflaming East and West to the point of annihilative war. Bond learns the interceptor rockets are being fired from Japan and, with the cooperation of the Japanese Secret Service, he tracks down Blofeld in his volcano mountain hideaway, blows the place up and short-circuits a very unlikely World War Three. Robert Robinson's prognosis on *Thunderball* seemed borne up definitively when Bosley Crowther wrote: 'There's so much of that scientific clatter – so much warring of super-capsules out in space and fussing with electronic gadgets – that this wayout adventure picture should be the joy and delight of the youngsters and . . . adults who can find release in the majestically absurd.'

Whatever slender grip the James Bond of *Dr No* had on dramatic reality was lost forever, it seemed, with the new movie. Connery, therefore, who drew and projected his strength from *real* strengths – from the adverse conditions of his childhood and his assiduous application to the classics – became redundant. James Bond, not Sean Connery, had become a big movie star. To Connery, the option of vacating the role was the best for everyone. As the movies were going, James Bond could well stand on his own feet. Any hunk who could move, talk and bed a woman could be screen Bond. 'It could have been different though,' Connery said. 'Had the producers not been so greedy today United Artists could belong to Connery, Broccoli and Saltzman.' But there would have been radical changes had that dream been realised. Greed aside, Connery made it clear he would have altered the superstructure of 007, re-introduced credible characters and gritty situations, humanising Bond again.

It didn't happen like that, so Sean Connery pocketed his quixotic dream and set off in '67 in search of a character.

Out of Bondage Connery had time to contemplate all sorts of unreached goals. His love for golf (which now had him playing off a handicap of thirteen) was one other source of frustration. 'I really adore the game,' he said. 'I considered turning pro, but I'm not sure it would have made me any happier. I'm an actor, and I love my job most.' Always a scribbler, he dabbled with storylines in Putney and started drafting a script he had toyed with for years – 'Macbeth, to be made in Scotland with Scottish actors; I'll direct it myself.'

'Writing, after football and golf, was his big thing,' says John Boorman. 'He liked to write poetry, though he didn't show it around. I suppose he'd read enough bad scripts to make him want to set records right. And, no doubt about it, he had the intellectual capacity to do great stuff.'

The blossoming opportunities of uncontracted idleness provided Connery with what was to develop into a most satisfying ongoing intellectual stimulus – an outlet for investment, financial and otherwise, in Scotland's future. The outlet came in the person of revolutionary Scottish industrialist Sir Iain Stewart, nationally known in the late sixties for his brave campaigns to reduce unemployment and rejuvenate Clydeside, specifically in his Fairfields Shipyard plan. Connery met Stewart, a Glaswegian, at a golfing society dinner in London. In roundabout chatter, the industrialist detailed his five-year plan for Fairfields, an outrageous labour-management experiment that had started with the support of George Brown at the DEA, Jim Callaghan at the Treasury and Ray Gunter at the Ministry of Labour. The plan, in essence, slackened potentially stifling union regulations and allowed a workers' voice in management. The real viablity of the plan was

167

never tested because in 1968 Stewart made the mistake of allowing Fairfields to enter the disastrous Upper Clyde Shipbuilders merger, a scheme that ended in bankruptcy in 15 months.* But, at the time, Connery was so intrigued by Stewart's rebel dream that he journeyed to Glasgow to examine procedures for himself and, without prompting, decided to make a documentary about the problems of Clydeside.

The Bowler and the Bunnet (a bunnet is the Lowlands Scots equivalent of the flat cap) was written and directed by Connery over a few weeks late in '67 and shown on Scottish Television. Efforts to sell it to regional independent television, even the BBC, failed, but the documentary was regarded as good of its kind and did serve to highlight the positive progress Stewart was making at Fairfields. Connery was especially proud of his little film because it spoke up for Scotland. 'Stewart was doing something at Fairfields that hadn't been done so successfully anywhere in the country, including England. He was bridging that terrible gulf between the bosses and the workers and he was breaking down the petty suspicions between unions. He even had carpenters doing painters' work when necessary and he had union men sitting in the boardroom. It was all working famously and production was going up . . . what the film did for me in personal terms was made me realise that part of me belonged to that kind of background . . . I just couldn't turn my back on it completely.'

The failure of Fairfields in UCS two years later was an industrial and social tragedy, but more than a little good had come from Connery's first personal venture into film-making. The friendship with the sagacious Stewart inspired a concept that was grander than union-management control.

The Scottish International Educational Trust, founded

*Stewart agreed to go into the UCS merger as deputy chairman because, he said, he was assured 'that the methods that had been successful at Fairfields would be used and the recommendations of the industry's working party report would be adopted.' This, however, did not transpire, and he resigned after two months, predicting the bankruptcy.

in 1970 to provide bursaries for bright but underprivileged Scots and supply cash for educational projects like the establishment of a drama chair at Strathclyde University, started life as a modest charity golf tournament set up by Connery along the lines of the famous American Bing Crosby Pro-Am. In 1968 during early preparation for the tournament Connery was announcing that 'part of the money raised is going to be used researching the reasons why the Scots leave Scotland. I've already talked to St Andrews' University about the research programme.' At the same time he was declaring his support for the Scottish Nationalists, while confessing he had never actually voted in his life. 'I was reminded of the return of the prodigal son,' says an Edinburgh friend with a grin. 'Sean had never actually got Scotland out of his blood, to give him credit, but he never gave any big indication till then of national pride. Of course everyone here was pleased.' Some interpreted Connery's sudden fervour as an anti-big-town reflex, but it would be naive to think he was recanting some heart-hurting heresy. 'Sean had wealth and time to do good after Bond,' says Robert Hardy. 'One got the impression he wished to advance himself and his causes.'

Following a firm restatement of his allegiance to the Scottish cause on an Eamonn Andrews TV show, Connery was formally approached by the National Party to stand as their candidate at the next election, representing an unspecified constituency. He rejected because 'I would not be so presumptuous as to sit for any political candidacy without sufficient work, background and knowledge . . . I suppose it would be easy enough to let lieutenants spoon-feed you, but I'm not familiar enough with the details across the country. I'd get found out.' In fact, having dallied with industrialists and politicians for a while – and snatched a good rest – Connery was gravitating back to movieland. He abhorred boredom and got restless when Cilento's lady friends came to call, or when the children threw tantrums. Charles Feldman's offer to bring him back to the big screen as Bond in the spoof *Casino Royale* was dismissed, as were a clutch of ridiculous

169

cardboard booby' spy stories. When at last one offer took his fancy it surprised no one that the subject was a western, intended for early '68 shooting in Mexico, called *Shalako*.

Edward Dmytryk, the director, chose Connery as 'the ideal' for Louis L'Amour's frontier scout hero and producers Euan Lloyd and Dimitri de Grunwald granted their blessing with a $1,200,000 cheque (to be cashed in over a nine month period) plus thirty percent of net profits. Connery was childishly enthusiastic about the project, though he cooled slightly when told Brigitte Bardot would be his co-star. Bardot's star-studded ego was well known to be bigger than her going price ($350,000 for *Shalako*, plus a cut in profits), and, true to form, she asked Lloyd to fix a meeting with Connery before she signed papers – 'to test the vibrations'. In his intimate biography of Bardot, Willi Frischauer suggests Connery's initial response was glum, but on meeting Bardot face to face at Deauville champagne spilled cheerily and hearts throbbed fast. Gunter Sachs, Brigitte's current husband 'feared the worst', and cleared out; but within a few days BB was back in his arms.

Shalako was not, as Honor Blackman, a co-star, describes it, a happy film. The threat of a labour strike in Mexico forced Lloyd to relocate the shoot in dusty old Almeria and events shuddered to an unpromising start when Bardot delayed filming by arriving belatedly, with snowy Rolls-Royce and entourage of photographers and hangers-on, to take up queenly residence at the Hotel Aquadulce. 'Once Sean was over that bad start he kept out of it,' Blackman says. 'He took a rented villa nearby, where he stayed with his family and made a point of concentrating on doing as good a job as possible under the circumstances.' The circumstances were not conducive to refreshing work. In her personal plot to remain the perennial teenager, Bardot brought to Almeria exactly the kind of press-heavy circus charade that Connery had hoped to see the back of with Bond. Bardot's open rows with former lover, actor Stephen Boyd, made matters worse; worse again were her threats to quit the location

170

before half her footage was in the can. 'Eddie Dmytryk's patience was truly remarkable,' says Blackman. 'Then, I guess we all deserve credit.'

Ten years before, the story of a true-as-an-arrow western hero despatched by the Army to guide a party of wealthy aristocrats out of raging Indian country would have encouraged Connery to barter his soul; now he almost regretted signing on. Satisfied enough with his own performance, he was relieved when the picture wrapped up only slightly over time. Returning to London, he awarded himself the gift of a new (well, second-hand) Jensen for endurance and self-control beyond the call of duty.

All the publicity promises – 'the most sensuous film BB has ever made', 'Connery and BB, the electrifying twosome' – were not upheld in the final screen cut. Lloyd had shrewdly prefinanced the film entirely by the unusual method of procuring advance guarantees of release from some 27–30 different countries, which was just as well. Reviewers clashed fiercely, divided between those who thought this first ambitious British western an out-and-out dud, and those who admired the motley of former Negro football star Woody Strode as an Indian chief, purring Honor Blackman as the aristocratic faithless wife and Eric Sykes as a French chef. No one said much about Bardot, and she herself conceded, '*Shalako* is Sean Connery's film. He carried the whole weight of it on his shoulders.' Marjorie Bilbow in *Screen International* declined the ritual baton: 'Connery seems so determined to erase all memories of James Bond that he allows the foreground figure of Shalako to fade into middle distance.'

Few kids in the Blue Halls would have been impressed.

CHAPTER THIRTEEN

A Sixties' Hangover

WITH BOND BURIED and the wound-licking spree of idleness and *Shalako*, the long-dreamt-of western, past, Connery slumped to a career stance that appeared something between defeatism and apprehensive torpor. 'He was, momentarily, completely unsure of himself,' an actor colleague swears. 'Everything he did, he questioned. I remember a friend visited him in Putney, where he'd had this German hot-and-cold water shower installed in the basement, and it had cost a few hundred quid. He agonised over it. A few hundred quid was a big deal! In Scotland his Dad could've lived for a year on a few hundred quid. Sean wasn't happy, and didn't know how to *get* happy. He smoked pot, but disliked it, found it turned him on but made him lethargic too. He tried to give up cigarettes and cut down on his drinking. He tried many things. One got the feeling that here was a man who wanted to retrace his steps, go back to the past – all this was evident in his fixation with doing good for Edinburgh's poor, all that – but he'd lost his way.'

Dennis Selinger, Connery's new agent-manager replacing Richard Hatton, who had retired to go into production, was concerned too. He believed Connery needed to capitalise on the lingering Bond boom, but work fast to establish himself as a separate, talented entity. At round table meetings in Selinger's office in central London the agent outlined his proposals: Connery must recognise that his non-Bond films had largely flopped and, out of Bondage, he could lose ground fast. He must not sit to wait for offers, he must go out and grab whatever was available, meet directors and moguls, *work*. 'I'd proved this with

172

Mike Caine,' Selinger says. 'If one wants to make international impact the surest system is to make as many films as possible. I told Sean, if one can do four or five movies a year *one* is bound to hit and that one can up your price and keep you on top. Sean wasn't too convinced. "But *The Hill* won't come along every week," I advised him. You must get out and at it.'

Very reluctantly Connery shambled back to work, taking on two offers that were to prove atrocious cul-de-sacs – *The Molly Maguires,* directed by Martin Ritt for Paramount, and the Italian-Russian co-production *The Red Tent.* To date, *The Molly Maguires* has lost about $10 million (negative cost, inflation adjusted) and *The Red Tent* about £9 million. Both rate among the twenty biggest box-office losers of all time. Connery had been keen on *The Molly Maguires,* a project first suggested to him by Marty Ritt while Ritt was directing *Hombre* and Connery was visiting his wife. Blacklisted from TV where he started his career during the McCarthyist drive of the early fifties, Ritt was enamoured of the idea of a movie about the abused, impoverished Irish miners in the Pennsylvania coal pits of the 1870s banding together (as the secret Molly Maguires) and taking murderous action against their brutal employers. The story of *The Molly Maguires,* as written by Ritt's lifelong friend Walter Bernstein, revolved round the infiltration of the Irish group by a management agent, McParlan (played by Richard Harris with thunderous vigour), who eventually befriends miners' leader Kehoe (Connery) and is won over by the sincerity of the oppressed. Though based on fact, the plot is pure fiction and somehow, in its grey-faced telling, reveals all the irksome weaknesses of arty analogy. The critics mostly disliked the film and found little to rejoice about in Connery's unsympathetic character; many disdained specious crusading, though Connery himself defended the wholesomeness of the venture, seeing it as an extension of his work-for-the-people on *The Bowler and the Bunnet.* The Molly Maguires were the indirect forerunners of free trade unionism, he claimed, and he was proud to be associated with so honest a film. While the picture was being made on location in

173

Pennsylvania (later at Paramount Studios, Hollywood), *On Her Majesty's Secret Service*, the sixth Bond, was in progress at Pinewood, with Australian newcomer George Lazenby portraying Bond. Connery temporarily declined comment on Bond developments but saw no significant loss of face in his own second-billing on *The Molly Maguires*. Queried about his declining popularity he said, 'They're paying me a million dollars for this picture. For that kind of money they can put a mule ahead of me.' In Pennsylvania he was moody, but generally good company; though he was ready to talk to the press publicists were advised that questions about a return to Bond were taboo. The weather was good, too good, during most of the shoot and he suffered dehydration – as he had done during the making of *You Only Live Twice* in Japan. The suffering eased some need for purgation within him and he bragged about doctors having to give him tea with whole lemons squeezed into it and salt crackers.

Ritt recognised the failure of his film just about as fast as Connery – though he certainly suffered worse for it. Later he admitted it 'went on its ass, didn't do any business at all, and though I wasn't completely without employment (after it), employment wasn't as accessible to me as it had been – *The Molly Maguires* was quite an expensive film!'

Apart from three slender weeks in Russia on *The Red Tent* early in '69, employment was no richer for Connery – though this was largely by his own choosing. What followed was a period of film inactivity which lasted almost two years. A colleague opines: 'Part of it was identity crisis, yes. Another part was the general late sixties hangover syndrome. All the icons were down. The Beatles were hobbling back from the Rishikesh, popping LSD, doing the drab, indulgent trampy thing *Let It Be*. And James Bond was flagging out too. Sean had been on this speeding merry-go-round for six years and when he jumped off everything was swirly. He was trying to get his feet, trying on various masks, I suppose. Like, we saw him for a while as the convert to "serious films" – that

174

was the general impression of *The Hill* and *The Molly Maguires* – but it didn't last.'

In the hiatus – whenever there was a hiatus for the mature Connery – business raised its head. Though part of his continuing association with Iain Stewart's pioneering interests arose from an almost hippie-trendy sense of social duty, many non-charitable, less altruistic investments were explored as well. The Fairfields friendship led to the establishment of a merchant bank, Dunbar & Co, with impressive panelled offices in Pall Mall, as well as a multitude of large-share interests in other companies. All the time Connery was professing himself a socialist, though not infrequently letting that particular mask slip. 'Golf, food and drink – that's what I enjoy,' he told the *Express*. 'And the only point in having money is to indulge them.' *France Soir*, the French newspaper, was indelicate enough to suggest Mr Connery had gone to seed and had been forced out of Bond by the producers because his waistline had thickened too much. Connery sued promptly. In the High Court David Hirst, QC, for Connery told the judge, 'It was asserted quite erroneously that the producers of the James Bond films had dispensed with his services because he was no longer fit to play the role of James Bond.' Connery had, in his own words, checked his waistline with a measuring tape, recorded an acceptable inch of flab and phoned his lawyer. On February 17, 1969 *France Soir* retracted its statement, apologised for libel and settled with Connery for an undisclosed sum. Connery was as effusively delighted as he had been when Warners were forced to palm out a couple of thousand dollars when *A Fine Madness* ran over schedule.

Having holidayed in Australia at Cilento's home and again, living hermit-like, looking after the 100 muscat grape vines just planted at the Spanish farm, Connery progressed to Leningrad and Moscow for *The Red Tent*. He liked Moscow, despite the fact that his hotel room was routinely bugged, but found Leningrad drab. At a top-class Leningrad restaurant he deplored the ineptitude of out-of-step dancers performing to a good balalaika band.

175

They were 'hopeless . . . they wouldn't have lasted ten minutes at the Dennistoun (Glasgow) Palais.' Russia was agreeable, but not the kind of place he'd like to call home. Deciding where exactly home should be became a contentious issue too. Suggestions that he was about to flee Britain and opt for tax exile in Bermuda or somewhere similar were dismissed, as were reports that he banked all his loot in Switzerland and had some personal grand plan for the future. 'Scotland would be as far as I'd consider moving,' he told a journalist, but among friends he aired his angry views on British taxes and weather. 'Because he loved to play golf whenever he could he sought the sun,' a friend says. 'But that wasn't the main reason he'd begun to contemplate emigration. The main reason was money. In Britain, because of the punitive taxes, he believed he was squandering by just sitting on his backside.' Ten years later Connery admitted that his finances during this period 'were in a mess. The accountants were unscrambling what they could. But the practical answer was to get out.'

Before all the vast changes of the early seventies *The Red Tent* unfurled. In concept an ambitiously mystical film, it failed through heavy-handed direction and a conservative, plodding acting approach that killed all the sense of wonder and intrigue intended. Peter Finch dominates the film as General Nobile, leader of the ill-fated trans-Arctic dirigible expedition, who is visited forty years after the event by the ghosts of the main participants. In the recreated story the dirigible breaks up in a blizzard and the survivors are scattered. A base comprising a red tent and items for survival is set up, but the chances of rescue are slim. Valeria (Claudia Cardinale), Nobile's fiancée, persuades Norwegian explorer Roald Amundsen (Connery) to search for the lost men and, in so doing, Amundsen perishes. Nobile is eventually rescued – before most of his men – and the question of the rightness of his behaviour develops and haunts him. Connery's fee for the film was not large, and though he received second billing it seemed hardly deserved. Roger Greenspun in the *New York Times* observed 'to have taken a situation with such potential

and to have made it as dull as Mikhail Kalatozov has
. . . must have taken great ingenuity.'

In November Connery's friend the journalist Roderick
Mann was dreamily imagining what a 'splendid year it
has been for Mr Sean Connery. Most of it has been spent
playing golf. And why not, when you think of it? What's
the point of working hard and making money if you're
not going to enjoy yourself?' Dennis Selinger was tugging
hard in the opposite direction when in between, to universal bewilderment, Connery was declaring his next projects – two 'long held ambitions' – a stage play he would
direct, and his own movie of *Macbeth*.

Diane Cilento was, in the instance of the stage play
anyway, the motivational source. It was she who had
introduced Connery to the work of Canadian playwright
Ted Allan Herman, whose *The Secret of the World* he had
hoped to direct after *You Only Live Twice*, and it was she
who was first approached to star in the new play of Herman's, *I've Seen You Cut Lemons*. Knowing Connery to
have admired Herman so much and understanding his
restive mood after *The Red Tent* debacle, Cilento suggested
to the producer that he engage her husband to direct the
play. Connery accepted and, with Cilento's agreement,
invited actor Robert Hardy in as male lead.

'We started rehearsals at a church hall in Putney, not
far from where Sean and Diane lived,' Hardy remembers.
'It was, of course, a joy to be working with them because
I admired them both for their separate talents – but I must
say I accepted the play against my instincts. It was too
difficult a work, the odds were heavily against it even
remotely succeeding.' The play was a two-hander – just
Hardy and Cilento as Canadian brother and sister – which
investigated at close-hand the frustrations and passions
of two people spiralling towards an incestuous involve-
ment. At rehearsals in the church hall Connery was never
less than positive-minded, but Hardy is not so sure about
the director's vision of likely success. 'Sean knew how
tricky it would be, but he had a flair that forced the best
out of a performance. Once he'd started, there was no
turning back.' Hardy is absolutely clear about Connery's

urge to give it his best. 'It's a condition not uncommon in our trade, where stars of great international réclame like Sean decide to go back to their roots. Sean had decided, though I doubt if he saw himself in the long term as a director. He just then felt the need to do it, to rebel against the frivolity of other areas of the business, to work *at the heart* of the craft.'

Prior to opening at Oxford and then going on tour, Connery asked Hardy to stay for a week at his Putney home to intensify rehearsals. Hardy found 'a big, empty house, quite attractive but with the bare necessities of furniture – though some interesting paintings. We rehearsed hard during the day and talked long into the night. In the end, I think, it helped our performances – and, God, we needed what help we could get.' Every morning Connery allotted a time for Hardy to utilise the house 'think tank', a zinc-lined fully closed-in sentry box which occupied a neat corner in the upstairs study. 'Sean believed sitting in here, totally shut up, concentrated the mind and conserved nervous energy. He used it, and claimed it worked. For myself, well, I didn't rush to install one in my own home.'

I've Seen You Cut Lemons opened late November to bad notices. The month-long tour took it to Newcastle and Manchester, thence to the Fortune Theatre in London where 'it hit the deck, but *good!*' Hardy was not surprised at all. 'I'd jumped in, eyes closed, nose held tight, feet together. I had the gravest reservations from the start, I suspect many of us had.' After five days the play was handed the Black Spot. Connery expressed only mild disappointment to his cast. 'When word came that we were to close Sean responded in the same positive way he had right through the setting-up. He didn't, like many directors, disappear. Backstage he gave us our little talking to. He said it wasn't our fault, and so on – all the kind things one can possibly deploy at such a sad time. The alternative attitudes and phrases are limited, of course,' Hardy laughs. 'But Sean took it genuinely well. He tried, he failed. I think we had all done our best with very, very tough material.'

Most critics felt the elaborate scaffold-design set by Sean Kenny dwarfed the players ridiculously and, like Hardy, that the play itself was unfit. Connery received a few lukewarm compliments, but every review, implicitly if not explicitly, called him back to James Bond.

Usurped by Roman Polanski's new *Macbeth*-in-planning, Connery's second major artistic departure was shelved.

Dennis Selinger's conviction in Connery's ability to transcend Bond continued and he was relieved when, at so low an ebb, a Sidney Lumet movie came along. Of all the directors Connery had worked with Lumet exemplified the qualities he most admired – discipline, efficiency in bringing the work in on time, care over the script. *The Hill* enshrined Connery's happiest professional memories so now, almost before he had read *The Anderson Tapes*, the bored, listless actor was straining to go. Selinger was pleased too because *The Anderson Tapes* was a move back towards 'popular' cinema, a frothy caper movie which in Lumet's hands would acquire at very least the veneer of indelible polish. The polish would appease Connery, the public at which the caper was aimed, and Selinger.

The Anderson Tapes, shot on location in New York to the tightest of schedules, was a resounding hit, rocketing Connery back into the American top ten box-office draws for 1971, a feat that might have seemed unreachable after *Shalako*. Once again, Lumet and Connery excited the best in each other and the same Roger Greenspun who had damned *The Red Tent* in the *New York Times* celebrated 'Sean Connery's laconic, attractive, beautifully subdued John Anderson' in a movie where 'the quality of professionalism appears in rather lovely manifestations to raise a by no means perfect film to a level of intelligent efficiency that is not so very far beneath the reach of art.' Greenspun accurately pinpointed the fact that *The Anderson Tapes* is a 'minor story': John 'Duke' Anderson, recently released from jail, visits his former lover Ingrid (Dyan Cannon), interestedly digests her new surroundings – a luxury apartment block where she is residing with a sugar daddy – and reckons the entire building

179

constitutes one abundantly-stacked safe for the cracking. He gathers a team of experts and, over a Labour Day weekend, attempts, almost successfully, to outwit police chief Delaney (Ralph Meeker) and strip the joint of treasures. For Greenspun the 'multiplicity of life' yielded by small characters made the movie, and indeed the best fun comes in flashed vignettes, where the racy wit of Connery's Duke points up the hilarity in corruption.

But even before the June '71 premiere of *The Anderson Tapes* the astounding announcement of a return to Bond-age had been made. In March, out of the blue, and catching even close friends by surprise, a press release stated that Connery had been talking with Broccoli and Saltzman again and a deal had been reached: Connery would return to the mink-lined prison world of 007 for a fee of $1.2 million, plus a percentage. Every cent earned would go to the newly-formed Scottish International Educational Trust, which had Sir Samuel Curran, Vice-Chancellor of Strathclyde University, as its chairman, Iain Stewart and Jackie Stewart, the racing driver, among its trustees, and had had its first financial shot in the arm the previous summer with the Connery two-day pro-am gold tourna-ment at Troon. The personal bait for Connery, it was stated, had been the bonus offer of United Artists support for any two films of his own choosing, to be made after the single, final Bond. Connery's very closest friends were stunned. One colleague says, 'He never told me; I read about it first. Did it seem out of character for him to reverse the pledge he had so solidly made a couple of years before? Well, put it this way: it had nothing to do with (George Lazenby's) failure as Bond; it could never have happened the year before; Sean had things to work out of his system – and the exercise strengthened him; he resumed Bond, I believe, with two equally important mo-tives – to help his charity and to restore his market posi-tion.' In the clear light of the aftermath of holiday and experiment, then, Connery assessed his values and saw that Selinger and other advisers were almost certainly right: everything, even his philanthropic concern, was dependent upon the manipulation of his standing Bond-

based success. Playing the long-haired poet with the Za-
pata moustache and the zinc-walled-hideaway was a be-
lated diversion, an extension of the madman of *A Fine
Madness*, an extension of tearaway Tommy. It would
always live within him, but it would, from now on, be
secondary to the disciplined sincerity he espoused before
all else.

It was a transformed Sean Connery who late in February
1971 signed with Eon, guided by the sauve charm of UA's
Bond fan David Picker, to make *Diamonds Are Forever*.
Gone was the pale-faced tension even uttering the word
'Bond' had induced, the recalcitrant urge to row with
Saltzman and Broccoli, the lion's mane of thinning hippie
hair, the confusion of purpose. Gone too was the pretence
of permanence in the relationship with Cilento. At the
High Court libel trial two years before Connery had given
his address as Curzon Street, a side-track of some significance to those close to him; now, he was overt in his
feelings about the marriage. He told friends it was over,
that he had true respect for Cilento, but they could never
be compatible. He bought a flat overlooking the Thames
at Chelsea Embankment, in a block where once Hitler's
ambassador von Ribbentrop had lived, and removed all
his possessions from Putney. Casual acquaintanceships
with women friends were more actively pursued, with
Connery stating, 'sex is still important to me'; but if intimate relations grew they did so in an atmosphere of rigid
discretion.

Contrary to the apparent consensus of jaundiced gibing,
On Her Majesty's Secret Service, had not, without Connery,
fallen on its face. True, in the series to date it was the
slowest earner at the box-office, but then *You Only Live
Twice*, its predecessor, with Connery, marked a decline
from *Thunderball*. Furthermore the kind of invidious comparison fledgling George Lazenby was subjected to, especially in the lesser journals, advanced a reputation for
the film which related not at all to its achievements. Far
and away the most human Bond story, rich in pathos and
irony, *OHMSS* sure-footedly took its place alongside *From
Russia With Love* as a triumph of British cinema – all credit

181

to breakneck direction by former editor Peter Hunt; Lazenby, excelling by instinct; and the splendid, endearing Diana Rigg.

As eulogy and lament for all that was best in Bond, indeed in sixties cinema, *OHMSS* would, everyone knew, take some beating. Moreover, its storyline effectively completed a Bond cycle: Richard Maibaum had started *Dr No* with the raw material of a boisterous, not-too-far-from juvenile fist-fighter policing the lions' lairs of the world; by *OHMSS* Bond was flawed, weathered, weakened by the business – a weary man given to melancholy, ultimately settling for the emotional shield of marriage. Guy Hamilton, who had been signed by Eon to make *Diamonds Are Forever* before Christmas '70, was amply aware of the need to reconstruct a Bond persona.

'I was under the impression we were going with a new actor after *OHMSS*,' Hamilton says. 'John Gavin was a possible, and there were others.* Myself, I suggested an affable gent called Burt Reynolds, but the producers said no, he's only a stunt man! Anyway, I worked on the script a little in London, and then dear Tom Mankiewicz (the writer) was called in to redevelop this Bond character. So, off to America we went – we knew America was to be our setting, having considered France and a few other places – and got down to some hard rebuilding. After *OHMSS*, which was slow and had lots of overage (extra, unused footage), we needed a fresh type of story – yes. By the time I was told Sean had signed with David Picker and Eon the script was already there, finished. Sure, it was quite a departure from old Bond. Above all the others it was larger than life, zany. But Sean came out to America in April and we had just a day or two before we started shooting, and he looked over what we had and agreed it was good. He did suggest alterations – attitudes and a

---

*John Gavin was contracted for *Diamonds Are Forever*. His pay-off, once Connery agreed to return, was about $50,000. Roger Moore was, according to Hamilton, 'in the offing right through negotiations'; but he was contractually tied to Sir Lew Grade for the TV series *The Persuaders*, co-starring Tony Curtis.

line here or there – but fundamentally he agreed that Bond must be exaggerated, expanded, after the kind of santurnine presence of before, especially *OHMSS*.'

Diamonds Are Forever was the first American Bond, ostensibly based at Pinewood but, because most of the shooting was in Nevada and California, utilising Universal Studios in Hollywood instead. Part of Eon's selection of America must have been triggered by the likelihood of most extensive press cover. And, from day one, the hoped-for fretful furore of the multi-media cavalcade was unleashed. Simultaneous with Connery's arrival at Las Vegas came the old bandwagon, journalists from everywhere (yes, even Japan again), this time fattened by the dark gossip that had surrounded the enigmatic personage of 'Bond' in retirement. Connery was strangely amenable, prepared to talk to most about anything – but there was some speculation among the discerning about the straightness of his replies. Though everybody knew his well-aired views about the decline in Bond script values he announced, straight-faced, that this was 'the best script I've ever had' – curious, that, because *Diamonds* positively emasculated the character as never before. Questioned about future prospects in light of the extra two-picture deal that went with Bond he stated, 'There's no doubt that Bond made me a success, and made it possible for me to do other things. But I won't stay an actor, that's for sure.' To others he mused on the possibilities of pursuing *Macbeth*, even in competition with Polanski, and to the few journalists who were old friends, he confided his business plans and true hopes for the Educational Trust. Baring his soul to writer Peter Evans he admitted that *Diamonds* was an act of enriching exorcism which would help his charity, help his businesses and, with luck, aid his career. He did not, he stressed, wish to make for himself 'another fortune – I don't want that kind of maniacal power'. Essentially Bond was the key catalyst. 'With this picture I'm finishing part of my life. I will have accomplished quite a few things . . . and bought a bit of breathing space to look at my life and decide what I'm going to withdraw from, reach for, what I really need.' Though tricksy answers to glib queries might have hinted at continuing inner conflict, there was none.

Hamilton found Connery very relaxed and clear about his acting future. He had laid down laws about this Bond with David Picker – the shoot must not run longer than 16 weeks: if it did a further $145,000 per week would be added to his salary – and he was anxious to progress to other films, intelligently-conceived popular films like *The Anderson Tapes*. Confident of the coming success of the Lumet movie Connery arranged a special private viewing, pre-premiere, in Vegas during the first weeks of *Diamonds*. Chorus lines from all the big Vegas shows were invited, as were many top-bill stars. Anyone who cherished reservations about Connery the actor in the wake of *The Red Tent* discarded them. All agreed *The Anderson Tapes* displayed shimmering talents.

As on *Goldfinger*, Hamilton's fine-art technique of knowing what he wanted to shoot and going unwaveringly at it satisfied Connery. 'With a limited number of days,' Hamilton says, 'one can't "have a bash", one has to clearly perceive the thing. All our problems were worked out before we shot a foot of film.' Saltzman and Broccoli prudently steered clear of the set and Connery was put up in the Presidential Suite of the best hotel in Vegas. 'Golf was his only outlet,' says Hamilton. 'We almost had it written into our contracts that we had this one day off per week to take a helicopter and fly to one of the great courses nearby. Sean unwound there. As for gambling, he didn't do much – threw a few dice maybe, tried the one-arm bandits. Basically he was there for the job, and his sights were set further away.' Rumours about a romantic tie with Jill St John began, but both stars anxiously evaded compromising off-the-set photographs by dining in private. St John had originally been assigned the part of Plenty O'Toole, a peripheral character devised by Hamilton, who would be Bond's only minor fling beyond the heroine, Tiffany Case. Hamilton thought she would be wasted as Plenty, but just right for the 'brassy, hard-nut Tiffany'. Some rejigging ensued and Lana Wood, raven-haired sister of Natalie, was placed as Plenty while St

John took the big role. 'The chemistry between Sean and Jill was undeniably interesting,' Hamilton believes. 'And that was important to me. One of my interminable gripes about Bond concerns the women. I've always felt Sean especially needed a strong co-lead, a woman who could answer up to him, appear equal in talent anyway.'

After nine weeks in America cast and crew made for Pinewood and location work in Europe. Connery remained cheery, though tired by the unrelenting schedule he had set himself. On the studio floor he looked slightly bored, slightly overweight. His toupee was streaked with grey and his eyebrows bushier than usual. He looked, one film worker commented, like 'Bond getting set for pension', but he was content enough. As time ran out the schedule tightened and Hamilton speeded up. Journalists were ejected and concentration fixed. Having forked out more than a million of the seven million dollar budget to their lead star, UA were unwilling to draw out the chequebook again. A record of a few days towards the end of filming indicates the pressure:

Thursday:	7.15 :	Car picks up Connery from home to take him to Pinewood.
	8.30 :	Filming of Metz' laboratory sequence starts.
	16.00 :	Filming completed. Connery, St John, Saltzman, Hamilton depart for Heathrow to fly to Frankfurt.
	19.55 :	Arrive Frankfurt. Greeted by press and fan crowds.
Friday:	7.00 :	Make-up & wardrobe call at hotel.
	8.00 :	Filming on set at Lufthansa jet at airport.
	14.00 :	Filming complete. Connery and St John lunch aboard jet.
	16.50 :	Depart for Amsterdam.
	20.30 :	Press conference in Amsterdam.
	22.00 :	Off duty.
Saturday:	12.00 :	Connery's call – after lie-in and late breakfast.

185

12.15 :	Filming Connery's drive to ren-dezvous with Tiffany.
16.30 :	Daylight shooting finished.
21.00 :	Night-time scenes outside Tiffany's apartment filmed.
Midnight :	Filming completed.

In John Boorman's words, brilliance often arises from adversity, but in the case of *Diamonds* an unblended script of disparate elements made the task tough for Connery and Hamilton. About three chapters of Fleming's novel formed the basis of the movie and clearly much more could have been powerfully used. Instead, a cocktail of tawdry razzmatazz and unctuous humour inflated a wind-bag story. Here, Bond masquerades as a diamond smug-gler, assisting another of like kind (St John), with the intention of unravelling the mystery of a diamond pipeline leading from Africa to middle America. He discovers Blo-feld (Charles Gray), his old enemy, to be masterminding yet another scheme to dominate the world, this time wielding the untouchable weapon of a laser-satellite pow-ered by diamonds.

Though the film did come in on schedule in August, set for Christmas release, pressure fractures were evident, even beyond the storyline. One continuity error that has a stunt trick car driving down a narrow alley on two wheels, going in balanced left and coming out tilted right, was laughable for all the wrong reasons. Yet even this glaring abuse of what Bond once was skipped the uncrit-ical, Connery-drunk fans' notice. Reviewers were less gul-lible. *Commonwealth* magazine pined for pure Fleming, while welcoming Connery, the essence of the series' suc-cess, back: 'The new film is . . . a bit early to have camp appeal; and script-writers Maibaum and Mankiewicz, along with director Guy Hamilton, seem unsure why they are making another Bond feature just now. Their one fresh idea is to throw in some self-parody . . . [not] much relief from two hours of Bondage, but all the film has to offer.'

By the time such reviews were circulating Connery was

too deeply involved in other matters – the promotion of *The Anderson Tapes* and preparation for a great new departure – to be much bothered. David Picker and Eon weren't much alarmed either. *Diamonds Are Forever* opened side-by-side in America and London at Christmas and caused tremors that shook box-office records everywhere. Film history was made when £6 million was grossed in twelve days world wide. In London alone the picture took more than £34,000 during the first week at the Odeon, Leicester Square. Po-faced newspapers reported staff arriving for work early in the morning finding 700 fans already queuing. 'The theatre telephone has been permanently blocked,' *Films Illustrated* recorded, 'and police have frequently been on the spot to cope with fisticuffs started by anti-queue jumpers.'

Historians and cynics agree: Bond had crested with *Thunderball* in which he was the establishment rebel-or-hero (choose your own) of sixties society. Outdated, jaded and back-tracking, the impossible had yet been accomplished: the ghost had risen in Las Vegas, rolled the bones and hit jackpot again. Nobody doubted that this freakish redoubled success was entirely due to the contribution of Sean Connery, token playing or not.

Declared box-office champion for 1971, the world lay like a carpet of gems for the picking at his feet. Older and wiser, he could now reshape his image in whatever way he desired, with UA backing to begin with, and bring to fruition the facets of potential versatility glimpsed before Bond. Predictably, to smash type, he turned, too soon, to an offbeat classic.

CHAPTER FOURTEEN

Micheline On Course

IT WAS, FOR Connery, the best of times and the worst of times, these mellow days after *Diamonds Are Forever*. The press allegations that the Educational Trust fund was a tax dodge device – which had naturally upset him more than a little – were exploded by the patent advance of the cause. Connery's insistence on having *The Anderson Tapes'* European premiere in Scotland had brought £5,000 into the Trust and the Troon golf tournament had produced another £17,000. This on top of the chunky $1 million dollars had already begun to assist young artists in need and, more ambitiously, had padded the backbone of a new social and industrial experiment of Sir Iain Stewart's. A new town in Scotland called Glenrothes in Fife, population 30,000 expected to rise to 75,000, was the site of investment. Money from the Trust, it was announced, would finance a training college for trade unions and management within the estate, the main object of which was to break down the barriers which can disrupt industry. A seminar at Glenrothes in which the plan was forged created so much interest that the Labour Party and the Tory government sent representatives north to examine Stewart's and Connery's methods.

Whilst stating he was still a socialist with nationalist interests at heart, Connery was eager to extend open arms to anyone keen on promoting his beloved Trust. 'If a good idea comes to the Trust I don't give a damn whether it comes from a Tory or a Communist.' Lest anyone doubt his true loyalties he expanded: 'I'm in favour of fragmentation in general. I don't believe in the Common Market or the United States or the Soviet Union – because there'll always be national differences and skirmishes . . . so Scotland should pull away somewhat after hundreds of years taking second place to England.'

While remaining active Vice-Chairman of the Trust he did not neglect his businesses. Dunbar & Co, the bank, thrived and, among other new investments, he became part-owner of a London garage. On the movie front he readied himself for the project he had chosen as the first of the UA-guaranteed twosome – a film version of John Hopkins's stage play *This Story of Yours*, a Royal Court success in 1960 which Connery had been planning anyway to revive for stage. He also formed a production company, Tantallon Films, and scouted for further properties. Everything was tinged with activity, optimism, hope. . .

But at home there were regrets and heartbreaks. Quietly preparing for divorce from Cilento he reflected on 'years of failure. What we had to do was step back and see just what we were doing to each other, to our lives, and the lives of our son and daughter. Our careers were incompatible, not us. You were offered a part you wanted to do but suddenly there are a hundred questions to settle: what is she doing? What is he doing? Who will look after the kids? Can they come? Who will look after the house? Interminable.' The split was amicable, with Connery arranging reasonable financial support through his own bank. All that really concerned Diane and himself, he made clear, was the effects of break-up on the children and 'making sure the future works for them . . . fortunately they know the situation, they're great.'

Hot on the heels of divorce agreement came the shock news in a phone call from Neil that Joe was dead. Less than four years before Connery had at last urged Effie and Joe out of Fountainbridge – and then only because the brewery had started demolishing next door properties. They had settled in a pretty gadget-equipped house in the quiet Edinburgh residential district of Newington, a considerable distance from the good memories. In retirement Joe had been endlessly restless: some days he went to the pictures, often to see his son on screen, on rainy days he

189

stayed in bed. 'He'd never been really sick a day in his life,' Neil says. 'Right up to the end he looked fine of fettle. It was custom for Mum and Dad to join myself and family for Christmas lunch. But this year Dad had phoned and said he'd a touch of 'flu, and wouldn't be round. I offered to bring food to their house, but he said no, he wasn't hungry. A few days later he was hospitalised for tests . . . then a doctor called me aside and spilled it out. He said, "Your father's got cancer, and he hasn't too long to live." At the time I just couldn't believe it. He was only 69, it seemed impossible.' Once informed, Sean Connery wanted to arrange the best medical care for Joe, if necessary moving him from Scotland; but the doctors advised that no better treatment could be had anywhere – Joe had no options. Within weeks, too few weeks, Joe was dead. By mistake the night sister phoned not Neil but Effie, now living alone, to break the sad news. Neil was appalled. 'It took mother from midnight till two in the morning to ring over the word – she was so distressed. The hospital had blundered with phone numbers, it was very unfortunate.' Roderick Mann, interviewing Connery a short time after Joe's demise found him 'quietened down'. Connery attributed the change to the events of the last year or so, especially his father's death. 'That was a great stopper for me,' he revealed. 'More than I can explain. I never thought it would happen. . . The Masai tribe say that you're not a man until your father dies. They may be right, but if it's true it is a pretty stiff price to pay.'

Joe's funeral interrupted production work on the new film, a venture that UA had grave doubts about underwriting. Ian Bannen, Sidney Lumet, Trevor Howard – all old friends of Connery's – were signed by Tantallon Films, steered by executive producer Denis O'Dell. 'It was a cracking play,' Bannen says, 'but presented problems in terms of commercial cinema. We – the people working on it – loved it, but it would be foolish to say we expected it to have anything like a Bond impact.' John Hopkins, who had once penned some twenty episodes of BBC's Z-Cars in two years, worked closely with Connery and his team. Over months the title switched from This Story of Yours to

Something Like the Truth, finally, unsatisfactorily to most, *The Offence*.

Connery detailed his outlook to Tony Crawley: '*The Offence* was *the* reason for going back to the Bond films . . . the premise was a picture that people (like Lumet, Bannen) could make and *participate* in . . . it was a sort of downbeat theme but the last forty minutes of it, quoting John Huston, is some of the best he's ever seen. . . It was the study in the disintegration of a policeman and his mind – aided by the terrible things policemen are exposed to, and a really destructive marriage. Sidney made a fantastic job of it, but I think he got a bit European on us.'

The Offence was a rogue movie, styled and performed miles from the mainstream of current cinema; a daring choice for a star actor at any time, but downright insane, on the face of it, after so big a popular hit as *Diamonds Are Forever*. Connery seemed to take fiendish pleasure in indulging himself at the expense of UA, declaring later that he had never imagined the movie would make a profit.

United Artists had allotted $1 million to the movie, which came in $80,000 under budget. In August 1981, eight years after release it first showed a profit.

In *The Offence* he played the savage Detective Sergeant Johnson, a man tainted by the cruelty of the criminal world, who breaks down while interrogating a child molester (Ian Bannen) and, in a mindless frenzy, kills him. Parallel with the story of the inner struggle which erupts into violence runs the account of home life, a strained, furious partnership of habit with Maureen (Vivien Merchant, impeccably self-controlled). Paradoxically, though *The Offence* was chosen with the serious intention of neutralising Bond identification, Connery's portrayal of Johnson, so large and verbose and strong he looms, produced an illusion of heroism – soiled perhaps, but no less honourable. In killing the rapist, in cracking up, Johnson is seen to be doing the decent thing: the balance of dialogue favours him. In that slight but significant way, Connery's purpose was frustrated with *The Offence*, though the movie itself displays a crystal, uniform brilliance that must have satisfied him.

Bannen remembers, 'We rehearsed it like a stage play, very tightly, then started a fast shoot at Twickenham. Sean was worried about only one aspect of the production – time. He wanted to bring the thing in in 28 days and save money. Otherwise, he was pleased with Hopkins's script and all the technical and acting people he had round him. There was a family feel, which was good, and I thought it one of his finest performances . . . though in that last scene of mine I suffered his true-to-life playing!' (Bannen, as criminal Baxter, is beaten to death by Johnson in a protracted scene: Bannen was heavily padded beneath his clothing.)

Though Connery defiantly pretended indifference to the world, he was hopeful that *The Offence* would make money, some money, *and* be seen too as an artistic success. As with *The Anderson Tapes*, he arranged a special showing at his business office near St James's Palace, to which he invited important friends, as well as cleaners and porters from the building. 'I tried to find out how people would react,' he said, 'the film's story is probably difficult to take. The cleaners and porters all said they liked the acting, but were not too forthcoming about the subject.' For Bannen, everything was right, barring the title. 'In Italy or somewhere I saw it go out as *In The Mirror, Darkly*, using the Shakespearian clip, and I thought that was much better. *The Offence* spelt out grimness.' Connery felt the film was maybe fifteen minutes overlong, but he trusted Lumet's decision on what to leave in. Because he had had huge creative control, he enjoyed making *The Offence* more than any movie to date, but he was enraged when UA, released the movie 'through the toilet', making no effort at all to push it on its most likely receptive markets (the film was never shown in France).

Critically *The Offence* scored. Sydney Edwards of the *Evening Standard* admired it, and Connery. Marjorie Bilbow liked the 'well constructed script and finely controlled acting. When any two characters are locked in spoken combat the film is both moving and intellectually stimulating.' But the box-office was sluggish and those, like

Selinger, interested in Connery's development, were worried. 'I think the fear might have been that Sean would persist in trying to mock Bond in the rest of his work,' suggests a colleague. But Connery was really most interested in assembling sound credits that would be a foundation for wider acceptance. After shooting *The Offence* he flew to Spain to unwind and take in some golf, but he brought a mountain of script treatments with him, leaving Selinger in no doubt that he was intent on working fast, as prescribed, to *build on* Bond. 'He was interested in a possible comedy,' says Selinger, and Connery himself went on record cataloguing his priority choices: comedies he liked – 'the only movies I never miss are the *Carry Ons*'. Spy stories did not interest him; John Hopkins had written, on commission for Tantallon, another screenplay, based on the life and adventures of the explorer Sir Richard Burton – but the second $1 million from UA would not cover such an expansive film. Connery had contacted Germaine Greer and asked her to try a script – her idea was about Australian Aborigines, and was instantly chucked aside. Connery quite liked Greer but found 'her mind worked on that outer cog. I feel the Aborigines were there thousands of years before us and they seem to have survived . . . so let them get on with it!' Despite the Playboy-financed Polanski *Macbeth* there was talk yet again of reviving Connery's screenplay, but that died down in Spain.

At this frantic time of project-searching, something entirely unexpected happened: at a golf tournament in Morocco Connery met a tousle-haired blonde artist called Micheline Roquebrune, an avid golfer and multi-linguist, and found friendship. Born in Nice and brought up in North Africa, Micheline was thirty-eight, had a young son from a previous marriage and was looking for companionship. The two were drawn together firstly by the shared interest in golf, but quickly formed a bond of trust. They were inseparable during their first summer together in Spain, but friends doubted the relationship would survive Connery's determination to stay single. 'His feelings about marriage were very mixed,' says one. 'From week

193

to week he contradicted himself. Now he wanted more children, now he wanted total freedom.' Connery himself told the press: 'I don't seem to have the equipment for marriage in terms of the contract as it exists today. But I'd like more children. And of course I'd want them to be by a woman who would bring them up properly. Who knows what will happen?'

For a year, in the eyes of the press and public almost nothing happened. Over Christmas '72 Micheline and Connery grew closer, but when he returned to Britain to launch *The Offence* he played his cards close to his chest and gave little hint of the lifestyle changes already on the horizon. On the spur of the moment he accepted an offer from adventurous director John Boorman, based in Ireland, to lead his futuristic fantasy movie *Zardoz*. Burt Reynolds, the director's first choice after their superb pairing on *Deliverance*, had cried off because of a hernia rupture, but Connery was overjoyed to be asked anyway. 'I located him on a golf course in Spain,' says Boorman, 'and sent out the script. Sean doesn't shillyshally. He read it over a weekend and agreed to do it immediately. He was in Ireland, sitting down with me for script talks within a couple of days. He was extraordinarily imaginative, supportive, assured. I knew instantly I had netted myself a bonus.'

Zardoz almost defies description in its unshowy but truly cosmic concept. Its subjective, near voyeuristic slant on a far future world where inhabitants of the bubble-covered Vortex cherish the secret of eternal life senselessly owes much, Boorman reckons, to his six years in America, where he directed smash-hits like *Point Blank* with Lee Marvin. 'It's about immortality being a fairy tale,' he says simply, 'and in America, in the crazed consumer-land, one sees this obsession with imagined permanence, this desire to perfect life and extend it.' After the success of *Deliverance*, with which Boorman won an Oscar nomination, he approached Warner Bros for finance. On the basis of his synopsis and demand for total artistic control he was turned down; Columbia followed suit. Finally 20th Century-Fox agreed a deal – 'not great, but one accepts and adapts oneself to restrictions in this business. Greatness often comes from excess. In *Zardoz* we ended up on a shoestring, but the pressures brought out the best in everyone, especially Sean. It was no hardship for him.'

As Zed, exterminator by decree, Connery plays the balancing spirit incarnate of nature, who breaks into the time-locked Vortex to confound the immortal elite and reintroduce the threat of their mortality. He has come from the polluted, ravaged world beyond the Vortex, and appears at once as god and demon to the Vortex people. Consuella (Charlette Rampling), among others, is eventually swayed by Zed's promise of natural ageing and death and joins him in escape from the bubble world. They live, breed and die together.

'No one part of the filming was harder than any other,' says Boorman. 'It was an enormously difficult film to do, with effects and all the rest. Because there was so much running round, it was physically taxing for the actors, particularly Sean, who was half-naked all the time. The final sequence, however, caused a stir. It involved a long, messy make-up sitting in order to show Sean and Charlotte growing older and older, till they die. Sean was very good and patient, but after the first make-up and shoot we found the film stock was faulty, so that necessitated a complete re-run. Sean was less philosophical about sitting through the make-up process again, but he held out. And we shot the sequence again, and it turned out fine. Then some young boy we had at the Studios accidentally exposed the film, destroying it. So I came to Sean and told him. His reaction was hilariously frightening. I mean, he took off! The poor kid was cursed to death. "Where is he?" Sean demanded to know. "If I get my hands on him I'll break his fucking neck!" And this boy was scuttling round the Studios for days, whispering, "Where's Connery? For God's sake, have you seen Connery?" ' More seriously Boorman relates, 'Sean had no patience with people who behaved unprofessionally. His goal was fulfilling the ambitions of the movie, fast and competently.'

Connery's Zed, given the dazzling distractions of photographic and directorial wizardry, was masterful and inspired Jan Dawson in the *Monthly Film Bulletin* to wax eloquent about the 'ferociously concentrated energy which imposes the character as both a physical and moral force and does much to dispel one's doubts about the apparent loose ends in the philosophical tapestry.' Dawson also saw the film as primarily 'visionary – its images speaking both louder and clearer than its occasionally pedantic dialogue'; fair comment, vaunting Connery's emergence as an energetic presence all the more.

Like *The Offence*, Connery found the stimulating artistry and relative critical success of *Zardoz* satisfaction enough, though he was mildly disgruntled by the bad business of both movies. *Zardoz* he judged, rightly, to be ahead of its time, but he did not regret a moment of the ten weeks he had spent in County Wicklow making the picture. On the contrary, Ireland had galvanised him into reorganising his domestic life. Before *Zardoz* premiered he was flying back from Spain to arrange the sale of his Chelsea Embankment flat and finalise divorce proceedings with Cilento.

'My decision to sell was a pollution thing,' he told the *Express*. 'After spending all those weeks in Ireland and then being in Spain, London seemed pretty ropey when I came back: all those car exhausts spewing out muck.' Allusions to another marriage were evident: 'Who knows? Permissive society or not, it's a rare bird who'll stay with you year in and year out if you don't marry her.' But might Micheline, his partner for a year now, be his second wife? Connery refused to comment. But one telling secret emerged: in London he had started to take Spanish language lessons, attending classes in a school above Dunbar & Co. The fact that Spanish and Arabic were second nature to Micheline was, to many, worthy of note.

A sense of anti-climax suffused the next films Connery hurried into during the winter-spring of '73–'74, though at least their popular targeting lent optimism to those who wondered about the dangers of his possible indulgent commitment to purely offbeat, long shot projects. *Ransom*, for Finnish director Casper Wrede, was a pedestrian affair in which Connery played a security chief in Oslo battling wits against a terrorist group led by Ian McShane which is holding a Boeing aircraft and the British Ambassador against the release of six political prisoners. The plot incidents, ranged like bean cans on a supermarket shelf, were eminently forgettable, the direction sadly lacking. Connery was efficiently heroic, stiffly assured – but apparently abandoned by director Wrede, who seemed to see snowbound Oslo as the real film pivot.

One actor off the movie felt, 'Wrede wasn't living up to whatever one might have expected from the man who made *One Day in the Life of Ivan Denisovich*. We the cast figured we were on an average movie, with average chances.' The schedule ran over, due to, among other unavoidable intrusions, acts of God. The snows melted too soon, and thousands of tons of salt-mix had to be brought in for continuity. Connery grinned and bore up. Minor altercations brightened the lives of snow-blinded actors longing for London. At one stage Connery threatened to walk off the picture because the canteen food was so bad. On another occasion his wit, honed by adversity, flew like a starry tracer-flare through the gloom. At a private showing of *Ivan Denisovich*, attended by cast principals and Wrede himself, no one knew that Alexander Solzhenitsyn, author of the book, was seated in the murk at the back of the theatre. As the film ended Solzhenitsyn stood up and applauded. Everyone turned to cheer the great man in turn. Connery watched the squat, bearded figure approach, the high domed forehead fringed with black stubbly hair. As the Russian drew almost into earshot Connery cracked, 'He's got his fucking head on upside down.' Wrede did not appear to hear, or chose not to. As for Solzhenitsyn – 'the Scots drawl probably saved him,' says a co-star from *Ransom*.

In April Connery repaired to Elstree Studios to embark on Agatha Christie's *Murder on the Orient Express*, a thirties' crime thriller immaculately dressed and costumed by Tony Walton. Sidney Lumet was the unusual choice of director, and as ever Connery attained his near-best under his old friend's control. As Colonel Arbuthnot of the Indian Army, en route home with his lover (Vanessa Redgrave), Connery falls suspect, along with a dozen others, for the vicious murder of Ratchett (Richard Widmark). The redoubtable Hercule Poirot, played to definitive perfection by Albert Finney, finally discovers a conspiracy of no less than *all* suspects to murder the man they held responsible for the death of a child many years ago. Though the film was a sizeable hit – 'a splendidly frivolous gift wrapped in glittering silver foil and tied with a big satin bow,' in the eyes of *Screen International* – Connery did not benefit as he might have done. The movie was star-heavy, featuring Ingrid Bergman, Anthony Perkins, John Gielgud, Michael York and others; so, Finney apart, even the most distinguished character acting assumed no better than cameo impact. In a BBC radio interview during filming Connery assessed his recent career casually, curiously expressing no disenchantment. He recognised the fact that most people still linked him with Bond, though Roger Moore had already taken over the mantle with reasonable success in *Live and Let Die*, and agreed that some of his post-Bond work had flopped. Work satisfaction was monumentally important to him, but he was learning to enjoy leisure without guilt. Future plans, he said, were vague – though that confession seemed not to bother him. Actor colleagues who met him on *Murder on the Orient Express* found him fit and tanned from frequent months in Spain and, in the words of one 'very bloody smug.'

Though officially still domiciled in Britain he had taken residence in Monaco, was applying for citizenship to ease tax pressures, and had swapped his farm in Spain for a villa near Marbella. 'It was all a very calculated process,' says an acquaintance, 'which, in retrospect we can see was leading up to a second marriage. Sean had lawyers working here to sort his affairs out, and Micheline standing by in Spain. His close friends, if they could be described as "close", were golfing people like Tommy Cooper, Bruce Forsyth and Jimmy Tarbuck. Eric Sykes saw a fair bit of him too, and they played together very regularly in Marbella.' To all intents, he was married to Micheline already, though he was loath to discuss any intimate business with any journalist, friendly or other-wise. Gigi was sixteen now, and going her own way in Diane Cilento's footsteps, but Jason and Micheline's younger son Stefan were settling in Spain, at the villa. Within a year of the divorce from Cilento, Connery was snugly back in a family unit, drawing fresh profound strengths from the stability of a peaceful home.

In the autumn he started work in Almeria, comfortably close to Micheline, on John Milius's *The Wind and the Lion*, earning his biggest cheque since Bond and his finest chance to achieve wide audience appeal. Privately he was happier than he'd been in a long time but, fearful of any disturbances of the secret calm, he presented a stony un-cooperative face to the press. When the *Daily Mail*'s Ann Kent visited him on location she discovered a sober, de-fensive man who 'gives you his "that's another stupid question you asked me" look.' He did, however, confide some surprising news. The lawyers working to 'sort out' his affairs in Britain had disentangled him from *all* his business concerns. 'It's the easiest thing in the world to start a business empire,' he groused, 'but it creates a chain reaction of secretaries, minutes, meetings . . . it just never stopped. I found I was a mogul without a structure to support my empire, every decision had to be mine and it became too much. Now I am dropping everything except the Trust and my film interests.' As news filtered back to Britain disbelief sounded from every quarter. Increasingly through his thirties and early forties Connery had prided himself on his ability to turn over a quick buck. Frequently the press had branded him 'businessman-actor', and it was an accepted fact in the City that most of his invest-ments, properly structured or not, had turned good. The warm friendship with Sir Iain still flourished. . . So why the sudden departure?

Those who pondered the apparently incomprehensible were forced to wonder too why Connery had chosen *The Wind and the Lion*. David Quinlan, the film writer, was one of many to consider him miscast from the start. *The Wind and the Lion* was a historical adventure story that aroused memories of *Gunga Din*, and Connery was to be the noble desert warrior who was last of the Barbary pirates – a muscle-rippling, heroic part as stoutly written as vintage Bond.

Theoretically Connery could have been making another *Offence*. United Artists' proffered $1 million was depleted by inflation, but the fund still stood to back a small film of Connery's choice and though Connery often denied it, there was so obviously plenty of modest properties around. Acquaintances began to speculate that Micheline was the force behind the changes – that Micheline had urged her man out of time-draining business management and had started to work on his career. But Connery had only recently said, 'I've never had a confidant, I've never needed one. Even when I was married I made my own decisions, by myself.' This remark had raised some eyebrows in Cilento's circle of friends. Had she not nurtured and advised the young movie-struck Connery? Hadn't she been responsible for his taking on Bond? Suggestions were made that Connery's spiky references to a friendless past arose from remarks Cilento had been making to the press about their years together. When divorce had been agreed upon Connery had phoned Diane and asked that neither should talk about their past; though this was settled on, Cilento had given interviews subsequently which irritated him. Connery told Ann Kent that it was unlikely he would marry again, which further confused the situation for probing onlookers.

Whichever way, Micheline's setting up home with Connery, coinciding with his abandonment of business concerns, assumed some importance in light of *The Wind and the Lion*. John Milius, famous for telling the cinema tales of *Dillinger* and *Jeremiah Johnson*, steered the movie to considerable box-office success, applying, by *Photoplay*'s reckoning, 'all the elements essential for big screen entertainment . . . there is romance, drama, large scale battles, pageantry and, above all, heroes.' In spite of the din and zip of the production, Connery's Berber leader Mulay El Raisuli, holding America to ransom by kidnapping an American woman (Candice Bergen) and her children, towers up like a colossus, a feat universally remarked upon.

The fact that the scales of historical truth (the film was based on a real-life incident that occurred in 1904) and exotic intrigue were perfectly balanced assured a wide appeal, both family audience and high-brow. Marjorie Bilbow acknowledged only 'relax-and-enjoy-it gusty entertainment to be taken no more seriously than a game of cowboys and Indians', while Vincent Canby in the *New York Times* contemplated what was possibly 'the most sappy movie ever made, as well as one of the shrewdest . . . a paean to opportunism of awesome proportions, and if interest in it is stirred up by current headlines, it is not inappropriate.'

By the time *The Wind and the Lion* opened in May '75 Connery was at work on the John Huston epic, *The Man Who Would Be King*, for which the portents glimmered bright. In the way of the movie business, though Milius's picture had yet to be valued at the box-office, word had it that he was hot again, and his fees were up. The tiny aberration that succeeded *Diamonds Are Forever* was as good as forgiven and the fan mail was pouring in once more. Dennis Selinger was getting happier, and Connery and his Micheline had special reason to smile too. At Christmas, in secret, in Casablanca they had tied the knot.

CHAPTER FIFTEEN

Hits

The Man Who Would Be King was a watershed in many respects. Crucially, it marked the end of critical assessment of everything Connery did in terms of transmutations of James Bond. In the film, playing adventurer Danny Dravot who became king of a remote Himalayan tribe, Connery finally outpaced Bond and created his richest character. In work terms, the movie was the milestone of altered outlook; with it he began an intensive spate of varied, non-stop projects that has lasted to today – a Selinger-inspired unflagging campaign that has yielded quite a few superb movies of massive audience appeal. Connery clearly recognised the dividing line: 'the definite swing', he told *Men Only*, started when Joe died. 'It really hit me. I changed offices, agents, accountants, lawyers, secretaries – even my wife!' Micheline became comforter and guide, but Connery still harboured resentment about a variety of wrong decisions over the last years. Quietly, from the serenity of life with Micheline and work with the much-admired Huston, the virulent bitterness was vented. Those few journalists who got past amiable film PR man Brian Doyle heard Connery's bald account of Britain's ills. The colossal taxes he had paid for ten years angered him and, up till the last, he said, he had been fighting to 'get out from under the umbrella of parasites headed by people like Healey – and if not him Barber, when he was Chancellor.' He expressed no admiration of British accountants and lawyers but assumed full responsibility for miscalculated film ventures. 'People have said I'm worth three for four million pounds,' he told writer William Hall, 'but that's rubbish.' He went on to outline losses in shares and anticipated the likelihood of being 'worth a million' once all affairs in Britain were sorted. His future, he made clear, would be films, films, films.

The Man Who Would Be King was a $7 million version of Kipling's boyish yarn which John Huston had originally written up more than twenty years before with the hope of getting Bogart and Gable together in rebel-ridden India. 'It kind of sat on a shelf,' Michael Caine says. 'First Bogie died, then Gable, and John didn't know what to do with it. Then, after all those years, John brought it to Dennis Selinger, saying he wanted Sean and me, because we were the big British names and I suppose he thought that would be nicely fitting for Kipling.' Selinger was more excited by the script than anything he had read in years. He contacted Connery and Caine immediately, confident that 'this was an important picture for Sean, something of real substance that could give him one hell of a spurt.' Connery liked the idea of working with Huston, and with his buddy Michael Caine. The added factor that location work was planned for Morocco, just across the neck of the Med from home, appealed too. Fees were negotiated – not great, but not bad by current standards for actors trailing the American elite of Redford and Brando. Connery and Caine were awarded a quarter of a million each, plus a percentage.*

Work began in the foothills of the Atlas Mountains, in an atmosphere of harmonious joy. 'Sean had married Micheline shortly before,' says Brian Doyle, 'and he reluctantly decided to announce it to a Scottish journalist during the film. In a matter of hours, of course, Fleet Street had it and there was a mighty fuss that didn't please him. Similarly with Bond. He'd say before a press conference, "Look, no questions on Bond, OK?" Then someone would ask the inevitable, and off he'd go, ram-

---

*Connery and Caine sued Allied Artists, the production overlords, for proper percentage returns in 1977. They won their court action and were reportedly enriched by $¼ million each. The counter-suit for $22 million, claiming libel, failed. Had it succeeded, Connery is in no doubt, it would have all but destroyed him.

bling on about why he'd quit, the possibilities of a return with the non-Broccoli project (*Warhead*) which was under discussion, the lot. He was really for the most part quite pleasant with journalists, but the myth of the surly, difficult slob was perpetuated, based on scraps.' Connery severed with Bond bluntly in a chat with William Hall. 'I say no (to a return) because I don't feel a great passion for it myself. If it was something that would give me a *zing* then I'd do it.' No mention of McClory or the upcoming collaboration with writer Len Deighton was made; at this point in time Bond was inessential to Connery's success. *The Man Who Would Be King* buzzed of quality from the first day's shoot.

'One of the things that worked right was the relationship Sean and I had as Danny and Peachy,' says Michael Caine, 'which was based, if you like, on the way we got on. There was humour in the script, but we wove in our own. Back at the hotels at night, or just before shooting during the day, we'd work out together some bit of business and go to John (Huston) and present him with it. More often than not he'd accept it, and say, Yeah, that's better than the script, do it. For instance, there's the little soldier routine we do at one point, marching into the palace, one-two, one-two, all haughty disdain – that was Sean and me injecting a bit of ourselves.' Huston was also impressed by each actor's confidence in the other. 'We decided we'd play to camera, emphasising each other's best lines – so in that way we orchestrated movement. And Sean was particularly good at that – anything physical, anything to do with grace of movement, he was terrific. . . He was great – a great *person* to work with, not only actor. He had no time for the appurtenances of success, none of your whose-dressing-room-is-biggest? I think the biggest hit element the movie had going for it was the fun of the whole escapade.'

Sharika, Caine's wife, was in the film too, so, complemented by Micheline, the foursome teamed happily after hours. There was much laughter and Huston thought the experience rewarding beyond expectations. Six years later, when the director was critically ill and believed to be dying, Caine and Connery visited him. 'It was uncanny,' Caine recalls. 'He recognised us, but he called us Peachy and Danny. He'd loved those damned characters so much, he'd lived with them in his head for so long.'

Huston, assisted in the writing by Gladys Hill, had considerably expanded Kipling's short story, embodying the author as narrator in the parable of two former Army sergeants, half-literate, striking a 'contrack' to cross the Himalayas and become the first Europeans to set foot in wildly primitive Kafiristan, where they will set themselves up as kings. Duly succeeding, they ultimately lose their hold over the tribesmen by revealing their humanness. Danny, the king, is killed trying to escape, and Peachy (Caine) survives to recount the adventure to Kipling (Christopher Plummer). In the *Monthly Film Bulletin* Tom Milne drew comparisons with Orson Welles's planned production of Conrad's *Heart of Darkness*, thematically similar. Though Welles would doubtless have explored the parables more fully, Milne opines, Huston 'does bring the conflict ignored by Kipling (sympathy for the underdog combined with support for imperialist authority) into the open. . . Here the film is beautifully served by the performances of Sean Connery and Michael Caine, very funny as twin incarnations of typically endearing Kipling ranker-rogues, identical in their sharp-witted, foul-mouthed opportunism. . .'

From the moment the film opened in December the seeds of predicted success sprouted hugely. *Photoplay* judged Caine and Connery 'inspired'; *Screen International* blared, 'Here's richness! A splendid all-rounder'; the *New York Times* chimed, 'Mr Connery and Mr Caine are two of (Huston's) nicest discoveries. The movie . . . looks lovely and remote and has just enough romantic nonsense in it to enchant the child in each of us.'

Escalating popularity totally removed from Bond, focused Connery's energies on yet more ambitious efforts. After the briefest snatched holiday waterskiing from his own beach at Marbella with Jason and Stefan ('actually I find the sport quite boring – give me golf'), Connery was entrenched in Richard Lester's tragicomic *Robin and*

Marian, shot entirely on the Plain of Urbassa (doubling for Sherwood Forest) near Pamplona, Spain – a favoured site Lester had picked and used to supreme advantage with his *The Three* (and *Four*) *Musketeers* the year before. 'It was an odd kind of new popularity,' a publicist suggests. 'I remember a handout for one of his post-Bond movies ran along the lines of – if you were a newsman in the sixties hoping to stitch together a headline, your racing certainties were Howard Hughes, Chairman Mao, the excesses of the Burtons and then old Bond. So Sean, no matter where he looked, drew attention. But by the time Roger (Moore) had done a couple of Bonds well enough, Sean had sloughed off the skin. He'd had those Spanish movies succeed, so he was in a different league. He wasn't newsworthy like your average flavour of the month. He was newsworthy like, say, Hoffman. Not quite up with the Brandos, but getting there, we felt.'

The Wind and the Lion and *The Man Who Would Be King* had been made back to back, so by the time Connery encountered Lester's film he was exhausted. He perked instantly when he read James Goldman's script. 'Not having worked with Sean before I can't say I imagined at all what his reaction would be,' Lester says. 'He wanted to see the script, naturally, but his response revealed no tiredness. He was enthused, as I had been four years earlier when the idea was offered to me.'

Years before a Columbia executive had come into Lester's Pinewood office with four cards on which were scribbled synopses of potential films. Riding high on the strength of absurdist comedies like the Beatles' films, Lester had 'jumped on the *Robin* one. I told him that was the picture I wanted to make and if he could go away and fix a deal, I was in.' Months later Goldman's script – 'beautifully done, and scarcely tampered with at all in the shooting version' – was submitted, and financing arrangements began. Lester thought of Connery first for the part of Little John (eventually played by Nicol Williamson). 'I thought that might be fun, off-centre casting . . . but then the notion of his taking on Robin grew and grew. The quality of innocence he can so well portray was food for thought.' Competition from other Robin Hood productions in planning threatened Lester's. Polish producer Wieslaw Kliszewicz opened discussions with British director Sidney Hayers to shoot a version starring Patrick Mower in England and Mel Brooks started sketching out a TV series in Hollywood. Undeterred, Lester laboured for the consummate version – and to that end secured the participation of Audrey Hepburn, agreeing to return to the cinema after seven years' absence. That coup effectively quelled competition, and proved decisive in winning Connery's signature. Appealing to Connery too was the quirky slant of Goldman's text. Though Lester's imprimatur assured a popular film, Connery was unashamedly attracted to 'a story about death, and dying. I had to find out what kind of man *is* Robin? Considering his later days will be something new.'

'So Sean's making a picture about Robin Hood dying?' a film executive is alleged to have said. 'How long will it take? He was ninety minutes dying in *The Offence*.'

Lester completed his film in an astounding six weeks, fully on location. 'I don't think I made many mistakes with it,' he says, 'but I regretted Ray Stark's (executive producer) decision to alter our working title. The title was *The Death of Robin Hood* and should have been left as such. In changing it we were inviting the kind of mindless technique many critics have of evaluating your movie *by the last one you made*. To me, *Robin* was not comedy – yet people asked me where were the jokes. Yes, there were humorous moments. Sean is an actor who looks for humour in his parts, to humanise characters – which is quite right. But *Robin* was straight, all of us saw it like that – and because of the connotations of the changed title it prompted the wrong reaction.'

But *Robin and Marian* was good enough to complete for Connery the hat-trick of critical successes begun with *The Wind and the Lion*. But although in Britain and Europe the film did fair business, it was not a box-office success in the American market. The heart of the story, Connery himself squarely judged, was wrong for America: Robin is in decline, returning disillusioned from the Crusades and ready to do battle again with the Sheriff of Nottingham (Robert Shaw) who, by order of King John (Ian Holm), is rounding up all higher clergy for exile. Maid Marian (Hepburn), now the abbess of a priory, is due for imprisonment but Robin's wrath is fired and he frees her, reactivates their love affair and, finally, tackles the Sheriff in single combat. Robin is gravely wounded and Marian sips poison to die by his side in a deftly handled, unsentimental concluding scene. Vincent Canby's contribution to the American salvos was ready to concede that Hepburn's and Connery's screen presences, 'the intensity of the images they project – are such that we are convinced that their late-August love is important and final.' By Connery's standards financially the film 'wasn't a success at all.'

'There were elements that hadn't been foreseen,' he told journalists at a press conference, principal of which was 'the Catholic response. She (Marian) was committing so many sins by committing suicide, killing me and living in sin.' Another difficulty for Americans was that 'their philosophy is very much in terms of solving problems, and that the good guy should never be over the hill, never in a state of deterioration.' The same explanation of failure as had been afforded to *The Offence* crowned the whole: 'I think it's more European to examine something like a myth-Robin and take him apart to see how the myth was realised in the first place . . . *Robin and Marian* was not an American-orientated film.'

The failure of the film financially was more than made up for by the hot attention Connery drew week by week, from all quarters. Robert Hardy considered his contribution 'a personal best' and took the trouble to write to Lester when he couldn't contact Connery. Pauline Kael in *The New Yorker* was unremitting in her praise: 'Sean Connery – big, fleshy, greying – is the most natural-looking heroic figure. He seems unrestrained, naked: a true hero . . . he's animal-man at its best.' Fred Zinnemann told me in conversation, '*Robin and Marian* drew my attention to Sean; his authority was memorable.' Frank Rich of the *New York Post* was greatly generous too, believing

Connery and Hepburn 'epitomise ideals of glamour and sophistication that have since passed out of our lives.'

On this winning streak it seemed Connery could do no bad. Richard Lester was not the only director who recognised and accepted the actor's saving grace presence in a movie. Lester wanted to use him again 'as soon as possible, as soon as the right script turned up' – and a number of popular directors felt the same. Offers came thick and fast, but Connery still displayed a vagrant propensity towards the unorthodox. He was pleased that *Robin and Marian* was accorded a citation of merit 'for excellence as family entertainment' by the Southern California Motion Picture Council, an award from the epicentre of the industry (and despite the fact that the movie was un-American), but he veered off immediately to a non-family entertainment – Richard C. Sarafian's *The Next Man*.

Sarafian's filmic vision is best demonstrated by his earlier *Vanishing Point* (1971), but *The Next Man* unfortunately combined all his ironic whimsy with liberal gushes of derivative tomfoolery. The humanitarian plot basis, with its agreeable dressing of high-risk intrigue, obviously engaged Connery's interest, but unending rewrites on an unsettled script stumped greatness, even novelty. Connery played a visionary Saudi Arabian minister determined to sign a pact with Israel for the co-production of petroleum and its by-products, for distribution at cost to poor nations. Lithe blonde Cornelia Sharpe was Nicole Scott, callous and amoral as Bond himself, assigned to kill the good Arab after first seducing him. The pompous edge to the hokum encouraged Vincent Canby to slam the makers as people 'whose talent for filmmaking and knowledge of international affairs would both fit comfortably into the left nostril of a small bee', and, for the first time ever, a Connery movie found no willing distributor in Britain. *The Next Man* was finally seen in Britain on Independent Television (network) in January 1982.

Sarafian and Connery were equally vexed by the critics' reaction. Much earnest labour had gone into the picture, and $4 million had been spent location-hopping from Nassau to London to Ireland to Munich, Nice and Morocco.

But, after a speedy opening at the Rivoli and other New York theatres, it was murdered noisily. Cornelia Sharpe, with her forty-nine costume changes, token nude scene and antagonistic calm took the brunt of most criticism. Deservedly: the script's attempt to maintain her at star-billing was agonisingly obvious, and the film would have been better had the chicanery been played with subtlety. Connery might have granted that, but he would not truck with one New York journalist's tack. In America to discuss offers with his Los Angeles agents, he read a review which boldly stated that Sharpe was only cast because she was the producer's girlfriend. Connery wasted no time in contacting the journalist by phone and threatening, very eloquently, to push her words down her throat. 'What did she say?' Roderick Mann later queried Connery; to which, without batting an eye, Connery replied, 'Nothing, she was speechless.'

This commendable quality of loyalty had always won Connery friends in the film business. Even those directors who stopped short, for whatever reasons, of using him, held him in high regard. John Schlesinger, whom Connery had approached in 1971 for a part in *Sunday Bloody Sunday* (Peter Finch was already cast, so Connery was turned down), frequently loaned out his Beverly Hills home to him; others went out of their way to enjoy his company. But, as Guy Hamilton says, 'Sean is not a social animal – though once admitted to his circle, people are inclined to stay there; Sean's ability to call a spade a spade makes him valued.' In Hollywood, Connery dined and drifted with Michael Caine, the writer Stanley Mann and a few notable expatriates. Pausing for breath before flying back to Britain to discuss possible new films he reflected on the fact that Spain was the dearest place on earth to him, Hollywood was good only for the best beef and lamb in the world and Britain – well, Britain had its values all mixed up. He told a columnist friend that he regretted not having been able to attend the premieres of his last three movies in Britain but 'the tax laws just won't allow it. If I stay in Britain for more than ninety days I'm subject to those crazy taxes. It's self-defeating, the government's making a big mistake. (The tax problems) only serve to discourage a major filmmaking in Britain. No big star will agree to risk a movie there that might conceivably overrun and land him in it. It's unfortunate, but I just don't want to.'

Back in Spain, too far from the risky realities of London and L.A., Connery signed swiftly to Joseph Levine's mammoth production of *A Bridge Too Far*, a $25 million reconstruction of Operation Market Garden, General Montgomery's outlandish attempt to terminate the Second War in a single coordinated thrust. Sir Richard Attenborough was signed to direct and the prestige ring of the endeavour, along with the quarter-million-dollar fee, convinced Connery he was on to a good thing. He was, in fact, the first of some dozen international stars to be signed and he was appalled when, weeks before shooting commenced in Holland, he read a newspaper account of Robert Redford's negotiated $2 million fee. 'At first I thought it was a mistake,' Connery said. 'Then I learnt it wasn't. Now, considering the size of my part in the picture, the salary I'd agreed on seemed fair. But when I found out how much others were getting – for the same amount of work and with no more acting ability – it became unfair.'

Connery's role was that of Major-General Roy Urquhart, whose job was to command the First Airborne Division's combat drop and push to consolidate the Rhine bridgehead at Arnhem, hopefully – but tragically not – with the support of General Horrocks's (Edward Fox) XXX Corps ground force. The part was meaty, and Connery vied for screen time only with Anthony Hopkins (as Lt. Col. Frost, the fighting hero of Arnhem Bridge). Incensed at press reports and the fuss surrounding Redford, James Caan and Elliott Gould, Connery met with Joe Levine and demanded fairer status. 'It had nothing to do with egotistical arrogance,' a friend contends. 'One of Sean's slogans after Bond had always been, pay me what I'm worth. Naturally he gathered that since Levine priced Redford so high, he deserved more. No shrewd producer, however well disposed towards him – and Levine was a pal – would deny him his worth.'

Levine agreed to increase Connery's salary by fifty percent rather than release him and the units moved to Deventer, 40 kilometers north of Arnhem, to commence a massive shoot. The logistical problems of mounting the film – assembling the 300-man production team and more than 100 actors, buying aircraft, tanks, guns from all over the world – were monstrous; but the end result, with superlative post-production – dubbing, music, cutting – made the undertaking worthwhile. Unlike *The Longest Day*, this movie (also based on a Cornelius Ryan book) knitted smoothly. Where Zanuck had corralled stars for 'star effect' in *The Longest Day*, Levine had employed the instantly recognisable faces as a means of punctuating the complex fabric of the story, making them, in their identifiableness, as necessary to narrative coherence as the screenplay itself.

While at Arnhem Connery steered clear of Marbella's temptations – 'When I'm working this hard I miss the golf . . . though I find ways to get round that' – and flew back to L.A. where, on October 31st, he swooped into the muddy mire of *Meteor*, $15 million of unmitigated disaster, directed by Ronald Neame, all about the attempts of an American and a Russian scientist (Connery and Natalie Wood respectively) to divert an earth-strike by a meteor. Elaborate special effects delayed the completion of the movie – which did not open till November 1979 – but Connery wasn't bothered. Before a quarter of the picture was shot at MGM Studios the cancer of defeat was about. 'It was one of those movies where you have to *try* hard,' commented an actor afterwards. 'When you have to try *that* hard, you know there's something amiss.' Expatriate old friends found Connery tired from three years of unbroken work, but coolly philosophical. He stayed again at Schlesinger's house, but this time had the company of Micheline and the children. En route the family had stopped off in Britain, where Connery had treated the boys, and Micheline, to a saunter down memory lane. He had collected Effie and driven to Fountainbridge to glance over 176 before the wrecking cranes moved in. To his surprise, he himself mirrored something of the boys' reaction. 15-year-old Jason found the place just 'interesting', where Stefan, two years his junior, thought it awful. 'I wanted them to see it,' Connery mused, 'but it really *was* a dump. A terrible place. No hot water, gas mantles on the landings. . .'

Micheline, who had seen many seedy, insect-infested hotel rooms in North Africa, aired her evaluation: 'What a dreadful place!' Effie had just smiled and hugged her son and whispered that it was really quite nice, unchanged; she didn't have to close her eyes to imagine what it was like all those years ago, with Joe out till all hours, toiling at the rubber mill, and Tommy stealing away, too young for dreams even, to kick football on the biggie.

In the Hollywood Hills, in the spring of '78, Connery relaxed and ruminated on the grey harsh past. Watching Micheline working with her oils and easel, painting Shakira Caine; the children, the scenery, dining with welcome visitors Ian Bannen and Richard Burton, snatching an hour's golf in eye-startling sun . . . in many ways, thinking of Fountainbridge, the new, secured life was hard to assimilate. He had certainly made the million he'd intended when he quit Britain for good – and well more. His career was stable, his services in demand, his company sought. And yet, and yet. . .

Fame had cost. Fame-seeking is a business of compromise. Connery had made the kind of fortune that would, in the words of a columnist, make a Clydeside trade unionist spit. Though the Trust remained, financed through Dunbar & Co, physically and emotionally Connery was many miles from the socialist experiments that had been dear to him. By '78, and that whistle-stop in Fountainbridge before demolition commenced, he knew there would never be any going back. He had found the good life he dreamed of when he peered wide-eyed into big star dressing-rooms in Pinewood more than twenty years before and, coloured by Micheline's magic, it was too sweet to let go. 'In himself he remained basically the

213

same,' Michael Caine says. 'Always a bit of the decent working man about him – like the time we were at a club in Los Angeles and this crowd of loud-mouths started to heckle the performer on stage. Sean wouldn't have it. He didn't call the manager or anything. He just did the bold thing and had a go at 'em. Very brave. But, you see, he wasn't offended himself – it wasn't that his cosy night out had been interrupted. He was upset for the performer on stage. He just couldn't take these rowdies, so he gave them a dose of their own medicine. Like any noble working man.'

In Hollywood writer-director Michael Crichton and producer Dino De Laurentiis offered Connery *The First Great Train Robbery* which he agreed to do, but withdrew from when informed the shoot would be at Pinewood. Schedules were reshuffled, Ireland's National (formerly Ardmore) Studios, were seen to be adequately equipped and a two-month filming run started in the summer of 1979. Weeks before he flew to Ireland, mulling over the new script at Schlesinger's house, Connery showed old loyalties again by inviting Ian Bannen aboard. 'Crazy,' says Bannen. 'It was about two o'clock in the damned morning and Sean threw me the script and said, "See if there's anything in it for you. I can't see it, but have a look." ' Bannen perused Crichton's racy script and declined. 'Sean was a very astute reader,' says Irish National Studios' director Seamus Smith. 'He had acquired a conversational range, an intelligence, an intellectual capacity that one might put on a par with, say, Peter Ustinov. He read all the time he was in Ireland. Whenever I saw him he had a book in his hands, not some trashy paperback, always something substantial. His way with scripts was remarkable, too. He could glance over an offered script and establish immediately whether it was right for him, or whoever. He was never brash, when one submitted something for his evaluation, just utterly, intelligently decisive.'

The First Great Train Robbery was a good choice at a good time in Connery's career. Crammed with fleeting images resoundingly redolent of Victorian life, it told the story of

214

the incorrigible crook, Pierce (Connery), who devises a plan to steal £25,000 of bullion being shipped to the troops in the Crimea, on the first leg of its journey – by train to Folkestone. Abetted by his mistress Miriam (Lesley-Anne Down) and Irish safe-cracker Agar (Donald Sutherland), Pierce gathers the four keys necessary to open the bullion safes, then tackles the train. The resultant episodes, where Pierce performs hair-raising carriage-top stunts on the moving locomotive, are among Connery's best action moments since James Bond. They were eminently memorable for Connery too. Seamus Smith recalls: 'Micheline wasn't around for all the shooting, and had she been there would have been trouble over the stunt sequence. Sean wanted to do it, but he was under the impression, as was Crichton, that the train which was an original 1870-built steam model would travel no more than about 30 mph. Of course, when the shooting was over and Sean stepped down from the carriage, all wind-washed, the helicopter pilot who'd been covering the shot flying alongside said, "No, mate, my instruments aren't likely to be wrong – and you were doing more than fifty!" Sean was, needless to say, shaken and stirred.'

After location shooting in Meath and Cork, Crichton transferred his cast to Pinewood for two London sequences, carefully limited so that Connery would not spend too many days 'under the umbrella'. Seamus Smith followed on to watch progress and found Connery demonstrated: 'remarkable stamina. One found it impossible not to admire the gusto he put into the picture. When Micheline wasn't around he doggedly kept his head down at golf. He ate well, enjoying good grub, and drank mostly wine. I got the feeling here was a contented man, ideally suited to the rigours of his chosen career.' Confusion of identification with Bond no longer troubled the mellow Connery. Smith recalls 'an awful, rainy afternoon, late-lunching with him at Pinewood's restaurant. The manageress came in, having picked up her children from school. Sean was off-duty, wearing a dirty anorak, bearded, without his toupee. But the kids instantly recognised him and came darting over, asking, "Can we have your autograph, Mr Bond?" Sean paused – and grinned. He seemed delighted to be recognised and cheerily responded to these children with their awe-struck expressions.'

Crichton's film lived up to all its promise, mixing pure escapism with visual sumptuousness, providing a fitting colourful epitaph for cinematographer Geoffrey Unsworth, whose last film it was. Gordon Gow in *Films and Filming* crystallised the specialness of the movie when he wrote 'charm is uppermost in this breezy film' and though *Time* and other notable journals picked out Lesley-Anne Down for the scene-stealing awards, Connery received his fair share too. Looking back on his recent career, *Films Illustrated* called him 'the most improved British actor of the decade' and everyone agreed that Connery had much to look forward to in the immediate future. 'He wanted to direct,' Seamus Smith says. 'Everybody knew that was a desire he'd long held. But he genuinely adored acting, and the parts were there for the taking like never before.'

'I haven't made too many mistakes,' Sean Connery told a press conference in 1981, 'but I made one with *Cuba*.' Late in '78, just weeks after finishing Crichton's film, Connery tirelessly hitched onto Richard Lester's new project, a love-and-war story about the last days of Batista's Cuba. His optimism had been undermined by grave doubts about the still unreleased *Meteor* and manifold signs of United Artists' indifference to promoting *The First Great Train Robbery*. In *Cuba* he blundered, settling for the two things he was instinctively most wary of – an unfinished script in the hands of an unsure director.

'Confidence is an actor's lifeblood,' says Robert Henderson. 'Take it away and you've got an actor in trouble.' Connery's choice of *Cuba* was to take him from the smoothest, happiest plateau of his career to the brink of disaster.

216

CHAPTER SIXTEEN

Misses

A CONSIDERABLE AMOUNT of Connery's undoing with *Cuba* was his own fault. Ever since the Bond days he had resisted long-shoot commitments on movies, believing a shorter, intense schedule allowed one the emotional intensity *plus* a detachment which made one more likely to achieve interesting screen results. The film most wasteful of time and energy had been the second last Bond, *You Only Live Twice* – a memory which still rankled. As late as '81 Connery was still cribbing that that 'took six months of my time, after two or three postponements – which meant it was almost a year out of my life . . . and if one film takes six months and the people who are supposedly producing it are so stupid they cannot programme it properly, then it leaves no room for flexibility (to make other movies).' Dennis Selinger's tactical scheme of fast-filming had shown itself worthy over four exciting years – pointing up Connery's own new belief that 'the more diverse the parts you play, the more stimulating it is and, in turn, the wider the experience, so there's even *more* you can play.' But speed-of-light transition from role to role entails real dangers – the very least, manifest on-screen exhaustion, as happened briefly during the mid-sixties; at worst, misconceived, rushed mishmash when the actor has too much control because of his stature.

Richard Lester had been eager to work with Connery again after *Robin and Marian*. Motivated by the same kind of loyalties, Lester believed he had 'come close to something really good' with *Robin*, but had crashed financially. Intending to make up to the actor he greatly admired, in 1977 he commissioned his friend the writer Charles Wood, a gifted 'character creator' who had worked on ten Lester films, to pen something special for Connery. Inspired by conversations with producer Denis O'Dell, mutual friend of Connery's and Lester's, who had himself spent some weeks in Cuba during the Castro take-over in 1960, the director chose this 'truly remarkable period' as the basis of what would be the Connery epic to end epics of the seventies. In a phone call outlining the proposal, Connery expressed enthusiasm. He thought the originality of the concept striking. It seemed 'extraordinary' to him that no filmmakers had raked the Cuban revolution in twenty years. Once excited, and trustingly fond of Lester, Connery was in. Once in, he was hurrying. The first treatment Charles Wood submitted he liked, and though he felt uneasy about the unfinished screenplay, he felt far more unhappy about the prospects of *Meteor* and vacuous career gaps looming ahead. Very fast, he negotiated *Cuba* with Denis O'Dell and production supervisors Alex Winitsky and Arlene Sellers. On the strength of recent achievements his fee rocketed to a fat million dollars, his biggest in some time. *The First Great Train Robbery* was well finished and nearly ready for release, and Connery was itchy to be on with further work, fatter cheques. He gave Lester a deadline: the film must start while the weather was right in Southern Spain, which would double for Cuba. September-October would be a good time.

But by October Wood's script was still unready. 'It was constant re-evaluation,' says Lester, 'because I felt we weren't reaching the proper balance between foreground characters and background history. We were risking falling between a romantic story involving uninteresting people, and a documentary-like survey of a ridiculous, fascist, sin-ridden Mafia-controlled city undergoing total change in a three-day revolution. I was under pressure to get rolling, but I was terrified of trivialising this fascinating time in recent world history.' Connery himself claims he postponed shooting twice because the script was not satisfactory. Eventually November 6th was declared as a start date – 'because we were running out of weather' – but this was pushed aside too. Logistically, for Lester, the

218

film was a nightmare. As on *Robin*, there would be no studio work, just ten weeks at 78 sites, ranging from the famous old cities of Jerez de la Frontera (where the sherry comes from), to Cadiz and picture-postcard Seville. The crew, organised under a plethora of assistant directors, numbered 160 – their job being to utilise multiple camera techniques in order to speed up the shooting and vary choice of sequences for editing, all designed to make the film fast, explosive and documentary-like. Finally, Connery's patience was spent. The umpteenth draft of the script was deemed acceptable, though Lester had reservations and was still scribbling amendments, and filming started on November 27th. Diana Ross had been first choice for Connery's love interest, but had dropped out late in the day, to be replaced by a coquettish but rather young-looking Brooke Adams, cast by Lester before he even met her.

The opening of *The First Great Train Robbery* in Britain a few weeks into shooting did nothing to cheer the ominous mood on location. United Artists had, as Connery anticipated, spared much on promoting *Robbery*, even though notices were excellent; why should he expect anything better from them with their *Cuba*? On set Connery was gruff and irritable, refusing to join a party of British journalists who had specially flown out for informal drinks after work, brutally fussy with the odd interviewer. 'But there were no tantrums,' Lester insists; 'Sean is too seasoned, too professional.' Good relationships with fellow actors Jack Weston and Brooke Adams ('He's hot, he's so *hot!*') were formed and, day by day, problems were tackled. 'But those problems, script apart, were too numerous,' Lester confesses. 'Problems like borrowing military hardware from the Spanish government, and it being taken back at the last minute; a key plane, the only one of its kind in Europe, crashing on us; the train for the last big sequence blowing up on *the first take* – we were snowed down.'

In January reports filtered back from Spain that two different endings were planned for the film and, according to *Screen International*, that 'Lester can often be heard speaking about fear. It seems that when he wakes up he is terrified of what lies before him. He worries about all the things that might go wrong.' At the same time Lester was putting a confident brave face on his difficulties. The open-ended script was no cause for alarm: 'It is lovely when films have their own organic growth,' he said from location. 'You let it develop and sometimes marvellous things happen.'

Cuba had Connery looking more Bondish than he had done since *Diamonds*. His hairpiece was thick and neat, the Gable moustache cropped to insignificance on his leaner, fitter face. The story is of a former British army Major (Connery) hired by Batista's people to teach his troops counterinsurgency as the storm builds in Havana. The Major meets a woman, Alexandra (Adams), whom he had an affair with fifteen years before. They are swept into the chaos of revolution but cannot agree on its likely outcome. While filming progressed the separate endings had Connery persuading Adams to leave as Castro takes over, or, against his convictions, deciding to stay with her to face the music. In the end a compromise was struck: Connery flees to Havana airport to get out of the country, leaving an air ticket for Alexandra, should she choose to follow. The effect was unfortunate after two hours of genuinely gripping action, after the intimacies, almost a cop-out. Marjorie Bilbow fairly castigated the whole, whilst admiring 'the way Lester keeps the pace going, fits the jigsaw pattern together, contrasts the squalor of poverty with the smug elegance of wealth.'

During the filming Connery never once complained of developments to Lester. 'I'm not a director who runs rushes, so there was nothing, in that way, to be discussed,' Lester says. Connery drove home whenever possible to Marbella, taking the wheel of his own Mercedes, refusing party gatherings. Quinn Donohue, the publicist, urged him to cooperate more fully with the press but his regular reply, bundling golf clubs out of the car during afternoon breaks, was 'Give me a break, eh? I've done my bit.'

Cuba came in on schedule and on budget, a laudable

220

accomplishment in the eyes of objective onlookers. Connery saw a rough cut, the unfinished edited version, but did not reveal his feelings to Lester. 'Only later it came back to me that he wasn't happy,' Lester says. 'He never said it to my face, but he was cross and he held me responsible for all that went wrong.' Lester emphasises that he was not sorry he made the movie. 'It works on a superficial level, the character interplay, all that, but the profundity I envisioned went out the window. There just wasn't *time* to get it.'

Unreasonably perhaps, Connery reflected on *Cuba* as a bad experience, a waste of time. Unforgiving, and admitting no blame himself, he dubbed it 'a fatal error . . . a case of patchwork'. In his opinion, he stated grimly, 'Lester hadn't done his homework.' Lester was understandably aggrieved and, though muted in defeat, later spoke words of defence for his product whilst confessing to me he doubted the breach of friendship was repairable. 'I haven't heard from Sean about the picture, but I take it his feelings are very strong.'

A shock of disillusionment – or just plain tiredness – rattled Connery after *Cuba*. It was the first long period of inactivity since 1972. Speculative projects were announced – a possible role in James Clavell's *Tai-Pan*, to be directed by John Guillermin for Filmways Productions (originally announced to star Steve McQueen), another possible in *Shogun* for ABC TV. All fell through, lost under another secretive blanket of domestic and business reshuffling. After a row with his Los Angeles agents, Connery quit Dennis Selinger and ICM's protective advice. Reviewing his business sallies of the mid-seventies he unearthed astounding miscalculations, bad judgements by himself, bad advice, unwise investments that had had the veneer of quality. He told the *Express* writer Victor Davis that while founding the Educational Trust and seeking ways, with Sir Iain Stewart, to improve the industrial atmosphere between men and management he had mistakenly assumed himself to be rich. The regretful irony was, that when he was writing over his $1 million plus to the Trust, he himself was running out of cash – 'thanks to mishandling, the fortune had turned out to be all figures and no substance.' Having remade a decent nest-egg, as he swore he would when he baled out, he was now taking time out to apply the lessons of the past and invest it well. Though he engaged a new agent in L.A., Connery declared, 'Nowadays I handle contracts myself – and I have a good lawyer. I think it was Erica Jong who said the difference between making a lot of money and being rich is a good lawyer.' In Los Angeles he purchased an apartment, and in Iowa a 600-acre pig and cattle farm. 'His intention,' says an acquaintance, 'was to resettle a part of himself near the hub of the film world. On *A Bridge Too Far*, for example, he had suffered the remoteness of Marbella: everyone else was raking in their millions while he was playing innocent golf, thinking, Oh, they won't try to swindle *me*. . . Sean always had some ongoing interest in the American scene, he realised that was necessary if an international reputation was to be maintained.'

Much as he guessed, Connery was in trouble, reputation-wise, when *Meteor* finally opened in November '79, followed weeks later by *Cuba*. The panning both movies received reverberated through the industry, amplified by the foul story of fouler takings on *The First Great Train Robbery*, whose progress around America was funereal. After the stock-taking holiday and part-move to the States, Connery sprung to action again, berating United Artists first of all for their weak-spined promotion of *Robbery*. He didn't need any agent to talk up for him – 'after all, it was me who made the film' – but went and saw the publicity-distribution people himself, pounding desks and demanding explanation. 'No satisfactory explanation came. . . United Artists owe me a bit, but I owe them some too, I suppose. I never did make that second picture for them, after *Diamonds*. . .'

With Natalie Wood, uninterestedly, he toured to promote the dreary Columbia *Meteor*, and was glad to get back to his L.A. flat to see Mike Caine and chat, in Caine's words, about anything but the bloody business. He spent a few days at the new farm in Iowa, and resolved to put Stefan and Jason to work there for a spell, to toughen them up. Back in L.A. he saw his friend the writer Roderick Mann and, over a flagon, reminisced. He would not be drawn on the failures of *Robbery*, *Cuba* and *Meteor* – nor the prospects of playing Daddy Warbucks in the upcoming film version of *Annie*, offered to him by Ray Stark, the producer. Yes, he liked the idea of hoofing in a musical again, and was taking singing lessons to loosen up the chords last fully tested with *There is Nothing Like a Dame*! – but that was as far as he would go in committing himself. Instead, he wanted to talk, as he always seemed to lately, about reversing personal financial failures.

Didn't Mann know the Chelsea Embankment flat had gone for £60,000? – too little – it was worth £300,000 today. And Dunbar & Co, still flourishing, was still dear to him – he held 80,000 shares. Plus shares in 'a number of banks in the Mid-West'. Aspects of the canny Connery, the screwball Scot who was always a bit of a maverick businessman emerged, during this hiatus, yet again.

Peter Hyams, distinguished new whiz kid director, at last urged Connery out of what colleagues described as 'his mini-retirement', with the offer of his hugely financed sub-*Star Wars* venture, *Outland*. Connery was jolted alive again by 'the story, the whole story. The setting of it and how it was (to be) constructed and designed and, obviously, as with any film, it had to be a viable part that I'd find stimulating.' With curious patriotic insistence disclaiming prior reluctance, Connery persuaded Hyams to relocate the shooting in Pinewood – 'partly because the technical facilities are so superior there (where *Star Wars* was made), but also because I haven't fully made a film there since 1974.' As a bonus perhaps just to try his hand again after the lull and regain confidence, he accepted a cameo part in Terry Gilliam's Monty Pythonesque, *Time Bandits* – an episodic bag of jokes, awkwardly interlinked but full of invention, which told the story of a boy's odyssey through holes in the fabric of time. As King Agamemnon, Connery was the only true heroic figure of the film, battling masterfully with the Minotaur till saved, by chance, by the boy (Craig Warnock). *Time Bandits* occupied a few days in Morocco, next door to Aloha Golf Course

223

and the stress-saving opportunity to bang a ball about with good pal James Hunt, now in retirement and living nearby.

Connery told colleagues he liked being back in front of the cameras, that sixteen months away had been too long. At the ritzy Marbella Club Hotel, where Loren and Bardot stopped off whenever cruising through, Connery was an occasional visitor, but everyone agreed that, even on holiday, he seemed more comfortable 'on the go'. Jackie, wife of high-living Prince Alfonso, the hotel owner and casual friend of the Connerys, comments, 'Dozens of the most beautiful women dally and flirt with him, but he doesn't give them the slightest chance.' Instead, even after years of close marriage, he skipped away alone with Micheline whenever possible. Together they played his favourite golf course – she off handicap seventeen, he now off a stunning nine. Given the choice, though, he claimed he would prefer to play with his men friends. Much as he adored Micheline, absence, he felt, was desirable. 'I couldn't possibly be with someone night and day. . . Whatever your situation, you should be parted for a lot of the time. I'll tell you why: if you've been away acting, painting, whatever, it's that marvellous exchange when you get back that counts for so much.'

The passion for golf which, friends contend, increasingly provided diversion from the strain and frustration of mishandling his own affairs – as he had done in rushing *Meteor* and, particularly, *Cuba* – immediately caused irksome inconvenience on *Outland*. Because he had, for the last four years, insisted on visiting St Andrews' and other Scottish courses for BBC TV pro-celebrity matches, his allowance for work days in Britain was reduced. *Outland* was a complicated endeavour that looked likely to swallow every minute of Connery's permitted ninety days, so for that reason at weekends he was forced to fly out of Britain aimlessly, to return for work on Monday morning. This 'nonsense restriction' appalled him, and he aired his views loud.Having brought work for 100 technicians to Pinewood, and inspired other investors planning space-age productions, he reckoned he was being 'penalised'.

The golf-playing would go on because 'there's no matching Scottish courses', but he objected to the 'paradoxical law that makes it difficult for a man to work as hard and often as he chooses to do. They (the government) seem to be more flexible (with) villains who break the law.' In occasional, terse interviews he concentrated on arguing forcefully about a scheme that would make the ninety days allowance a personal one, permitting British stars like Roger Moore, Mike Caine and himself the freedom to bring in multi-million dollar productions; the stars would then pay taxes on their British earnings alone. There lingered a muffled echo of Iain Stewart works' management idealism but, as before, it made much sense. And, as before, few listened, let alone gave latitude for the testing. Connery, once again, grew tired of driving, and withdrew. He focused all on *Outland*.

On set, opinion was divided among those who found Connery 'shaky, unsure of himself when disasters struck' (a fellow actor) and those, like the script girl, who greeted 'a feeling of strength when he's around'. Peter Hyams, whom Connery admired for his 'working to programme' – unlike the Bond producers – found 'an actor so consummate that he can convey a breaking heart without his head [moving] an inch to left or right if the technicalities of the scene forbid it.' The set, techniques and story of *Outland* were innovative and controversial. In telling his lean tale of the manipulation of labour by drugging workers on the futuristic mining base Con-Amalgamate 27, on Jupiter's moon Io, Hyams employed new film devices like Introvision, and a story principle purportedly based on Fred Zinnemann's *High Noon*. Where Gary Cooper was the moral marshal single-handedly confronting corruption and cowardice in the Wild West in Zinnemann's 1952 film, Connery was O'Niel of the Federal Security Service, investigating the labour unrest on Io and challenging the might of mine boss Sheppard (Peter Boyle). Some late sequences of *Outland* mimicked *High Noon* visually, but Fred Zinnemann took exception to the publicity campaign launched by Warner Bros or their agents, aggressively framing the new movie an an updated *High Noon*.

'It was ill-advised and wrong,' says Zinnemann. 'I saw *Outland* and naturally observed similarities in isolated incidents; but the pictures were *totally* different in mood and meaning.' Connery himself, as he had done before, tripped into the hyperbole. After filming he was, he said, 'most conscious of the *High Noon* aspects' and that Hyams had not tried to disguise the fact that his picture was based on Zinnemann's.

'What was clever,' Connery said, 'was setting it in space – a frontier town. *That* was what appealed to me in the first place.' Connery vocally supported all that Hyams aspired to for a variety of honest reasons, not least of which must have been his desire to hype the project and make it work at the box-office, thereby regaining lost ground. 'But he truthfully believed in it,' says film writer Tony Crawley. 'He set out to promote it more actively than anything he'd done in years because, he said, it was a novel and worthwhile space venture, a new cinematic departure. He greatly admired what George Lucas and Spielberg had been doing in their movies but he made a big point that here (in *Outland*) was a space movie he could understand. His kind of futurology.' Connery asserted, 'Space fantasy doesn't appeal to me . . . in the end I get lost among all those laser beams and hurtling spaceships.' He believed, he said, that what was depicted in *Outland* was a 'logical extension of known technology'. He also dearly liked the way Hyams dealt with human issues in a world of technology amok.

Connery's creative input in *Outland* was far greater than in any movie, with the exception of *The Offence*, to date. He participated, with Hyams, in set design and vetted all the actors, deeming it vital to 'have mainly people with good faces (who) had a certain look about them . . . rather like Western pioneers.' He wanted Colleen Dewhurst for his assistant Dr Lazurus, but she was working in theatre so he settled for Hyams's choice of Frances Sternhagen instead. Introvision, the complicated camera effects technique related to simple old back projection, and launched by Tom Naud, John Eppolito and former giants RKO, made an impressive debut at Pinewood's Stage J, creating the illusion of vast backgrounds and lending the picture a uniqueness that was a boon no one had quite foreseen.

As time ran out and Connery's 90-day deadline drew near, nerves shredded. Numerous incidents filtered through the Pinewood production offices – stories of Connery's ever shortening temper, moderated by a self-aware humour that could transform deadly situations into marvellous mirth. Real anger only ever flared when technicians blundered or shambled on 'programmed plans'. Once, suspended from a harness to pretend outer space weightlessness, Connery found his spacesuit communications system was not working. He signalled to the crew to lower him to the ground and impolitely told the unit 'to get *everything* set to shoot before you put that harness round my balls.' Pinewood oldtimers mused that the maestro hadn't changed much in twenty years. 'When he went in to tell Broccoli and Saltzman what he wanted for Bond and *Dr No*,' an old trouper says, 'he fucked and blinded, and lay the record straight. That's Sean. He only knows how to talk truth.'

Encouraged by the rough cuts of *Outland* and the continuing popularity of space films, Connery resigned himself to another unbroken run at some oddball, but potentially popular, films. Richard Brooks, whom he knew for many years, brusquely offered him a part in his personal-statement *Wrong is Right* (later changed for European release to *The Man with the Deadly Lens*), but Connery cautiously prised the script from the director before agreeing to go. The fact that Brook's abiding reputation is one of awkward self-sufficiency, Connery was understandably flattered when his collaborative cooperation was called upon in trimming the overweight 280-page screenplay and reshaping major characters. Connery said goodbye to British friends at Pinewood – to favourite actor chum Ralph Richardson, and Roger Moore – and flew straight to location for Brooks in New York. The busy, dedicated aura was serving him well, because before the end of spring he was negotiating with Fred Zinnemann for a new and special movie, and producing a documentary about Edinburgh, free of charge, to promote the tourist

227

attractions of his home town. July's premiere of *Time Bandits*, which really wasn't a Connery film at all but bannered his name conspicuously, delighted him. Though erudite journals turned up their noses, and the Monthly Film Bulletin sniffed, '*Time Bandits* strains for a comparable absurdity (with *Monty Python's Flying Circus*)', audiences queued in good numbers and a quick cult status was bestowed by virtue of the Palin-Gilliam-Cleese link, alchemic in campus America.

It was mid-'81, Connery was beginning to experience the upswing of new demand and talk of Bond revival was thick in the air. Approaching the twentieth anniversary of the *Dr No* breakthrough, it seemed the right time to recap. Being at Pinewood again had, he told journalists, given rise to warm nostalgia: it was there, on Stage D, James Bond had first introduced himself to the film world, from there the journey to wealth and wisdom began. And yet, all these years later, he had to admit he had never actually sat through an entire completed Bond movie – other than those demanded of him at the few premieres, and the two Roger Moores he had sneaked in on. Once in L.A., he told Roderick Mann, he did slip home after a night on the town with Richard Burton and Mike Caine to find *Dr No* running on TV. He took a beer from the fridge, kicked off his shoes and slumped in a chair to watch it alone. He liked it well enough . . . but fell asleep halfway through. For the admirers, Connery-Bond was an institution, the epitome of hedonism, the enviable face of the best steamy dreams. For Connery, Bond was, had always been, merely graft.

Box office anaemia struck *Time Bandits* around the time of the European premiere of *Outland*, rigged by Connery for Edinburgh again, with proceeds to the Trust, in August. Columnists worldwide started to rank Gilliam's picture alongside recent Connery flops on their file cards. Alerted, Connery momentarily vigorously shouldered *Outland* forward, but to no avail. It was much praised in Europe, celebrated especially for its projection of Connery-the-hero with resonances that were significant in today's morally bemused world. But in America it was seen as anachronistic – despite Introvision, a backward step after *Star Wars* and *The Empire Strikes Back*. Connery was dejected, and the signs showed painfully, instantly. He was completing Zinnemann's *Five Days One Summer* at the Bernina Range of mountains, round the corner from St Moritz, when *Outland* was launched and flew home directly to help with the push. Alan Ladd Jr's new company whose flagship *Outland* was (and which was behind Zinnemann's film) were disappointed when, in Edinburgh, Connery granted only three interviews. Returning to Switzerland, he concentrated on finalising his five months' work commitment for Zinnemann with glum determination.

For Zinnemann, a double Academy award-winning director with a thirty-year record of excellence, Connery was 'never less than remarkably professional. He was not difficult, had no star ego, no moods. One felt he had only one objective – to get on with the picture and do what was best for it.' Typically, nothing of the creeping insecurity that was the legacy of so many recent hapless choices revealed itself to Zinnemann. Ten months before, when Connery was finishing *Outland* at Pinewood Zinnemann had first contacted him with the invitation to star in what was for the director the realisation of a long-held dream – a movie about mountain climbing in the thirties. As a young man Zinnemann's favourite pastime was hiking through Europe's mountainland, but not until now had he found the story, and location, that could sustain a film. 'Sean was my first and only choice of actor because no one else could undertake the hazardous exercises required, and yet was mature and yet again *could* act,' Zinnemann asserts. With the Ladd Company's Sandy Lieberson as go-between, the initial approach and discussions were fixed before Connery's departure to start Brooks's picture. But the deal had not been finally settled till spring. In June, as soon as *The Man with the Deadly Lens* was in the can, Connery, along with the other principals of the cast, began mountain-climbing training at Pontresina. There, in the same high-profile creative spirit of all post-*Cuba* work, Connery took part in script revision and

229

preparation, carefully plotting his own role – though not, as one might imagine, to Zinnemann's annoyance.

'Sean was constructive,' the director swears. 'The story was one I'd read, in short-story form, thirty years before, and it needed quite a lot of development and imagination to make it work for cinema. We had a very fine young writer, Michael Austin, but Sean had thoughts and concepts, ninety-five percent of which were worthy of assimilation.' Each day for a fortnight, after mountain training that Connery found hair-raising and a bit crazy, director and actor locked themselves away to polish Austin's script. When in mid-June shooting started Zinnemann was pleasantly pleased with 'a production that was memorable for . . . relatively few troubles. Working at altitudes of ten to thirteen thousand feet was often not easy, but there were no big disputes.'

Betsy Brantley, the North Carolina newcomer, cast to play the young woman obsessively in love with the married doctor twenty-five years her senior, posed inevitable problems. 'Obviously there are difficulties when you place an actor of Sean's experience opposite a girl without the range, like Miss Brantley,' Zinnemann says. 'I can best explain the problem by telling you that the second film I ever did had to do with a black detective and a senile dog. The black detective had trouble learning his lines and needed seven or eight takes. The dog, on the other hand, was only good for one take – then he ran away to hide. All this had to be done in four weeks. So one learns to gear oneself against such disparities and *make* things fit. Sean was as helpful with Betsy Brantley as could have been expected of him. He's a very fine actor, and he didn't let me down.'

The stresses of coping with arduous, freezing rock climbs and inexperienced actors cannot have helped lift the sombre pall after *Outland*, but Connery still showed vestiges of apparent confidence – or was it loyalty again? – when, three weeks after Edinburgh, he attended the Deauville Film Festival on a $15,000 expense chit from Warners, to beat the drum about Hyams's film. *Outland* opened the festival and attendants were later treated to a retrospective of his earlier films, coincidentally side-by-side with a Lana Turner retrospective. Turner showed up to queen over the event, and even dined with the former close friend. They were pictured together brushing shoulders, grinning wide – but neither would comment on their controversial and mysterious past. 'Through Turner's stay and her packed Press conflab,' wrote Tony Crawley, who sat with pad-on-knee in awe, 'she gave the kind of glitzy performance that can only be described by one of her film titles: *Imitation of Life*.' Connery, for his part, was life itself – an accurate mirror image of all that had been whirling round him professionally and personally these last tough months. He was curt but courteous, impatient but grimly dedicated, voicing concern but brave-faced throughout.

To discerning onlookers at the Connery Deauville press conference, it seemed here was a star actor who was floundering, but hanging in.

CHAPTER SEVENTEEN

Looking Forward

'IN THE HOUSE by the sea at Marbella we have an excellent garden and I find myself looking at it more. Perhaps it is trying to tell me something. To slow down? I don't know. . . When I was twenty-five I thought everything would be perfect when I reached the age of forty. Now that I'm fifty I'm putting my estate totally in order, and I don't know whether that's a preparation for living or dying. . .'

It might almost have been James Bond talking. Early in the Fleming novel *You Only Live Twice*, the penultimate work, James Bond sat in Queen Mary's Rose Garden in Regent's Park and contemplated: 'the state of your health, the state of the weather, the wonders of nature – these are things that rarely occupy a man's mind until he reaches the middle thirties.' Only in middle-age, Bond mused, does a man cease taking the world for granted.

As a throwover from his rough beginnings, Connery had never taken anything for granted. He had, in his words, worked his ass off since he was a child in order to accumulate possessions and a good professional reputation. But middle-age did find him reassessing the value of back-breaking endeavour and very seriously reappraising the future. Maritally he had been very fortunate. Diane Cilento had been a good career navigator for the time she was around and Micheline, as different in personality as could be imagined, was the ideal companion for years that were both rockier and richer. Micheline – 'a right good 'un,' to Ian Bannen – proved exactly the kind of buoy-marker Connery needed. Unlike Cilento, her artistic ambitions were not home distractions: she liked to build

232

her sunny nest and look after the children and cook meals. Stefan and Jason, temperamentally different themselves, grew close and secure under Micheline's protective guidance. Jason was enrolled at Gordonstoun – a universe away from Darroch – but deserted the academic world to follow his father onto the boards. At eighteen he was appearing in the Perth Theatre's seasonal *Aladdin*, playing Who Flung. Stefan, meanwhile, was reportedly developing an interest in golf, with space aplenty around Marbella to practice his five-irons, and had begun business college studies. With gentle encouragement from Sean, Micheline did begin to showcase her work, giving exhibitions in Europe and America, featuring her portraits of King Hussein, notable directors like John Huston and, rarely, her husband.

Against this serene domestic backcloth, Sean Connery acknowledged the demarcation point that turned him over to middle-age. The immediate adjacent anxiety, common to all actors who, like Connery, know the relative ephemerality of their art, was that of surviving the transition from young lead to character actor. Bestowed with extraordinarily youthful attributes – agility, grace, creased but strangely ageless features – Connery, like Cary Grant, had managed to extend his natural life as a romantic lead. *The Man with the Deadly Lens* and *Five Days One Summer* were the pictures that irreversibly brought Connery out of all youngblood guises while still, apparently, allowing him the badge of archetypical heroism. In a closing scene in *The Man with the Deadly Lens* Connery ritually enacts the dawn of a new acting age when, as go-getting TV journalist Hale shuttling from presidents to kings to tell it as it is, he prepares to parachute from a plane – and at the last second whips off the scanty toupee that was almost unnoticeable in the first place. It's a moment of black comedy that properly evokes a laugh and a sigh, almost subliminally reminding us of the gap between the man and the image, a gap that existed with *Dr No* and before, but that now lies too exposed and demands a different kind of bridging.

Though abstracted somewhat by the miscalculation of recent films, Connery did seem conscious and decided, from *Outland* on, to involve himself more in the rethreading of a maturer image. His pernickety way with scripts, his insistence on some artistic control, his unshakable single-mindedness – all spoke of preparation for a new era, a time when Sean Connery and not some 'stupid producer' would coin a versatile and reusable screen persona. Clearly the gutsy hero, moral or amoral, apposite or anachronistic, had been stretched to the limits. . .

And yet, when friends were saying so and bright-eyed critics were keenly taking up the paper chase laid by the actor and preparing to forgive *Meteor* in exchange for the promises of the redoubtable Mr Zinnemann, James Bond crashed out of yesterday and pulled Sean Connery back into a ball-breaking harness. Kevin McClory's *James Bond of the Secret Service*, which was later to become anybody's *Warhead*, which in turn became Schwartzman's *Never Say Never Again* stole on the scene so gradually that by the time the world had the news for sure, Connery's professional dilemma and his uneasy but sure move towards consolidating a new image was dwarfed to insignificance.

Was anyone surprised by the 1982 return to Bondage? 'I don't think so,' says Irish National Studios director Seamus Smith, 'because Sean wasn't embarrassed by Bond per se. Few actors have a better audience understanding, and by the early eighties the continued huge success of Roger Moore's Bond dangled in front of Sean like a carrot.' Brother Neil, who himself had briefly dabbled with films,* wasn't surprised; Robert Hardy wasn't; Ian Bannen wasn't. All are equivocal in expressing their understanding of the move. It is evident though that Connery sought advice from people he admired professionally before leaping in again – a revelation of some importance about a man who prides himself on his capacity to stand alone.

*As well as appearing on Scottish TV, Neil made two films: *Operation Kid Brother*, directed by Alberto Demartino (UA, 1968) and *The Body Stealers*, directed by Gerry Levy (Tigon, 1969). Neither was greatly popular and Neil is now back at his old job, plastering, in Edinburgh. He is contemplating a return to TV work.

234

Repeatedly in the future the question will be asked: what primarily motivated Connery to resume Bond? Did he turn back the clock solely for money? Or to appease an audience frustrated by half-cocked efforts over two or three years? Vital in evaluating events, perhaps, is a decision he made during 1980 when, in Hollywood, he was taking dancing and singing lessons to prepare for the Daddy Warbucks role in *Annie*. Ray Stark, the producer, was sure Connery was perfectly suited to the part and, in the enthusiasm of his certainty, began phoning the actor every day or so to find out how lessons were progressing and whether he was ready to sign the contract. Connery could not make up his own mind. Finally, in spite of enjoying the work-outs, he announced that he was being 'pressured' by Stark and pitched the whole business aside. 'I was bugged,' he said. 'I wouldn't make a decision until I was sure I could do it well enough. I didn't want to take it on and then find I was going to be dubbed.' Albert Finney assumed the role and, under John Huston's direction, scored a considerable hit with it.

The *Annie* part, had Connery taken it, would have represented the first real departure from what writer Neil Sinyard calls 'the acceptable face of heroism in an anti-heroic age' which Connery so often so doggedly pursued. *Annie* might have brought Connery back to the amorphous vacuum of pre-Bond, back to *On The Fiddle*, and demanded of him to fill the void. Faced with that likelihood (and it should be remembered that Connery more than once openly wished for comic or musical parts during early Bond), he swung away and, instead, settled on a course that would bring him the dead end of *The Man with the Deadly Lens* and the inevitable corollary of Bond. One acting acquaintance concedes the point: 'Sean maintains he hasn't enough money to retire, which may be true if you consider his lifestyle – any wealthy man's lifestyle. He also has a genuine need, like most dedicated actors, to gratify an audience. Put the two together and you've got a good reason why he should fall back on Bond after all these years. Fear made him turn down *Annie* – maybe the fear of reaching the boundary of his talent, of

235

coming to the non "heavy" part that he couldn't handle. Which is a shame, because Sean could have coped with *Annie*, he could have been great.'

Having spent the first part of '82 golfing worldwide – he wrote to Craigie Veitch at one stage telling him, 'As usual, I've got one foot in an airport lounge and one foot on a plane' – Connery put the post-production finishing touches on his second documentary, *Sean Connery's Edinburgh*, before winding up for Bond. The 35-minute documentary had consumed no more than a few days of his time but, costing £3,000 a minute, most of it borne voluntarily by the district council, it looked more than promising. Already it had international bookings for the Commonwealth Games in Brisbane in the autumn, as well as Melbourne, Auckland and Sydney. The premiere would be during the Edinburgh Festival, and Warner Bros were considering taking it for wider cinema release. Connery was greatly happy with the diversion and the fact that it garnered plaudits from unusual but esteemed quarters. Increasingly he was talking of occupying himself with more director work, possibly documentary. 'One thing he didn't want,' says Ian Bannen, 'was to return to theatre. He said all that shouting gave him a headache and hurt his throat.'

Always disciplined, Connery abruptly went into training to play 007 once his fee was confirmed, commencing with dance-movement classes under Peggy Spencer, often BBC *Come Dancing* judge and tutor to Nureyev for the movie *Valentino*. Location work began in the South of France on September 27th, with plans to return to Elstree around Christmas for studio interiors. Connery was satisfied with the arrangement. He had rationed his days in Britain not only to permit English studio work on *Never Say Never Again*, but because he intended to keep closely in touch with Edinburgh, where Effie was seriously ill, having suffered severe paralysis after a stroke the previous summer. The heart-calling old patriotism had awakened too with the unexpected honorary Doctor of Letters degree conferred by Herriot-Watt University, undoubted reward for the burgeoning glory of his Educational Trust.

By '82m £300,000 of Trust grants had assisted countless artists, scholars and under-privileged institutions and, by Connery's estimate, some £50,000 per year was continually going out. 'I'm pleased with it,' he stated coyly in a BBC TV interview. 'Maybe it's not much to do for a country one owes so much to, but it's a gesture. It's something anyway.'

Before heading for the French location, he flew to Edinburgh by private jet to visit Effie at the Infirmary and see Neil and play golf at St Andrew's with *South Pacific* pal, producer-actor Michael Medwin. John Brady, one of the old mates from Oxgangs Rovers and the biggie, still living a spit away from the Fountain, did not expect to see him. In a voice devoid of resentment, rather brimming with admiration and a kind of unself-conscious pride, he says, 'Sean made it, didn't he? Fountainbridge is very far away to him now. But, no, he hasn't lost touch. I haven't seen him for quite a bit but my wife and I were thinking of dropping by when we were in America on holidays. There'd be no problem. Tommy doesn't change. . .'

Terence Young, the director responsible for lighting the Bond touchpaper, contends that, with the probable exception of Lassie, no actor has been changed so little by success as Sean Connery. Others, from Michael Hayes to Guy Hamilton speak of his *natural* talents, his relaxation, his lack of ego trappings.

'What is he like as a friend?' I asked Michael Caine over paper cartons of tasteless tea on a noisy, floodlit film set.

'Ordinary.' The direct, rheumy eyes squint plaintively and the large hands spread. 'I wish I could say more, or less,' Caine twinkles. 'But Sean's just an ordinary bloke who likes his job and gets on with it.'

Therein lies the story, beginning and end. In 1973, divorcing from Diane Cilento, Connery made a solemn vow never to talk to anyone about his personal life. His loyalties have been tried and tested enough to explain forever his resistance to press grilling. Evaluating his own talents he grunts evasively, 'I may not be qualified to be an actor, but I'm damned sure not qualified to be anything else.' Future plans, he told a German magazine during *Five Days*

One Summer, might be reduced to 'a little living, a little work, support my children and die quickly and without pain.'

Ultimately, to those who know him, James Bond, past or future, is irrelevant – of as much consequence as the proverbial sparrow's tears. Sean Connery, the echoes swell, is just a decent bloke who made good. 'A nice wee lad,' Fountainbridgers will tell you. Somehow, walking down the cobbled byways of Auld Reekie, talking to the scattered few who were left behind as the tenements fell, even luminous Oscar pales. Sean Connery has seen the glories of the gutter and the gutters of glory. One imagines he hungers for no greater honours.

CHAPTER EIGHTEEN

Postscript: Never Again?

The code of in-production secrecy that keeps the film world buoyed and commercially viable added greatly to the drama of Connery's acknowledged arrival at middle age. *Never Say Never Again,* filming through the winter-spring of '82-'83, stirred surprising clouds of impenetrable mystery. Initially, for the most obvious of reasons—a reluctance to rile the competing Broccoli—advance publicity of the behind-the-scenes variety was doused. Actors participating were reportedly sworn to solemn secrecy and Warner Bros, the contracted distributors, made it clear from the start that a running 'no comment' was the order of the day. Rumours started to circulate, wry rumours that confused the general interpretation of Connery's motives in returning. Most popular on the grapevine was the hint of a grotesque spoof, some elaborate put-down of Broccoli's Bond that would inevitably, most said, be tinged with personal vitriol. The casting of English comedian Rowan Atkinson as 'a bumbling British agent' was seen by some as an accurate pointer to the likelihood of spoof, as was the cast listing of Alec McGowan as 'Algy the Armourer,' antithesis of pure-bred macho man Bond-name.

Connery made no effort to allay fears—or perhaps hopes. Along with Schwartzman and Kevin McClory (now serving the quiet role of executive producer, the money-getter), he remained noncommittal when, in desperation, a double-pronged attack was mounted by the opposing camp. The trustees of Ian Fleming's estate took Broccoli's side in a High Court bid during mid-production for an injunction to stop the movie. Mr Justice Goulding, the London judge, rejected the appeal on the basis that it would be unfair to hinder a production so far advanced. He acknowledged the fact that the dispute would be further tried in the High Court at the end of '83 and rejected the plea by Mr Sam Stamler, QC, that a victory then would be useless, 'merely closing the stable door too late.' Journalists' efforts to prise a comment from Connery failed. In truth, thanks to the efficient smokescreen created by the film's publicists/anti-publicists, just about no one knew the physical location of Connery or *Never Say Never Again*. All indications were that Connery himself was the architect of this unusually hard shell of secrecy and that his reasons were as tangled and multi-faceted as those that brought him back to Bondage.

The sequence of locations led from the Casino at Monte Carlo to Villefranche-sur-mer, London and finally the Bahamas. Little by little energetic film journalists sketched out a likely scenario that appeared to reduce Broccoli's argument, which stated the movie was not a remake of the permitted *Thunderball*. The elements of the original *Thunderball* seemed properly present: the cast had American Revlon model Kim Basinger as Domino, Bond's girl ally; Blofeld and Largo, the old arch villains, were represented by strong character actors Max Von Sydow and Klaus Maria Brandauer; the stolen nuclear bomb plot was intact; even Largo's versatile enemy-base yacht was here, generously loaned for the purpose by real-life billionaire Adnan Kashoggi. The odd modification was noted. Nicaraguan beauty Barbara Carrera became Fatima Blush, a beautiful psychopath absent from book and film of *Thunderball*, but allegedly outlined by Fleming and McClory in their late '50s discussions about possible Bond film plots.

One of the first journalists to crack the location trail and confront Connery was the *Daily Mail's* Margaret Hinxman, the critic. She found him comfortably at Monte Carlo, 'back playing his one-time *bête-noir* and *alter ego*. . . shooting his cuffs with deceptive nonchalance.' Bluntly seeking his reasons for returning to Bond, Hinxman reported the predictable cautious response: Well, what's wrong with changing one's mind? Connery would not be drawn into serious anal-

240

ysis. Instead he offered the bald mechanism of his decision-making process: 'I thought about it for a long time. Then I talked it over with my wife, and we decided, Why not? She thought up the title, which I like.' The title was important, he believed. 'It pre-empts all the bullshit that will be written about my coming back to Bond. There's room for two Bonds. Roger plays it his way, I play it mine. I'll be ten years older and greyer than I was in *Diamonds Are Forever*. But Bond's an interesting character. There's a lot more I can do with him.' For the first time some brutal candour was applied to the issue of ageing while prancing in a young hero's harness. 'I'm fifty-two. There's nothing particularly daring about playing your age. I've done it before—in *Robin and Marian* and *Murder on the Orient Express*. It's absurd to cling to what you were in your youth. It's the difference, say, between Burt Lancaster and Kirk Douglas. Lancaster plays his age, looks his age and has given some memorably fine performances on the screen. Douglas strives to stay young. But he seems gaunt, a shadow of his former self. It's a little sad.'

All reports from the set commended Connery's mature portrayal of Bond and, bit by bit, 'personal statement' spoof speculation abated. Though the script, no one denied, was in constant turmoil. Barbara Carrera, who had agreed to do the film with director Kershner before seeing a printed word, confessed to her disappointment with the first draft submitted. 'I've been scared at times,' she said. 'The first time I saw the script I wasn't at all happy with it, and it was almost too late.' Richard Schenkman, prime mover of the international James Bond fan clubs and a friend of McClory's, visited Nassau and observed a week of rain-washed chaos. 'Irvin Kershner was under a black cloud and was trying to save a schedule knocked all to hell . . . Connery's glib humour and creative interest can quickly turn to vociferous anger if he thinks people, including the director, are being inefficient or noncommunicative. He blew up when he realised ten minutes of rehearsal time had been lost because Kershner hadn't told everyone that he had changed his mind about something.' Kershner, for his part, stayed loyal. Sixteen years before he had directed Connery in *A Fine Madness* and come to hugely admire him. 'He's done some wonderful things

241

recently . . . *The Man Who Would Be King,* for instance, was superb. Unlike many American actors of his status, he's not afraid to take risks.' Kershner perhaps cast the clearest light on the true heart of *Never Say Never Again* when he mused on the risks he shared with Connery. He was not, he said, overawed by the challenge of precedents; he was serious about the film but, as Schenkman relayed, wanted 'to make it fun. The action is important and the film has lots of action but it also has people. I've got wonderful performers . . .'

By mid summer of '83, *Never Say Never Again* was fully in the can and Sean Connery had again slipped the chains of Bond-age. In London he oversaw post-production with Kershner and indicated willingness to participate in lively promotion— a gesture of great significance when one considers the trials of earlier Bond association. Already '83 was a landmark year. In March he had snuck in six days work on a medieval legend film, *Sword of the Valliant,* which had earned him one million dollars—about $21,000 for every hour he worked, one of the highest hourly rates in movie history. The cachet of success- ful Bond—or maybe just a return to acting form and a simpler working vision—had begun to pay off.

Whatever the box-office would decree for it, *Never Say Never Again* had rewarded Connery amply. Once again, the evidence suggests, he could happily look the doppleganger in the eye. Content enough to stay in the fray in this Day of the Sequel? Only time will tell. But the famous last-frame-of-the-movie tag lingers: *James Bond will be back.* And for half the world's movie-goers there has only ever been one James Bond.

Filmography

NO ROAD BACK (Great Britain; RKO-Radio, 1956)

Director: Montgomery Tully. Producer: Steve Pallos. Screenplay: Charles A. Leeds and Montgomery Tully, from the play *Madame Tic Tac* by Falkland L. Cary and Philip Weathers. Photography: Lionel Banes. Editor: Jim Connock. Music: John Veale. Art director: John Stoll. Running time: 83 minutes. In black & white. Certificate A.
Production company: Gibraltar Pictures.

John Railton	Skip Homeier
Clem Hayes	Paul Carpenter
Beth	Patricia Dainton
Inspector Harris	Norman Woodland
Mrs Railton	Margaret Rawlings
Marguerite	Eleanor Summerfield
Rudge Harvey	Alfie Bass
Spike	Sean Connery
Sergeant Brooks	Robert Bruce
Garage Man	Philip Ray
Night Watchman	Thomas Gallagher
The dog Rummy	Romulus of Welham

HELL DRIVERS (Great Britain; Rank, 1957)

Director: Cy Endfield. Producer: S. Benjamin Fisz. Executive producer: Earl St John. Screenplay: John Kruse and Cy Endfield. Photography: Geoffrey Unsworth. Editor: John D. Guthridge.

243

Music: Hubert Clifford. Art director: Ernest Archer. Running time: 108 minutes. In black & white and VistaVision. Certificate A.
Production company: Aqua Film Production.

Tom	Stanley Baker
Gino	Herbert Lom
Lucy	Peggy Cummins
Red	Patrick McGoohan
Cartley	William Hartnell
Ed	Wilfrid Lawson
Dusty	Sidney James
Tinker	Alfie Bass
Scottie	Gordon Jackson
Jimmy	David McCallum
Johnny	Sean Connery
Pop	Wensley Pithey
Tub	George Murcell
Ma West	Marjorie Rhodes
Blonde	Vera Day
Mother	Beatrice Varley
Assistant manager	Robin Bailey
Spinster	Jean St Clair
Chick	Jerry Stovin
Doctor	John Horsley
Nurse	Marianne Stone
Barber Joe	Ronald Clarke

TIME LOCK (Great Britain; British Lion, 1957)

Director: Gerald Thomas. Producer: Peter Rogers. Screenplay: Peter Rogers, from the play for television by Arthur Hailey. Photography: Peter Hennessy. Editor: John Trumper. Music: Stanley Black. Art director: Norman Arnold. Running Time: 73 minutes. In black & white. Certificate A.
Production company: Romulus. A Beaconsfield Production.

Dawson	Robert Beatty
Lucille Walker	Betty McDowall

Steven Walker	Vincent Winter
Colin Walker	Lee Patterson
Evelyn Webb	Sandra Francis
George Foster	Alan Gifford
Inspector Andrews	Robert Ayres
Howard Zeeder	Victor Wood
Max Jarvis	Jack Cunningham
Dr Foy	Peter Mannering
1st Police Officer	Roland Brand
2nd Police Officer	David Williams
Reporter	Larry Cross
Dr Hewitson	Gordon Tanner
Foreman	John Paul
Bank Customer	Donald Ewer
1st Welder	Murray Kash
2nd Welder	Sean Connery

ACTION OF THE TIGER (Great Britain; MGM, 1957)

Director: Terence Young. Producer: Kenneth Harper. Screenplay: Robert Carson, based on the book by James Wellard. Photography: Desmond Dickinson. Editor: Frank Clarke. Music: Humphrey Searle. Art director: Scott McGregor. Running Time: 93 minutes. In Technicolor CinemaScope. Certificate U. Production company: Claridge Film Production.

Carson	Van Johnson
Tracy	Martine Carol
Trifon	Herbert Lom
Henri	Gustavo Rocco
Kol Stendho	Jose Nieto
The Countess	Helen Haye
Mara	Anna Gerber
Security Guard	Anthony Dawson
Mike	Sean Connery
Katina	Yvonne Warren

ANOTHER TIME, ANOTHER PLACE (Great Britain; Paramount, 1958)

Director: Lewis Allen. Producers: Lewis Allen and Smedley Aston. Executive producer: Joseph Kaufman. Screenplay: Stanley Mann, from the novel by Lenore Coffee. Photography: Jack Hildyard. Editor: Geoffrey Foot. Music: Douglas Gamley. Art director: Tom Morahan. Running Time: 95 minutes. In black & white and VistaVision. Certificate A.
Production company: A Kaydor Production.

Sara Scott	Lana Turner
Carter Reynolds	Barry Sullivan
Kay Trevor	Glynis Johns
Mark Trevor	Sean Connery
Jake Klein	Sidney James
Alan Thompson	Terence Longdon
Mrs Bunker	Doris Hare
Brian Trevor	Martin Stephens

DARBY O'GILL AND THE LITTLE PEOPLE (USA; Walt Disney, 1959)

Director: Robert Stevenson. Producer: Walt Disney. Screenplay: Lawrence Edward Watkin, suggested by H. T. Kavanagh's *Darby O'Gill* stories. Photography: Winton C. Hoch. Editor: Stanley Johnson. Special photographic effects: Peter Ellenshaw and Eustace Lycett. Technical advisor: Michael O'Herlihy. Music: Oliver Wallace. Songs: *Wishing Song* by Lawence Edward Watkin and *Pretty Irish Girl* by Oliver Wallace. Assistant director: Robert G. Shannon. Running time: 90 minutes in original release; 89 minutes in 1978 re-release. In Technicolor. Certificate U.
Production company: Walt Disney Productions.

Darby O'Gill	Albert Sharpe
Katie	Janet Munro
Michael McBride	Sean Connery
King Brian	Jimmy O'Dea

246

Pony Sugrue	Kieron Moore
Sheelah	Estelle Winwood
Lord Fitzpatrick	Walter Fitzgerald
Father Murphy	Dennis O'Dea
Tom Kerrigan	J. G. Devlin
Phadrig Oge	Jack McGowran
Paddy Scanlon	Farrell Pelly
Molly Malloy	Nora O'Mahoney

Note: Sean Connery leaving dance: Jim Lilburn

TARZAN'S GREATEST ADVENTURE (Great Britain; Paramount, 1959)

Director: John Guillermin. Producer: Sy Weintraub. Screenplay: Berne Giler and John Guillermin, from a story by Les Crutchfield, based on the characters created by Edgar Rice Burroughs. Photography: Skeets Kelly. Editor: Bert Rule. Art director: Michael Stringer. Running time: 84 minutes. In Technicolor. Certificate U.
Production company: Solar Films.

Tarzan	Gordon Scott
Slade	Anthony Quayle
Angie	Sara Shane
Toni	Scilla Gabel
O'Bannion	Sean Connery
Kruger	Niall MacGinnis
Dino	Al Mulock

THE FRIGHTENED CITY (Great Britain; Anglo Amalgamated, 1961)

Director: John Lemont. Producers: John Lemont and Leigh Vance. Screenplay: Leigh Vance. Photography: Desmond Dickinson. Editor: Bernard Gribble. Music: Norrie Paramor. Songs: *Marvellous Lie* and *I Laughed at Love*; lyrics by Bunny Lewis, music by Norrie Paramor. Assistant director: Basil Rayburn. Running time: 98 minutes. In black & white. Certificate A.
Production company: A Zodiac Production.

247

Waldo Zhernikov	Herbert Lom
Det. Inspector Sayers	John Gregson
Paddy Damion	Sean Connery
Harry Foulcher	Alfred Marks
Anya	Yvonne Romain
Sadie	Olive McFarland
Ogle	Frederick Piper
Hood	John Stone
Alf Peters	David Davies
Tanky Thomas	Tom Bowman
Nero	Robert Cawdron
Sanchetti	George Pastell
Supt. Carter	Patrick Holt
Avril	Sheena Marsh
Frankie Farmer	Patrick Jordan
Moffat	Arnold Diamond
Tyson	Jack Stewart
Security Officer	Martin Wyldeck
Warder	John Baker
Wally	Kenneth Griffiths
Salty Brewer	Douglas Robinson
Wingrove	Robert Percival
Barmaid (Riviera)	Marianne Stone
TV Announcer	John Witty
Informer	J. G. Devlin
Hatcheck girl	Julie Shearing
Pretty secretary (Wingrove)	April Wilding
Sophie Peters	Vanda Godsell
Asst. Commissioner	Bruce Seton
Myra	Yvonne Ball
Title scene thug	Kenneth Warren
Alf's 1st thug	Stephen Cato
Alf's 2nd thug	James Fitzpatrick
Head waiter (Taboo club)	Neal Arden
Miss Rush	Joan Haythorne

Publican	Stuart Saunders
Lippy Green	John Maxin
Lord Buncholme	Tony Hawes
Rover driver	Joe Wadham
Clarissa	Penelope Service
Billy Agnew	Walter Brown
Basher Preeble	Maurice Bush
Pianist (Taboo club)	Norrie Paramor
Choreographer (Taboo club)	Malcolm Clare
Pretty girl (Taboo club)	Yvonne Buckingham
Cigarette girl (Taboo club)	Eve Eden

ON THE FIDDLE (Great Britain; Anglo Amalgamated, 1961)
USA title: *Operation Snafu*

Director: Cyril Frankel. Producer: S. Benjamin Fisz. Screenplay: Harold Buchman, from the novel *Stop at a Winner* by R. F. Delderfield. Photography: Edward Scaife. Editor: Peter Hunt. Music: Malcolm Arnold. Art director: John Blezard. Running Time: 97 minutes. In black & white. Certificate A.
Production company: S. Benjamin Fisz.

Pedlar Pascoe	Sean Connery
Horace Pope	Alfred Lynch
GP/CPT Bascombe	Cecil Parker
Trowbridge	Wilfred Hyde White
Cooksley	Stanley Holloway
Mrs Cooksley	Kathleen Harrison
Flora McNaughton	Eleanor Summerfield
Doctor	Eric Barker
Air Gunner	Terence Longdon
T/Sgt Buzzer	Alan King
Iris	Ann Beach
Hixon	John Le Mesurier
1st Airman	Victor Maddern
Huxtable	Harry Locke
Sister	Viola Keats

Pope	Peter Sinclair
Lil	Edna Morris
Sergeant	Thomas Heathcote
P.C.	Jack Lambert
Ticket Collector	Cyril Smith
Baldwin	Simon Lack
Sgt Ellis	Graham Stark
WAAF Corporal	Jean Aubrey
WAAF Sergeant	Miriam Karlin
Cpl. Gittens	Bill Owen
Lancing	Ian Whittaker
Cpl. Reeves	Harold Goodwin
Mavis	Barbara Windsor
Dusty	Kenneth Warren
Lady Edith	Beatrix Lehmann
US Snowdrop	Gary Cockrell

THE LONGEST DAY (USA; 20th Century-Fox, 1962)

Directors: Ken Annakin (British exteriors); Andrew Marton (American exteriors); Bernhard Wicki (German episodes); Darryl F. Zanuck (American interiors). Producer: Darryl F. Zanuck. Screenplay: Cornelius Ryan, based on his book. Additional episodes written by: Romain Gary, James Jones, David Pursall and Jack Seddon. Photography: Jean Bourgoin, Henri Persin and Walter Wottitz; Guy Tabary in charge of helicopter shots. Editor: Samuel E. Beetley. Music: Maurice Jarre. Thematic music: Paul Anka. Assistant directors: Bernard Farrel, Louis Pitzélé, Gerard Renateau and Henri Sokal. Supervisor of special action: John Sullivan. Running time: 108 minutes. In black & white. Certificate A.
Production company: Darryl F. Zanuck.

RAF pilot	Richard Burton
Capt. Maud	Kenneth More
Lord Lovat	Peter Lawford
Major John Howard	Richard Todd

Brig. General Parker	Leo Genn
British Padre	John Gregson
Private Flanagan	Sean Connery
Briefing Officer	Jack Hedley
Private Watney	Michael Medwin
Private Clough	Norman Rossington
Admiral Ramsey	John Robinson
Group Capt. Stagg	Patrick Barr
RAF officer	Leslie Phillips
RAF pilot	Donald Houston
Private Coke	Frank Finlay
Lieutenant Walsh	Lyndon Brook
Ronald Callen	Bryan Coleman
General Montgomery	Trevor Reid
Air Chief Marshal Leigh-Mallory	Simon Lack
Air Chief Marshal Tedder	Louis Mounier
Wren	Sian Phillips
Lt. Col. Vandervoort	John Wayne
Brig. General Cota	Robert Mitchum
Brig. General Roosevelt	Henry Fonda
Brig. General Gavin	Robert Ryan
Destroyer Commander	Rod Steiger
U.S. Ranger	Robert Wagner
Private Dutch Schultz	Richard Beymer
Major-General Haines	Mel Ferrer
Sgt. Fuller	Jeffrey Hunter
U.S. Ranger	Paul Anka
Private Martini	Sal Mineo
Private Morris	Roddy McDowall
Lieutenant Sheen	Stuart Whitman
Captain Harding	Steve Forrest
Col. Tom Newton	Eddie Albert
General R. O. Barton	Edmond O'Brien
U.S. Ranger	Fabian
Private John Steele	Red Buttons

251

Lieutenant Wilson	Tom Tryon
Major-General Smith	Alexander Knox
U.S. Ranger	Tommy Sands
Captain Frank	Ray Danton
General Eisenhower	Henry Grace
Private Harris	Mark Damon
Private Wilder	Dewey Martin
Colonel Caffey	John Crawford
Joe Williams	Ron Randell
Lieutenant-General Bradley	Nicholas Stuart
Rear-Admiral Kirk	John Moillon
Janine Boitard	Irina Demick
Mayor of Colleville	Bourvil
Father Roulland	Jean-Louis Barrault
Commander Philippe Kieffer	Christian Marquand
Madame Barrault	Arletty
Mother Superior	Madeline Renaud
Sergeant de Montlaur	Georges Riviere
Rear-Admiral Jaujard	Jean Servais
Alexandre Renaud	Georges Wilson
Louis	Fernand Ledoux
Jean	Maurice Poli
Housekeeper	Alice Tissot
Naval captain	Jo D'Avra
Major-General Blumontritt	Curt Jurgens
Field-Marshal Rommel	Werner Hinz
Field-Marshal von Rundstedt	Paul Hartmann
Sergeant Kaffeeklatsch	Gert Frobe
Major Pluskat	Hans Christian Blech
Major-General Max Pemsel	Wolfgang Preiss
Lieutenant-Colonel Ocker	Peter Van Eyck
Colonel Priller	Heinz Reincke
General Erich Marcks	Richard Munch
General Hans von Salmuth	Ernst Schroeder
Captain Ernst During	Karl Meisel

252

Lieutenant-Colonel Meyer	Heinz Spitner
Aide to Lt.-Col. Meyer	Robert Freytag
Colonel General Jodl	Wolfgang Luckschy
Captain Hellmuth Lang	Til Kiwe
Major-General Dr. Hans Speidel	Wolfgang Buttner
Frau Rommel	Ruth Hausmeister
Manfred Rommel	Michael Hinz
Colonel Schiller	Paul Roth
Sergeant Bergsdorf	Hartmut Rock
Luftwaffe General	Karl John
Luftwaffe Major	Dietmar Schonherr
Lieutenant Fritz Theen	Reiner Penkert

Note: Sean Connery uncredited in some publicity handouts.

DR NO (Great Britain; United Artists, 1962)

Director: Terence Young. Producers: Harry Saltzman and Albert R. Broccoli. Screenplay: Richard Maibaum, Johanna Harwood and Berkely Mather, from the novel by Ian Fleming. Photography: Ted Moore. Editor: Peter Hunt. Production designer: Ken Adam. Art director: Syd Cain. Music: Monty Norman. *James Bond Theme* played by The John Barry Orchestra. Assistant director: Clive Reed. Running time: 105 minutes. In Technicolor. Certificate A.
Production company: Eon Productions.

James Bond	Sean Connery
Honey Rider	Ursula Andress
Dr No	Joseph Wiseman
Felix Leiter	Jack Lord
M	Bernard Lee
Professor Dent	Anthony Dawson
Quarrel	John Kitzmiller
Miss Taro	Zena Marshall
Sylvia	Eunice Gayson
Miss Moneypenny	Lois Maxwell

Puss-Feller	Lester Prendergast
Major Boothroyd	Peter Burton
Strangways	Tim Moxon
Girl Photographer	Margaret LeWars
Jones	Reggie Carter
Duff	William Foster-Davis
Playdell-Smith	Louis Blaazer
Sister Rose	Michele Mok
Mary	Dolores Keator
Sister Lily	Yvonne Shima

FROM RUSSIA WITH LOVE (Great Britain; United Artists, 1963)

Director: Terence Young. Producers: Harry Saltzman and Albert R. Broccoli. Screenplay: Richard Maibaum and Johanna Harwood, from the novel by Ian Fleming. Photography: Ted Moore. Editor: Peter Hunt. Art director: Syd Cain. Set dresser: Freda Pearson. Music: John Barry. Title song: Lionel Bart, sung by Matt Munro. Assistant director: David Anderson. Stunt work arranged by Peter Perkins. Running time: 116 minutes. In Technicolor. Certificate A.
Production company: Eon Productions.

James Bond	Sean Connery
Tatiana Romanova	Daniela Bianchi
Kerim Bey	Pedro Armendariz
Rosa Klebb	Lotte Lenya
Red Grant	Robert Shaw
M	Bernard Lee
Sylvia	Eunice Gayson
Morzeny	Walter Gotell
Vavra	Francis de Wolff
Train Conductor	George Pastell
Kerim's girl	Nadja Regin

254

Miss Moneypenny	Lois Maxwell
Vida	Aliza Gur
Zora	Martine Beswick
Kronsteen	Vladek Sheybal
Belly dancer	Leila
Foreign agent	Hasan Ceylan
Krilencu	Fred Haggerty
Rolls chauffeur	Neville Jason
Benz	Peter Bayliss
Mehmet	Mushet Auaer
Rhoda	Peter Brayham
Boothroyd	Desmond Llewelyn
Grant's masseuse	Jan Williams
McAdams	Peter Madden

WOMAN OF STRAW (Great Britain; United Artists, 1964)

Director: Basil Dearden. Producer: Michael Relph. Screenplay: Robert Muller, Stanley Mann and Michael Relph, from the novel by Catherine Arley. Photography: Otto Heller. Editor: John D. Guthridge. Production designer: Ken Adam. Music: Muir Mathieson. Assistant director: Clive Reed. Miss Lollobrigida's clothes by Dior. Running time: 117 minutes. In Eastman Colour. Certificate A.
Production company: Novus Production.

Maria	Gina Lollobrigida
Anthony Richmond	Sean Connery
Charles Richmond	Ralph Richardson
Thomas	Johnny Sekka
Baines	Laurence Hardy
Fenton	Danny Daniels
Third Executive	A. J. Brown
Yacht Captain	Peter Madden
Lomer	Alexander Knox

First Executive	Edward Underdown
Second Executive	George Curzon
Judge	Andre Morell
Chauffeur	Robert Bruce
Wardress	Peggy Marshall

MARNIE (USA; Rank UK, 1964)

Director: Alfred Hitchcock. Producer: Alfred Hitchcock. Screenplay: Jay Presson Allen, from the novel by Winston Graham. Photography: Robert Burks. Editor: George Tomasini. Sets: Robert Boyle and George Milo. Music: Bernard Herrmann. Assistant director: James H. Brown. Running time: 130 minutes. In Technicolor. Certificate X.
Production company: Universal International.

Mark Ruthland	Sean Connery
Marnie	'Tippi' Hedren
Lil Mainwaring	Diane Baker
Sidney Strutt	Martin Gabel
Bernice Edgar	Louise Latham
Cousin Bob	Bob Sweeney
Mr Ruthland	Alan Napier
Sam Ward	S. John Launer
Susan Clabon	Mariette Hartley
Sailor	Bruce Dern
First detective	Henry Beckman
Rita	Edith Evanson
Mrs Turpin	Meg Wyllie

GOLDFINGER (Great Britain; United Artists, 1964)

Director: Guy Hamilton. Producers: Harry Saltzman and Albert R. Broccoli. Screenplay: Richard Maibaum and Paul Dehn, from the novel by Ian Fleming. Photography: Ted Moore. Editor: Peter Hunt. Production designer: Ken Adam. Art director: Peter Murton. Music: John Barry. Title song: lyrics by Leslie Bricusse

256

and Anthony Newley, music by John Barry, sung by Shirley Bassey. Assistant director: Frank Ernst. Action sequences by Bob Simmons. Running time: 109 minutes. In Technicolor. Certificate A.
Production company: Eon Productions.

James Bond	Sean Connery
Pussy Galore	Honor Blackman
Goldfinger	Gert Frobe
Jill Masterson	Shirley Eaton
Tilly Masterson	Tania Mallet
Oddjob	Harold Sakata
M	Bernard Lee
Solo	Martin Benson
Felix Leiter	Cec Linder
Simmons	Austin Willis
Miss Moneypenny	Lois Maxwell
Midnight	Bill Nagy
Capungo	Alf Joint
Old lady	Varley Thomas
Bonita	Nadja Regin
Sierra	Raymond Young
Smithers	Richard Vernon
Brunskill	Denis Cowles
Kisch	Michael Mellinger
Mr Ling	Bert Kwouk
Strap	Hal Galili
Henchman	Lenny Rabin
Q	Desmond Llewelyn

THE HILL (Great Britain; MGM, 1965)

Director: Sidney Lumet. Producer: Kenneth Hyman. Screenplay: Ray Rigby, based on the original play by Ray Rigby and R. S. Allen. Photography: Oswald Morris. Editor: Thelma Connell. Technical advisor: George Montford. Assistant directors: Frank Ernst and Pedro Vidal. Running time: 123 minutes. In

black & white. Certificate X.
Production company: A Kenneth Hyman Production.

Joe Roberts	Sean Connery
R. S. M. Wilson	Harry Andrews
Harris	Ian Bannen
George Stevens	Alfred Lynch
Jacko King	Ossie Davis
Monty Bartlett	Roy Kinnear
Jock McGrath	Jack Watson
Williams	Ian Hendry
M.O.	Sir Michael Redgrave
Commandant	Norman Bird
Burton	Neil McCarthy
Walters	Howard Goorney
Martin	Tony Caunter

THUNDERBALL (Great Britain; United Artists, 1965)

Director: Terence Young. Producer: Kevin McClory. Screenplay: Richard Maibaum and John Hopkins, based on the original treatment by Jack Whittingham, Kevin McClory and Ian Fleming. Photography: Ted Moore. Editor: Peter Hunt. Production designer: Ken Adam. Art director: Peter Murton. Music: John Barry. Title song: lyrics by Don Black, music by John Barry, sung by Tom Jones. Assistant director: Gus Agosti. Underwater sequences: Ivan Tors Underwater Studios Ltd. Underwater director: Ricou Browning. Underwater cameraman: Lamar Boren. Action sequences by Bob Simmons. Running time: 130 minutes. In Technicolor Panavision. Certificate A.
Production company: Eon Productions.

James Bond	Sean Connery
Domino	Claudine Auger
Largo	Adolfo Celi
Fiona	Luciana Paluzzi
Felix Leiter	Rik Van Nutter

M	Bernard Lee
Paula	Martine Beswick
Count Lippe	Guy Doleman
Patricia	Molly Peters
Q	Desmond Llewelyn
Miss Moneypenny	Lois Maxwell
Foreign Secretary	Roland Culver
Pinder	Earl Cameron
Palazzi	Paul Stassino
Madame Boiter	Rose Alba
Vargas	Philip Locke
Kutee	George Pravda
Janni	Michael Brennan
Group Captain	Leonard Sachs
Air Vice Marshal	Edward Underdown
Kenniston	Reginald Beckwith

A FINE MADNESS (USA; Warner-Pathe, 1966)

Director: Irvin Kershner. Producer: Jerome Hellman. Screenplay: Elliott Baker, based upon his novel. Photography: Ted McCord. Editor: William Ziegler. Music: John Addison. Assistant director: Russell Llewellyn. Running time: 104 minutes. In Technicolor. Certificate A.
Production company: A Pan Arts Production.

Samson Shillitoe	Sean Connery
Rhoda	Joanne Woodward
Lydia West	Jean Seberg
Dr Oliver West	Patrick O'Neal
Dr Vera Kropotkin	Colleen Dewhurst
Dr Menken	Clive Revill
Dr Vorbeck	Werner Peters
Daniel K. Papp	John Fiedler
Mrs Fish	Kay Medford
Mr Fitzgerald	Jackie Coogan

Ms Tupperman	Zohra Lampert
Miss Walnicki	Sue Ane Langdon
Leonard Tupperman	Sorrell Booke
Mrs Fitzgerald	Bibi Osterwald
Chairwoman	Mabel Albertson

YOU ONLY LIVE TWICE (Great Britain; United Artists, 1967)

Director: Lewis Gilbert. Producers: Harry Saltzman and Albert R. Broccoli. Screenplay: Roald Dahl. Additional story material: Harold Jack Bloom. Based on the novel by Ian Fleming. Photography: Freddie Young. Editor: Thelma Connell. Production designer: Ken Adam. Art director: Harry Pottle. Music: John Barry. Title song: lyrics by Leslie Bricusse, music by John Barry, sung by Nancy Sinatra. Second Unit director: Peter Hunt. Technical advisor: Kikumaru Okuda. Underwater cameraman: Lamar Boren. Aerial cameraman: John Jordan. Action sequences by Bob Simmons. Assistant director: William P. Cartlidge. Running time: 116 minutes. In Technicolor Panavision. Certificate A. Production company: Eon-Danjaq.

James Bond	Sean Connery
Aki	Akiko Wakabayashi
Tiger Tanaka	Tetsuro Tamba
Kissy Suzuki	Mie Hama
Osato	Teru Shimada
Helga Brandt	Karin Dor
Miss Moneypenny	Lois Maxwell
Q	Desmond Llewelyn
Henderson	Charles Gray
Chinese girl	Tsai Chin
M	Bernard Lee
Blofeld	Donald Pleasence
American President	Alexander Knox
President's aide	Robert Hutton
SPECTRE 3	Burt Kwouk
SPECTRE 4	Michael Chow

SHALAKO (Great Britain; Warner-Pathe, 1968)

Director: Edward Dmytryk. Producer: Euan Lloyd. Screenplay:
J. J. Griffith, Hal Hopper and Scot Finch, from the screen story
by Clarke Reynolds, based on the novel by Louis L'Amour.
Photography: Ted Moore. Editor: Bill Blunden. Special effects:
Michael Collins. Music: Robert Farnon. Musical director: Muir
Mathieson. Title song: lyrics by Jim Dale. Art director: Herbert
Smith. Running time: 113 minutes. In Technicolor Franscope.
Certificate A.
Production company: Kingston Films. A Dimitri de Grunwald
Production.

Shalako	Sean Connery
Irina Lazaar	Brigitte Bardot
Bosky Fulton	Stephen Boyd
Sir Charles Daggett	Jack Hawkins
Frederick von Hallstatt	Peter Van Eyck
Lady Daggett	Honor Blackman
Chato	Woody Strode
Mako	Eric Sykes
Henry Clarke	Alexander Knox
Elena Clarke	Valerie French
Rojas	Julian Mateos
Buffalo	Donald Barry
Chato's father	Rodd Redwing
Loco	'Chief' Elmer Smith
Hans	Hans De Vries
Peter Wells	Walter Brown
Marker	Charles Stainaker
Luther	Bob Cunningham
Hockett	John Clark
Johnson	Bob Hall

THE MOLLY MAGUIRES (USA; Paramount, 1969)

Director: Martin Ritt. Producers: Martin Ritt and Walter Bern-

stein. Screenplay: Walter Bernstein, suggested by a book by Arthur H. Lewis. Photography: James Wong Howe. Editor: Frank Bracht. Script supervisor: Marvin Weldon. Second Unit director: Oscar Rudolph. Second Unit photography: Morris Hartzband. Technical advisor Mine Operations: Joseph Lawrence. Music: Henry Mancini. Songs: *Eileen Aroon, Cockles and Mussels* and *Gary Owen*, all traditional Irish songs. Assistant director: James Rosenberger. Running time: 125 minutes. In Technicolor. Certificate A.
Production company: A Martin Ritt Production.

James McParlan	Richard Harris
Jack Kehoe	Sean Connery
Mary Raines	Samantha Eggar
Davies	Frank Finlay
Dougherty	Anthony Zerbe
Mrs Kehoe	Bethel Leslie
Frazier	Art Lund
Frank McAndrew	Anthony Costello
Father O'Connor	Philip Bourneuf
Mr Raines	Brendan Dillon
Mrs Frazier	Frances Heflin
Jenkins	John Alderson
Bartender	Malachy McCourt
Mrs McAndrew	Susan Goodman

THE RED TENT (Italy/USSR; Paramount, 1969)

Director: Mickail K. Kalatozov. Producer: Franco Cristaldi. Screenplay: Ennio De Concini and Richard Adams. Photography: Leonid Kalashnikov. Editor: John Shirley. Second Unit director: Igor Petrov. Music: Ennio Morricone. Assistant director: Valerj Sirovsky. Running time: 121 minutes. In Technicolor. Certificate U.
Production company: A Vides Cinematografica, Rome-Mosfilm, Moscow Coproduction.

General Nobile	Peter Finch

Amundsen	Sean Connery
Valeria	Claudia Cardinale
Lundborg	Hardy Kruger
Biagi	Mario Adorf
Romagna	Massimo Girotti
Zappi	Luigi Vannucchi
Malmgren	Edward Marzevic
Viglieri	Boris Kmelnizki
Trioani	Juri Solomin
Behounek	Juri Vizbor
Mariano	Donatas Banionis
Cecioni	Otar Koberidze
Samoilovich	Grigori Gaj
Chuknovsky	Nikita Mikhalkov
Kolka	Nicolai Ivanov

Note: Original Italian release title; *La Tenda Rossa.*

THE ANDERSON TAPES (USA; Columbia-Warner, 1971)

Director: Sidney Lumet. Producer: Robert M. Weitman. Screenplay: Frank R. Pierson, based on the novel by Lawrence Sanders. Photography: Arthur J. Ornitz. Editor: Joanne Burke. Technical consultant: Roger G. Battie, Script supervisor: Nick Sgarro. Music: Quincy Jones. Assistant director: Alan Hopkins. All electronic devices are authentic and provided by The William J. Burns International Detective Agency, Inc. Video and tape recorders, cameras and related equipment by Ampex Corporation. Running time: 99 minutes. In Technicolor. Certificate AA. Production company: A Robert M. Weitman Production.

Anderson	Sean Connery
Ingrid	Dyan Cannon
Haskins	Martin Balsman
Delaney	Ralph Meeker
Angelo	Alan King
The Kid	Christopher Walken

Parelli	Val Avery
Spencer	Dick Williams
Everson	Garrett Morris
Pop	Stan Gottlieb
Jimmy	Paul Benjamin
Psychologist	Anthony Holland
Werner	Richard B. Schull
Dr Rubicoff	Conrad Bain
Miss Kaler	Margaret Hamilton
Mrs Hathaway	Judith Lowry
Bingham	Max Showalter
Mrs Bingham	Janet Ward
Jerry Bingham	Scott Jacoby
Longene	Norman Rose
Mrs Longene	Meg Miles
O'Leary	John Call
D'Medico	Ralph Stanley
Vanessi	John Braden
Nurse	Paula Trueman
First Agent	Michael Miller
Johnson	Michael Prince
Papa Angelo	Frank Macetta
Eric	Jack Doroshow
Eric's friend	Michael Clary
Receptionist	Hildy Brooks
Doctor	Robert Dagny
TV watcher	Bradford English
Judge	Reid Cruckshanks
Sync man	Tom Signorelli
Detective A	Carmine Caridi
Sergeant Claire	Michael Fairman
Detective B	George Patelis
Detective C	William Da Prato
Private Detective	Sam Coppola

DIAMONDS ARE FOREVER (Great Britain; United Artists, 1971)

Director: Guy Hamilton. Producers: Harry Saltzman and Albert R. Broccoli. Screenplay: Richard Maibaum and Tom Mankiewicz. Based on the novel by Ian Fleming. Photography: Ted Moore. Editors: Bert Bates and John W. Holmes. Production designer: Ken Adam. Art directors: Jack Maxsted and Bill Kenney. Music: John Barry. Title song: lyrics by Don Black, music by John Barry, sung by Shirley Bassey. Stunt arrangers: Bob Simmons and Paul Baxley. Assistant directors: Derek Cracknell and Jerome M. Siegel. Miss St. John's costumes by Donfeld. Running time: 120 minutes. In Technicolor Panavision. Certificate A.
Production company: Eon Productions.

James Bond	Sean Connery
Tiffany Case	Jill St. John
Blofeld	Charles Gray
Plenty O'Toole	Lana Wood
Willard Whyte	Jimmy Dean
Saxby	Bruce Cabot
Mr Kidd	Putter Smith
Mr Wint	Bruce Glover
Leiter	Norman Burton
Dr Metz	Joseph Furst
M	Bernard Lee
Q	Desmond Llewelyn
Shady Tree	Leonard Barr
Miss Moneypenny	Lois Maxwell
Mrs Whistler	Margaret Lacey
Peter Franks	Joe Robinson
'Bambi'	Donna Garratt
'Thumper'	Trina Parks
Doctor	David de Keyser
Sir Donald Munger	Lawrence Naismith
Mr Slumber	David Bauer

THE OFFENCE (Great Britain; United Artists, 1972)

Director: Sidney Lumet. Producer: Denis O'Dell. Screenplay: John Hopkins based on his own stage play. Photography: Gerry Fisher. Editor: John Victor Smith. Music: Harrison Birtwhistle. Assistant director: Ted Sturgis. Running time: 112 minutes. In colour. Certificate X.
Production company: Tantallon Films.

Det. Sergeant Johnson	Sean Connery
Cartwright	Trevor Howard
Maureen	Vivien Merchant
Baxter	Ian Banen
Jessard	Derek Newark
Panton	John Hallam
Cameron	Peter Bowles
Lawson	Ronald Radd
Hill	Anthony Sagar
Lambeth	Howard Goorney
Garrett	Richard Moore
Janie	Maxine Gordon

ZARDOZ (Great Britain; Fox-Rank, 1974)

Director: John Boorman. Producer: John Boorman. Screenplay: John Boorman. Photography: Geoffrey Unsworth. Editor: John Merritt. Production designer: Anthony Pratt. Design and story associate: Bill Stair. Special effects: Jerry Johnston. Music: David Munrow. Assistant director: Simon Relph. Costumes by Christel Kruse Boorman, made by La Tabard Boutique, Dublin. Running time: 104 minutes. In DeLuxe Panavision. Certificate X. (Original running time: 105 minutes.)
Production company: John Boorman Productions.

Zed	Sean Connery
Consuella	Charlotte Rampling
May	Sara Kestleman
Avalow	Sally Anne Newton

266

Friend	John Alderton
Arhur Frayn	Niall Buggy
George Saden	Bosco Hogan
Apathetic	Jessica Swift
Star	Bairbre Dowling
Old scientist	Christopher Casson
Death	Reginald Jarman

RANSOM (Great Britain; British Lion, 1974)
USA title: *The Terrorists*

Director: Casper Wrede. Producer: Peter Rawley. Screenplay: Paul Wheeler. Photography: Sven Nykvist. Editor: Thelma Connell. Art director: Sven Wickman. Music: Jerry Goldsmith. Assistant director: Bernard Hanson. Running time: 94 minutes. In Eastman Colour. Certificate A.
Production company: A Peter Rawley Production.

Nils Tahlvik	Sean Connery
Petrie	Ian McShane
Captain Denver	Norman Bristow
Bert	John Cording
Mrs Palmer	Isabel Dean
Ferris	William Fox
Joe	Richard Hampton
Palmer	Robert Harris
Lookout pilot	Harry Landis
Hislop	Preston Lockwood
Bernhard	James Maxwell
Shepherd	John Quentin
Barnes	Jeffry Wickham
Second pilot	Sven Aune
Matson	Knut Hansson
Donner	Kaare Kroppan
Police inspector	Alf Malland

Female housekeeper	Noeste Schwab
Male housekeeper	Kare Wicklund
Poison	Knut Wigert
Air hostesses	Froeydis Damslora
	Inger Heidal
	Brita Rogde

MURDER ON THE ORIENT EXPRESS (Great Britain; EMI, 1974)

Director: Sidney Lumet. Producers: John Brabourne and Richard Goodwin. Screenplay: Paul Dehn, from the novel by Agatha Christie. Photography: Geoffrey Unsworth. Editor: Anne V. Coates. Production designer and costumes by: Tony Walton. Art director: Jack Stephens. Music: Richard Rodney Bennett. Orchestra of the Royal Opera House, Covent Garden, conducted by: Marcus Dods. Assistant director: Ted Sturgis. Running time: 127½ minutes. In Technicolor. Certificate A. Production company: A John Brabourne-Richard Goodwin Production.

Hercule Poirot	Albert Finney
Mrs Hubbard	Lauren Bacall
Bianchi	Martin Balsam
Greta	Ingrid Bergman
Countess Andrenyi	Jacqueline Bisset
Pierre	Jean-Pierre Cassel
Col. Arbuthnott	Sean Connery
Beddoes	John Gielgud
Princess Dragomiroff	Wendy Hiller
McQueen	Anthony Perkins
Mary Debenham	Vanessa Redgrave
Hildegarde	Rachel Roberts
Ratchett	Richard Widmark
Count Andrenyi	Michael York
Hardman	Colin Blakely
Doctor	George Coulouris

Foscarelli	Denis Quilley
Conceirge	Vernon Dobtcheff
A.D.C.	Jeremy Lloyd
Chief attendant	John Moffatt

THE WIND AND THE LION (USA; Columbia, 1975)

Director: John Milius. Producer: Herb Jaffe. Screenplay: John Milius, based loosely on actual events. Photography: Billy Williams. Editor: Bob Wolfe. Production designer: Gil Parrondo. Special effects: Alex Weldon. Music: Jerry Goldsmith. Assistant director: Miguel A. Gil. Running time: 119 minutes. In Metrocolor Panavision. Certificate A.
Production company: A Herb Jaffe Production. Production services by Claridge Associates/Persky-Bright.

Raisuli	Sean Connery
Eden	Candice Bergen
T. Roosevelt	Brian Keith
Hay	John Huston
Gummere	Geoffrey Lewis
Jerome	Steve Kanaly
Chadwick	Roy Jenson
Bashaw	Vladek Sheybal
Dreighton	Darrell Fetty
Wazan	Nadim Sawalha
Sultan	Mark Zuber
Von Roerkel	Antoine St. John
William	Simon Harrison
Jennifer	Polly Gottesman
Alice Roosevelt	Deborah Baxter
Gayaan	Luis Bar Boo
Ugly Arab	Aldo Sambrell
Edith	Shirley Rothman
Lodge	Larry Cross

269

Sketch artist	Ben Tatar
Japanese General	Akio Mitamura
1st aide	Frank Gassman
2nd aide	Leon Liberman
3rd aide	Allen Russell
Secretary	Michael Damian
Root	Alex Weldon
Diplomat	Howard Hagan
1st Secret Serviceman	Arthur Larkin
2nd Secret Serviceman	James Cooley
3rd Secret Serviceman	M. Ciudad
Marine sergeant	Rusty Cox
Quentin	Jack Cooley
Kermit	Chris Aller
Mountain man	Rupert Crabb
1st reporter	Charles Stalnaker
2nd reporter	David Lester
3rd reporter	Paul Rusking
1st station man	Carl Rapp
Gummere's aide	Jim Mitchell
Station woman	Anita Colby
Torres	Ricardo Palacois
U.K. military advisor	Robert Case
Pock-faced Arab	Felipe Solano
Miss Hitchcock	Audrey San Felix
Decapitated Arab	Charley Bravo
Philippe	Eduardo Bea
Chef	Juan Cazalilla

THE MAN WHO WOULD BE KING (USA; Columbia-Warner, 1975)

Director: John Huston. Producer: John Foreman. Screenplay: John Huston and Gladys Hill, based on the short story by Rudyard Kipling. Photography: Oswald Morris. Editor: Russell Lloyd. Second Unit director: Michael Moore. Production de-

signer: Alexander Trauner. Art director: Tony Inglis. Special effects: Dick Parker. Sculptor: Giulio Srubek Tomassy. Music: Maurice Jarre. Assistant directors: Bert Batt, Michael Cheyko and Christopher Carreras. Costumes: Edith Head. Running time: 129 minutes. In colour Panavision. Certificate A.
Production company: Persky-Bright/Devon. For Allied Artists/Columbia.

Daniel Dravot	Sean Connery
Peachy Carnehan	Michael Caine
Rudyard Kipling	Christopher Plummer
Billy Fish	Saeed Jaffrey
Kafu-Selim	Karroum Ben Bouih
District Commissioner	Jack May
Ootah	Doghmi Larbi
Roxanne	Shakira Caine
Babu	Mohammed Shamsi
Mulvaney	Paul Antrim
Ghulam	Albert Moses
Sikh soldier	Kimat Singh
Sikh soldier 2	Gurmuks Singh
Dancers	Yvonne Ocampo
	Nadia Atbib
Officer	Graham Acres

With the Blue Dancers of Goulamine

ROBIN AND MARIAN (USA; Columbia-Warner, 1976)

Director: Richard Lester. Producer: Denis O'Dell. Executive producer: Richard Shepherd. Screenplay: James Goldman. Photography: David Watkin. Editor: John Victor Smith. Production designer: Michael Stringer. Art director: Gil Perondo. Music: John Barry. Assistant director: Jose Lopez Rodero. Fight arrangers: William Hobbs and Ian McKay. Stunt sequences by Miguel Pedregosa, Joaquin Parra. Running time: 107 minutes. In colour. Certificate A.
Production company: Raster. For Columbia.

Robin Hood	Sean Connery
Maid Marian	Audrey Hepburn
Sheriff of Nottingham	Robert Shaw
King Richard	Richard Harris
Little John	Nicol Williamson
Will Scarlett	Denholm Elliott
Sir Ranulf	Kenneth Haigh
Friar Tuck	Ronnie Barker
King John	Ian Holm
Mercadier	Bill Maynard
Old Defender	Esmond Knight
Sister Mary	Veronica Quilligan
Surgeon	Peter Butterworth
Jack	John Barrett
Jack's apprentice	Kenneth Cranham
Queen Isabella	Victoria Merida Roja
1st Sister	Montserrat Julio
2nd Sister	Victoria Hernandez Sanguino
3rd Sister	Margarita Minguillon

THE NEXT MAN (USA; Harris Films, 1976)

Director: Richard C. Sarafian. Producer: Martin Bregman. Executive producer: Emanuel L. Wolf. Screenplay: Mort Fine, Alan R. Trustman, David M. Wolf and Richard C. Sarafian, from a story by Alan R. Trustman and David M. Wolf. Photography: Michael Chapman. Editor: Aram Avakian and Robert Q. Lovett. Production designer: Gene Callahan. Art director: Stuart Wurtzel. Music: Michael Kamen. Songs: *The Next Man Theme*, by Michael Kamen; Frech lyrics by Rosko Mercer, sung by Robert Fitoussi; *Stay with Me* sung by Tasha Thomas. Stunt co-ordinator: Louie Elias. Runnng time: 107 minutes. (16 mm film.) In Technicolor.
Production company: Artists Entertainment Complex.

Khalil Abdul-Muhsen	Sean Connery
Nicole Scott	Cornelia Sharpe

272

Hamid	Albert Paulsen
Al Sharif	Adolfo Celi
Justin	Marco St. John
Frank Dedario	Ted Beniades
Fouad	Charles Cioffi
New York Security Men	Jaime Sanchez
	James Bullett
Ghassan Kaddara	Salem Ludwig
Yassin	Roger Omar Serbagi
Hafim Othman	Tom Klunis
Abdel-Latif Khaldoun	Armand Dahan
Atif Abbas	Charles Randall
Devereaux	Ian Collier
Salazar	Michael Storm
Conglomerate Chairman	Maurice Copeland
Zolchev	George Pravda
Russian Economics Minister	Alex Jadokimov
Andy Hampsas	Stephen D. Newman
TV interviewer	Holland Taylor
Mrs Scott	Peggy Feury
Mr Scott	Patrick Bedford
Japanese diplomat	Toru Nagai
Japanese U.N. delegate	Ryokei Kanogogi
Federal Security Agents	Bill Snickowski
	Lance Hendrickson
U.N. reporters	Camille Yarborough
	Thomas Ruisinger
	Edward Setrakian
	Jack Davidson
Press Room reporters	Robert Levine
	William Mooney
Waldorf manager	John McKay
Auctioneer	Robert Wooley
London assassin	Bob Simmons
Ibn Sidki	Tony Ellis

Ibn Sidki's wife	Jamila Massey
London street dancer	Jim Norris
Arab at Parke Bernet	Joe Zaloom
Khalil's driver	Richard Zakka
British attaché	Jamie Ross
Nicole's Irish chauffeur	David Kelly
Customs man	Bill Golding
Socialite	Diane Peterson
Assassin in Saudi Arabia	Mohammed Sedrihini
Le Club	Patrick Shields
Junkanoo dancer	Tony Carroll

A BRIDGE TOO FAR (USA; United Artists, 1977)

Director: Richard Attenborough. Producers: Joseph E. Levine and Richard P. Levine. Screenplay: William Goldman, based on the book by Cornelius Ryan. Photography: Geoffrey Unsworth. Editor: Antony Gibb. Production designer: Terence Marsh. Art directors: Stuart Craig, Alan Tomkins and Roy Stannard. Second Unit director: Sidney Hayers. Aerial photography: Robin Browne. Parachute cameramen: Dave Waterman and John Partington-Smith. Chief technical advisor: Kathryn Morgan Ryan. Military advisers: Colonel J. L. Waddy O.B.E. and Co-lonel Frank A. Gregg, U.S.A. Music: John Addison. Assistant directors: Steve Lanning, Roy Button, Peter Waller and Geoffrey Ryan. Running time: 180 minutes. In Technicolor Panavision. Certificate A.
Production company: Joseph E. Levine Production.

Underground leader	Siem Vroom
Underground leader's wife	Marlies Van Alcmaer
Underground leader's son	Eric Van't Wout
Field Marshal Von Rundstedt	Wolfgang Preiss
General Blumentritt	Hans Von Borsody
Cafe waitress	Josephine Peeper
Lieutenant General Browning	Dirk Bogarde
Major General Maxwell Taylor	Paul Maxwell

Major General Urquhart	Sean Connery
Brig. General Gavin	Ryan O'Neal
Major General Sosabowski	Gene Hackman
Field Marshal Model	Walter Kohut
Capt. 'Harry' Bestebreurtje	Peter Faber
German sentry	Hartmut Becker
Major Fuller	Frank Grimes
R.A.F. Briefing Officer	Jeremy Kemp
Lieutenant Colonel Mackenzie	Donald Pickering
Brigadier Lathbury	Donald Douglas
Lieutenant Cole	Peter Settelen
Major Steele	Stephen Moore
Lt. General Horrocks	Edward Fox
Lt. Col. J.O.E. Vandeleur	Michael Caine
Lt. Col. Giles Vandeleur	Michael Byrne
Lt. Col. Frost	Anthony Hopkins
Private Wicks	Paul Copley
Captain Glass	Nicholas Campbell
Staff Sergeant Dohun	James Caan
Colonel Sims	Gerald Sim
U.S.Private	Harry Ditson
Organist	Erik Chitty
Vicar	Brian Hawksley
Corporal Hancock	Colin Farrell
Major Carlyle	Christopher Good
Private Morgan	Norman Gregory
Corporal Davies	Alun Armstrong
Private Dodds	Anthony Milner
Private Clark	Barry McCarthy
Sergeant Matthias	Lex Van Delden
Lieutenant General Bittrich	Maximilian Schell
Major General Ludwig	Hardy Kruger
Irish Guards Lieutenant	Sean Mathias
German Private	Tim Beekman
British Padre	Edward Seckerson

Kate Ter Horst	Liv Ullmann
Jan Ter Horst	Tom Van Beek
Colonel Stout	Elliott Gould
Lieutenant Cornish	Keith Drinkel
Old Dutch lady	Mary Smithuysen
Hans, her son	Hans Croiset
Captain Grabner	Fred Williams
German Lieutenant	John Peel
Sergeant Clegg	John Judd
Trooper Binns	Ben Cross
British Medical Officer	Hilary Minster
Private Andrews	David English
Sergeant Towns	Ben Howard
Captain Cleminson	Michael Graham Cox
R.A.F. Met. Officer	Denholm Elliott
U.S. Sergeant	Peter Gordon
U.S. Medical Colonel	Arthur Hill
Lieutenant Rafferty	Garrick Hagon
U.S. Engineer	Brian Gwaspari
Grenadier Guards Lieutenant	Stephen Rayment
British Corporal	Tim Morand
Private Gibbs	James Wardroper
Colonel Barker	Neil Kennedy
Private 'Ginger' Marsh	John Salthouse
Glider Pilot	Jonathan Hackett
Regimental Sergeant Major	Stanley Lebor
Private Vincent	Jack Galloway
Private Long	Milton Cadman
'Taffy' Brace	David Aucker
Doctor Spaander	Laurence Olivier
Colonel Weaver	Richard Kane
Private Stephenson	Toby Salaman
British Staff Colonel	Michael Bangerter
Grenadier Guards Colonel	Philip Raymond
Boat truck driver	Myles Reithermann

Major Cook	Robert Redford
U.S. Captain	Anthony Pullen
U.S. Padre	John Morton
U.S. Lieutenant	John Ratzenberger
German Lieutenant	Patrick Ryecart
Captain Krafft	Dick Rienstra
Sergeant Whitney	Ian Liston
Private Gordon	Paul Rattee
Sergeant Tomblin	Mark Sheridan
Sergeant Macdonald	George Innes
Grenadier Guards Major	John Stride
British Medical Orderlies	Nial Padden
	Michael Graves
Private Simmonds	Simon Chandler
Private Archer	Edward Kalinski
Corporal Robbins	Shaun Curry
Sergeant Treadell	Sebastian Abineri
Corporal Merrick	Chris Williams
Flute player	Andrew Branch
British Staff Major	Anthony Garner
Dutch priest	Feliks Arons
Dutch villagers	Bertus Botterman
	Henny Alma
Elderly Dutch couple	Johan Te Slaa
	Georgette Reyevski
Young Dutch couple	Pieter Groenier
	Adrienne Kleiweg

THE FIRST GREAT TRAIN ROBBERY (Great Britain; United Artists, 1978)
USA title: *The Great Train Robbery*

Director: Michael Crichton. Producer: John Foreman. Screen-

play: Michael Crichton, based on his own novel. Photography: Geoffrey Unsworth. Editor: David Bretherton. Production designer: Maurice Carter. Art director: Bert Davey. Music: Jerry Goldsmith. Assistant directors: Anthony Waye, Gerry Gavigan and Chris Carreras. Running time: 110 minutes. In Technicolor Panavision. Certificate AA.
Production company: Starling Productions. Presented by Dino De Laurentiis.

Edward Pierce	Sean Connery
Agar	Donald Sutherland
Miriam	Lesley-Anne Down
Edgar Trent	Alan Webb
Henry Fowler	Malcolm Terris
Sharp	Robert Lang
Clean Willy	Wayne Sleep
Burgess	Michael Elphick
Emily Trent	Pamela Salem
Elizabeth Trent	Gabrielle Lloyd
Harranby	James Cossins
McPherson	John Bett
Station dispatcher	Peter Benson
Maggie	Janine Duvitski
Woman on platform	Agnes Bernelle
Police constable	Frank McDonald
Trent's butler	Brian De Salvo
Rail guard	Joe Cahill
Shepherd	Pat Layde
Executioner	Derek Lord
Elderly woman on train	Rachel Burrows

Note: Film dedicated to the memory of the late Geoffrey Unsworth.

METEOR (USA: Columbia-EMI-Warner, 1979)

Director: Ronald Neame. Producers: Arnold Orgolini and Theodore Parvi. Executive producers: Sandy Howard and Gabriel Katzka. Screenplay: Stanley Mann and Edmund H. North, from

278

a story by Edmund H. North. Photography: Paul Lohmann. Editor: Carl Kress. Production designer: Edward Carfagno. Art director: David Constable. Special effects: Glen Robinson and Robert Staples. Technical Advisor (Jet Propulsion Laboratories): John Small. Technical Advisor (NASA): Doug Ward. Music: Laurence Rosenthal. Stunt co-ordinator: Roger Creed. Assistant director: Daniel J. McCauley. Running time: 107 minutes. In color Panavision. Certificate A.
Production company: A Sandy Howard/Gabriel Katzka/Sir Run Run Shaw Presentation.

Dr. Paul Bradley	Sean Connery
Tatiana Donskaya	Natalie Wood
Harold Sherwood	Karl Malden
Dr. Alexei Dubov	Brian Keith
General Barry Adlon	Martin Landau
Sir Michael Hughes	Trevor Howard
Secretary of Defence	Richard Dysart
The President	Henry Fonda
Easton	Joseph Campanella
Jan	Katherine DeHetre
Alan	James Richardson
Manheim	Bo Brundin
Hunter	Roger Robinson
Mrs Bradley	Bibi Besch
Watson	John McKinney
Mason	Michael Zaslow
Tom Easton	John Findlater
Bill Frager	Paul Tulley
Michael McKendrick	Allen Williams
Russian Premier	Gregory Gay
Hawk-faced Party Member	Zitto Kazann
Yamashiro	Clyde Kusatsu
Coastguard Officer	Burke Byrnes

CUBA (USA; United Artists, 1979)

Director: Richard Lester. Producers: Arlene Sellers and Alex

Winitsky. Executive producer: Denis O'Dell. Screenplay: Charles Wood. Photography: David Watkin. Editor: John Victor Smith. Production designer: Gil Parrondo. Art director: Denis Gordon Orr. Second Unit photography: Robert Stevens. Music: Patrick Williams. Assistant directors: David Tringham, Roberto Parra, Steve Lanning, Javier Carrasco. Running time: 122 minutes. In Technicolor Panavision. Certificate AA.
Production company: An Alex Winitsky-Arlene Sellers Production.

Robert Dapes	Sean Connery
Alaxandra Pulido	Brooke Adams
Gutman	Jack Weston
Ramirez	Hector Elizondo
Skinner	Denholm Elliott
General Bello	Martin Balsam
Juan Pulido	Chris Sarandon
Faustino	Alejandro Rey
Therese	Lonette McKee
Julio	Danny De La Paz
Miss Wonderly	Louisa Moritz
Press agent	Dave King
Don Pulido	Walter Gotell
Colonel Rosell Y Leyva	Earl Cameron
Dolores	Pauline Peart
Maria	Anna Nicholas
Jesus	David Rappaport
Carillo	Tony Matthews
Cecilia	Leticia Garrado
Gary	John Morton
Spencer	Anthony Pullen Shaw
Ramon	Stefan Kalipha
Painter	Raul Newney
Girl in arcade	Eva Louise

TIME BANDITS (Great Britain; HandMade Films, 1981)

Director: Terry Gilliam. Producer: Terry Gilliam. Executive producers: George Harrison and Denis O'Brien. Screenplay: Michael Palin and Terry Gilliam. Photography: Peter Biziou. Editor: Julian Doyle. Production designer: Millie Burns. Art director: Norman Garwood. Special effects supervisor: John Bunker. Models: Val Charlton, (asst.) Carol De Jong, Jean Ramsey, Alix Harwood and Behira Thraves. Sculptors: Geoff Rivers Bland and Laurie Warburton. Special optical effects: Kent Houston, Paul Whitbread, (asst.) Tim Ollive, Dennis De Groot, Peerless Camera Co. Second Unit director: Julian Doyle. Music: Mike Moran. Greek dance music: Trevor Jones. Songs and additional material: George Harrison. Song: *Me and My Shadow* by Rose Jolson, Dreyer, arranged by Trevor Jones. Assistant directors: Simon Hinkley, Guy Travers, Mark Cooper and Chris Thompson. Costumes: Jim Acheson and Hazel Côté. Running time: 113 minutes. In Technicolor. Certificate A.
Production company: HandMade Films.

Robin Hood	John Cleese
King Agamemnon	Sean Connery
Pansy	Shelley Duvall
Mrs Ogre	Katherine Helmond
Napoleon	Ian Holm
Vincent	Michael Palin
Evil Genius	David Warner
Supreme Being	Ralph Richardson
Ogre	Peter Vaughan
Randall	David Rappaport
Fidgit	Kenny Daker
Wally	Jack Purvis
Og	Mike Edmonds
Strutter	Malcolm Dixon
Vermin	Tiny Ross
Kevin	Craig Warnock
Kevin's father	David Baker
Kevin's mother	Sheila Fearn

Compere	Jim Broadbent
Reginald	John Young
Beryl	Myrtle Devenish
Hussar	Brian Bowes
1st refugee	Leon Lissek
Lucien	Terence Bayler
Neguy	Preston Lockwood
Theatre manager	Charles McKeown
Puppeteer	David Leland
The Great Rumbozo	John Hughman
Robber leader	Derrick O'Connor
2nd robber	Declan Mulholland
3rd robber	Neil McCarthy
Arm wrestler	Peter Jonfield
Robert	Derek Deadman
Benson	Jerold Wells
Cartwright	Roger Frost
Baxi Brazilia III	Martin Carroll
Horseflesh	Marcus Powell
Bull-headed warrior	Winston Dennis
Greek fighting warrior	Del Baker
Greek Queen	Juliette James
Giant	Ian Muir
Troll father	Mark Holmes
Fireman	Andrew McLachlan
Voice of TV announcer	Chris Grant
Voice of Supreme Being	Tony Jay
Sureme Being's face	Edwin Finn

OUTLAND (USA; Columbia-EMI-Warner, 1981)

Director: Peter Hyams. Producer: Richard A. Roth. Executive producer: Stanley O'Toole. Screenplay: Peter Hyams. Photography: Stephen Goldblatt. Editor: Stuart Baird. Production designer: Philip Harrison. Art director: Malcolm Middleton.

Special effecs: John Stears. Optical effects supervision: Roy Field. Music: Jerry Goldsmith. Assistant directors: David Tringham and Bob Wright. Running time: 109 minutes. In Technicolor Panavision. Certificate AA.
Production company: The Ladd Company.

O'Niel	Sean Connery
Sheppard	Peter Boyle
Lazarus	Frances Sternhagen
Montone	James B. Sikking
Carol	Kika Markham
Ballard	Clarke Peters
Sagan	Steven Berkoff
Tarlow	John Ratzenberger
Pau O'Nile	Nicholas Barnes
Lowell	Manning Redwood
Mrs Spector	Pat Starr
Nelson	Hal Galili
Hughes	Angus MacInnes
Walters	Stuart Milligan
Cane	Eugene Lipinski
Slater	Norman Chancer
Fanning	Ron Travis
Morton	Anni Domingo
Hill	Bill Bailey
Caldwell	Chris Williams
Spota	Marc Boyle
Yario	Richard Hammat
Rudd	James Berwick
Worker	Gary Olsen
Nurse	Isabelle Lucas
Prostitute	Sharon Duce
Man 1	P. H. Moriarty
Maintenance woman	Angelique Rockas
Female prostitute (Leisure Club)	Judith Alderson

Male prostitute	
(Leisure Club)	Rayner Bourton
Man 2	Doug Robinson
Dancers at	
Leisure Club	Julia Depyer
	Nina Francoise
	Brendon Hughes
	Philip Johnston
	and Norri Morgan

THE MAN WITH THE DEADLY LENS (USA; Columbia, 1982)
USA title: *Wrong is Right*

Director: Richard Brooks. Producer; Richard Brooks. Executive producer: Andrew Fogelson. Screenplay: Richard Brooks, based on the novel *The Better Angels* by Charles McCarry. Photography: Fred J. Koenekamp. Editor: George Grenville. Production designer: Edward Carfagno. Art director: Karl Hueglin. Music: Artie Kane. Assistant director: Alan Hopkins. Running time: 117 minutes. In Metrocolor. Certificate A.
Production company: Richard Brooks Production.

Patrick Hale	Sean Connery
President Lockwood	George Grizzard
General Wombat	Robert Conrad
Sally Blake	Katherine Ross
Philindros	G. D. Spradlin
Homer Hubbard	John Saxon
Rafeeq	Henry Silva
Mallory	Leslie Nielsen
Harvey	Robert Webber
Mrs Ford	Rosalind Cash
Helmut Unger	Hardy Kruger
Hacker	Dean Stockwell
King Awad	Ron Moody

Erika	Cherie Michan
Abu	Tony March

FIVE DAYS ONE SUMMER (USA; Warner Bros, 1982)

Director: Fred Zinnemann. Producer: Fred Zinnemann. Executive producer: Peter Beale. Screenplay: Michael Austin, based on the short story by Kay Boyle. Photography: Giuseppe Rotunno. Editor: Stuart Baird. Production designer: Willy Holt. Art directors: Gérard Viard and Bob Cartwright. Second Unit director: Norman Dyhrenfurth. Mountain consultant: Hamish McInnes. Music: Elmer Bernstein. Assistant director: Anthony Waye.Costumes by Emma Porteous. Running time: 100 minutes approx. In colour.
Production company: A Ladd Company Production.

Douglas	Sean Connery
Kate	Betsy Brantley
Johann	Lambert Wilson
Sarah	Jennifer Hilary
Kate's mother	Isabel Dean
Brendel	Gerard Buhr
Jennifer Pierce	Anna Massey
Gillian Pierce	Sheila Reid
Dieter	Georges Claisse
Georg	Terry Kingley
Old woman	Emilie Lihou
Van Royen	Jerry Brouwer
French students	Marc Duret
	Francois Caron
	Benoist Ferreux
Maclean	Alexander John
Horse taxi driver	Michael Burrell
1st hut guardian	Frank Duncan
Choreographer	D'Dee

285

NEVER SAY NEVER AGAIN (USA; Warner Bros, 1983)

Director: Irvin Kershner. Producer: Jack Schwartzman. Executive producer: Kevin McClory. Based on *Thunderball,* by Ian Fleming, Jack Whittingham and Kevin McClory. Photography: Douglas Slocombe. Editor: Ian Crafford. Production designer: Philip Harrison. Art director: Michael White with Les Dilley. Computer video electronics supervisor: Rob Dickenson. Special effects supervisor: Ian Wingrove. Assistant director: David Tomblin. Sean Connery's make-up artist: Ilona Herman. Running time: 100 minutes approx. In colour.
Production company: Woodcote Productions.

James Bond	Sean Connery
Domino	Kim Basinger
Ernst Blofeld	Max Von Sydow
Largo	Klaus Maria Brandauer
Fatima Blush	Barbara Carrera
Felix Leiter	Bernie Casey
M	Edward Fox
Moneypenny	Pamela Salem
Armourer	Alec McGowan

Index

287

289

291

Monroe, Marilyn, 84
Monty Python's Flying Circus, 228
Moonraker, 9, 110
Moore, Kieron, 5, 92, 93, 96
Moore, Roger, 9, 11-12, 13, 17, 111, 182, 198, 206, 225, 227, 228, 234, 241
Moore, Ted, 128
More, Kenneth, 68
Morgan, Elaine, 73, 74
Mosley, Leonard, 149
Mower, Patrick, 207
Moxon, Tim, 118
Munro, Janet, 92, 93, 94
Murray, Ruby, 94

Nand, Tom, 226
Neagle, Anna, 47
Neal, Patricia, 163
Neame, Ronald, 212
Newman, Paul, 139, 159
Niven, David, 107
Nolan, Margaret, 140
Norman, Monty, 119
Nureyev, Rudolf, 236
Nurse Edith Cavell, 47

Oakes, Philip, 129
O'Casey, Sean, 138
O'Conaires of Munster, 20
O'Conaire, Padraic, 20
O'Connerys of Waterford, 21
O'Dell, Denis, 190
Occupussy, 9, 17
O'Dea, Jimmy, 93, 97, 136
O'Dell, Denis, 218
O'Dowda, Brendan, 94
O'Herlihy, Michael, 5, 92, 93, 94, 95
Olivier, Laurence, 8, 139
O'Neal, Patrick, 160
One Day in the Life of Ivan Denisovich, 197
O'Neill, Eugene, 68
On Her Majesty's Secret Service, 160, 174, 181-82, 183
On the Night of the Fire, 33
Osborne, John, 110
O'Sullivan, Michael, 23, 41
O'Toole, Peter, 137

Palance, Jack, 69
Palin, Michael, 228
Pallos, Steven, 71
Paluzzi, Luciana, 159

Paul, Gloria, 154
Pawnbroker, The, 147
Pearson, Mrs, 75
Peper, William, 133
Perdesatt, Fiona, 5
Perilli, Pat, 5
Perkins, Anthony, 198
Persuaders, The, 182
Peters, Molly, 5, 116, 130, 155, 156, 158
Peyton Place, 85
Piccadilly Incident, 47
Picker, David, 111, 181, 182, 184, 187
Pirandelli Luigi, 99
Pleasence, Donald, 164, 166
Plomer, William, 114
Plummer, Christopher, 205
Point Blank, 194
Polanski, Roman, 179, 183, 193
Poldark, 134
Porteous, Ian, 5
Powell, Dily, 159
Powell, Michael, 32
Power, Tyrone, 83
Pressburger, Emeric, 32
Proust, Marcel, 58, 60
Psycho, 134

Quare Fellow, The, 99
Quayle, Anthony, 98, 100
Quinlan, David, 199
Quigly, Isabel, 149

Rakoff, Alvin, 5, 69-70, 72, 73, 74, 75, 76, 77, 82
Rampling, Charlotte, 195
Ramsay, Alan, 19
Rank, J. Arthur, 32
Ratoff, Gregory, 110
Rattigan, Terence, 106
Rattle of a Simple Man, 146
Rawlings, Margaret, 71
Red Beret, The, 111
Redford, Robert, 203, 211
Redgrave, Michael, 112
Redgrave, Vanessa, 197-98
Reed, Carol, 32, 146
Reeve, Christopher, 13
Relph, Michael, 134
Remembrances of Things Past, 58
Reynolds, Burt, 182, 194
Ribbentrop, J. von, 181
Rich, Frank, 208

294